Togo

WORLD BIBLIOGRAPHICAL SERIES

General Editors:
Robert G. Neville (Executive Editor)
John J. Horton

Robert A. Myers   Hans H. Wellisch
Ian Wallace   Ralph Lee Woodward, Jr.

John J. Horton is Deputy Librarian of the University of Bradford and currently Chairman of its Academic Board of Studies in Social Sciences. He has maintained a longstanding interest in the discipline of area studies and its associated bibliographical problems, with special reference to European Studies. In particular he has published in the field of Icelandic and of Yugoslav studies, including the two relevant volumes in the World Bibliographical Series.

Robert A. Myers is Associate Professor of Anthropology in the Division of Social Sciences and Director of Study Abroad Programs at Alfred University, Alfred, New York. He has studied post-colonial island nations of the Caribbean and has spent two years in Nigeria on a Fulbright Lectureship. His interests include international public health, historical anthropology and developing societies. In addition to *Amerindians of the Lesser Antilles: a bibliography* (1981), *A Resource Guide to Dominica, 1493-1986* (1987) and numerous articles, he has compiled the World Bibliographical Series volumes on *Dominica* (1987), *Nigeria* (1989) and *Ghana* (1991).

Ian Wallace is Professor of German at the University of Bath. A graduate of Oxford in French and German, he also studied in Tübingen, Heidelberg and Lausanne before taking teaching posts at universities in the USA, Scotland and England. He specializes in contemporary German affairs, especially literature and culture, on which he has published numerous articles and books. In 1979 he founded the journal *GDR Monitor*, which he continues to edit under its new title *German Monitor*.

Hans H. Wellisch is Professor emeritus at the College of Library and Information Services, University of Maryland. He was President of the American Society of Indexers and was a member of the International Federation for Documentation. He is the author of numerous articles and several books on indexing and abstracting, and has published *The Conversion of Scripts and Indexing and Abstracting: an International Bibliography*, and *Indexing from A to Z*. He also contributes frequently to *Journal of the American Society for Information Science*, *The Indexer* and other professional journals.

Ralph Lee Woodward, Jr. is Professor of History at Tulane University, New Orleans. He is the author of *Central America, a Nation Divided*, 2nd ed. (1985), as well as several monographs and more than seventy scholarly articles on modern Latin America. He has also compiled volumes in the World Bibliographical Series on *Belize* (1980), *El Salvador* (1988), *Guatemala* (Rev. Ed.) (1992) and *Nicaragua* (Rev. Ed.) (1994). Dr. Woodward edited the Central American section of the *Research Guide to Central America and the Caribbean* (1985) and is currently associate editor of Scribner's *Encyclopedia of Latin American History*.

VOLUME 178

Togo

Samuel Decalo

Compiler

CLIO PRESS

OXFORD, ENGLAND · SANTA BARBARA, CALIFORNIA
DENVER, COLORADO

British Library Cataloguing in Publication Data

Togo. – (World Bibliographical
Series; vol. 178)
I. Decalo, Samuel.   II. Series
016.96681

ISBN 1–85109–160–2

ABC-CLIO Ltd.,
Old Clarendon Ironworks,
35A Great Clarendon Street,
Oxford OX2 6AT, England.

————

ABC-CLIO Inc.,
130 Cremona Drive,
Santa Barbara,
CA 93116, USA

Designed by Bernard Crossland.
Typeset by Columns Design and Production Services Ltd., Reading, England.
Printed and bound in Great Britain by Bookcraft (Bath) Ltd., Midsomer Norton.

THE WORLD BIBLIOGRAPHICAL SERIES

This series, which is principally designed for the English speaker, will eventually cover every country (and many of the world's principal regions), each in a separate volume comprising annotated entries on works dealing with its history, geography, economy and politics; and with its people, their culture, customs, religion and social organization. Attention will also be paid to current living conditions – housing, education, newspapers, clothing, etc. – that are all too often ignored in standard bibliographies; and to those particular aspects relevant to individual countries. Each volume seeks to achieve, by use of careful selectivity and critical assessment of the literature, an expression of the country and an appreciation of its nature and national aspirations, to guide the reader towards an understanding of its importance. The keynote of the series is to provide, in a uniform format, an interpretation of each country that will express its culture, its place in the world, and the qualities and background that make it unique. The views expressed in individual volumes, however, are not necessarily those of the publisher.

VOLUMES IN THE SERIES

Contents

Contents

Introduction

Togo is a small country in West Africa with an area of 21,620 square miles; it has a 32-mile long coastline and extends 320 miles inland. Situated between Benin and Ghana, Togo, which occupies two-thirds of the territory of the original German colony, has a northern border with Burkina Faso, for which it provides access to the sea.

Geographically, Togo has six naturally distinct regions. The sandy beaches and inland lagoons of the coast, the largest being Lac Togo, give way to the Ouatchi plateaux to their immediate rear, while further north lies the higher Mono tableland, which is drained by the Mono River and its tributaries. The fourth area is dominated by a mountain range, which dissects the country in a south-west, north-east direction and is part of neighbouring Benin's Atakora mountains that end in Ghana's Akwapim hills. It is here that Togo's highest altitude, Pic Baumann, is found, climbing to a height of 986 metres. Travel further north leads to the sandstone Oti plateau, through which the Oti river, a tributary of the Volta river, flows, and from there to the granite regions of Dapaong in the far north.

The country is heavily vegetated with grasslands. The highest rainfall (approximately 180 centimetres annually) falls at Kpalimé, 120 kilometres in the interior, while the coast is rather dry, recording only 65 to 90 centimetres of rain per year. The north has one rainy season between April and July (115 centimetres per year) while in the south there are two rainy seasons between April and July and October and November.

Togo has a population of 3.85 million (1993), comprising between eighteen and thirty different ethnic groups (depending upon one's classification). The largest and most important of these are the Ewe (and other Adja-related groups) who reside in the south and form forty-four per cent of the population, followed by the Kabre (and related groups) in the north who make up twenty-seven per cent. Prior to colonial rule most groups had little contact with each other. State formation was retarded and most entities, apart from a few small kingdoms in the north, were decentralized groups of villages under pressure from the Ashanti in the Gold Coast and the Fon in Benin. This meant that the region was a power vacuum, a weak neutral zone between the territory of the two other strong neighbouring West African states.

The first Europeans to arrive on the Togolese coast were the Portuguese navigators, João de Santarem and Pedro Escobar, between 1471 and 1473. It was not until the 19th century, however, that the stretch of coast from Accra to Lagos became an area of contention between a number of colonial powers, including France, Great Britain, and Germany. The main town in the region was Aného (then better known as Petit Popo), a Mina slave-port where various European agents were established. However, the town did not become a popular port of call because of the alleged sharp middlemen practices of local traders and the more plentiful supply of slaves at Ouidah (Benin) and along the Gold Coast.

The colony's name derived from the small coastal village of Togo where on 4 July 1884 the German Imperial Commissioner, Gustav Nachtigal, signed a protectorate agreement with Chief Mlapa III. Progress inland from the coast was slow, punctuated by resistance from indigenous groups, especially in the north. Germany's slow advance resulted in the frustration of one key imperial goal which was to reach the Niger river. The colony's borders were finally fixed in a number of conferences with the other colonial powers and ratified in the Treaty of Paris of 1897.

As was the case elsewhere in Africa, coastal elements developed at a much earlier date and at a faster pace than insular groups. In Togo the 120 different Ewe clans, the Mina and other related groups were the first to come into contact with Europeans, taking advantage of opportunities for advancement and ascending politically and administratively during the colonial era. By contrast, the northern population opposed the colonial intrusion, fought the penetration of their territory, and were in turn left undeveloped by the German and subsequent French administration. The differing reactions to modern influences and the growing socio-economic disparities between northern and southern ethnic groups drove a wedge of inter-ethnic hostility and resentment between them that contributed to the growth of regionalism and the rise of antagonistic regional political parties in the pre-independence era.

Although German colonial rule was authoritarian and brief, lasting only thirty years, until August 1914, it was during this era that much of Togo's infrastructure was built. A road system was established, Lomé's breakwaters and wharf were constructed, and just prior to the

First World War, the colony's third railroad was completed (later expanded by the French), facilitating the transport of cash crops to the coast. The agrarian expansion of Togo made the colony the first in West Africa to balance its own budget (1906). Despite similar German educational efforts, the harshness of their administration led to considerable opposition to their rule, Ewe migration to the Gold Coast, and a welcome to Allied troops when the First World War broke out.

Togo's conquest in 1914 by an Anglo-French force was the first Allied victory of the war and took only eighteen days to effect. After the war the occupying powers were granted League of Nations mandates over the partitioned territory, with the resultant division of the Ewe group into Gold Coast, British and French Togoland. It was this that lay at the root of the Ewe 'problem' that occupied the attention of the United Nations Trusteeship Council after the Second World War. The nationalist aspirations of the Ewe clans translated into several unification movements in the Gold Coast and French Togo, one of which was the *Comité de l'Unité Togolaise* (CUT) of Sylvanus Olympio, Togo's future president.

The Ewe objective of unification within one political entity was never realized, due to a variety of factors, such as: mutual Anglo-French suspicions as to each other's colonial ambitions; different decolonization policies within their respective trusteeships; inter-clan jealousies among the Ewe; and personality clashes among their leaders. With the approaching independence of Ghana, Britain informed the United Nations that she could no longer maintain her duties in British Togoland (governed from the Gold Coast), and a 1956 plebiscite on the future of the territory saw the majority of the people (but not the Ewe) opting for unification with the soon-to-be independent Ghana. France, suspicious of Britain's intentions and Kwame Nkrumah pan-Africanism, resisted calls to conduct a similar plebiscite. Instead, French Togo moved towards independence under the conservative pro-French Nicolas Grunitzky after a referendum in which the French administration supported such separatism, aided by a CUT boycott. Grunitzky's power-base lay in the alliance of his PTP party with the UCPN, led by northern chiefs, which dislodged the CUT – with active French support – from its dominant political position in the territory (1945-1951). His Autonomous Republic (1956-1958) collapsed, however, and his political allies were defeated in 1958 when a United Nations supervised vote confirmed Ewe political strength and brought a dramatic CUT/Olympio victory.

The entrenchment of the CUT saw the settling of old scores, and the emergence of an authoritarian system. Less than two years after independence a single-party state was declared, with some of Olympio's closest associates (especially from JUVENTO, the CUT's former youth wing) in prison, and scores of others in self-imposed exile in Ghana.

Under Olympio's leadership the emphasis was on settting Togo on a non-aligned course, one requisite of which was financial independence from France. As a fiscal conservative Olympio succeeded in balancing Togo's budget from local resources, including a plethora of taxes and austerity measures that antagonized many groups, including the Ewe who had originally supported the CUT. His clashes with Nkrumah led to the closure of the Ghanaian border, damaging the livelihood of Lomé's traders, while his friction with Lomé's Archbishop alienated him from a segment of the Ewe intellectual elite. Olympio's austerity policies and anti-military stances finally led to the 1963 ex-servicemen confrontation and coup, and his cold-blooded murder by Eyadema.

Other African states were disapproving of the coup which was the first to occur in West Africa. Olympio's murder was traumatic and barely relieved by the transferral of power to Grunitzky and Antoine Meatchi (as vice-president) and the May elections in which Togo's resurrected parties united to form a joint electoral list. From the outset the new regime was not popular; in the north feelings were in favour of a Meatchi presidency, while in the south the government was viewed as identical to the one ousted in 1958. The regime was promptly paralysed by a tug-of-war for supremacy between the two leaders at the top, while relations with Ghana remained poor, continuing to adversely affect local trade. The continued weak economy was sapped by new expenditures for an army that had been tripled in size to accommodate the perpetrators of the 1963 coup.

Grunitzky was also the target of plots sponsored from within and without his cabinet. The most serious of these erupted in November 1966 when, after a cabinet crisis, popular demonstrations, supported by the CUT, which was now the PUT, marched on the capital calling for his ouster and the establishment of a PUT government. The riots were quelled by the army which felt that they could not allow the government they had elevated to power to be ousted. Two months later, however, on the fourth anniversary of Olympio's murder, the army itself ousted Grunitzky's regime. After a brief military interregnum, General Gnassingbe Eyadema, the acknowledged murderer of Olympio, moved into the vacuum. He established his own authoritarian regime, which remains in place to this day, although it was forced to partly democratize in 1991.

The Togolese economy

The country's economy experienced three periods of growth: the first was during the German colonial era (followed by deep stagnation between 1920 and 1940); the second after the Second World War; and the third sparked off by the temporary (1974) boom in global phosphate prices. During the colonial era, German efforts to transform Togo into a model self-sufficient colony (*Musterkolonie*) brought about economic advances in the southern part of the country. There, a plantation economy developed that resulted in increased exports of coffee, cocoa, palm products and cotton, benefiting from the construction of Togo's three railway lines. During this period Togo made great advancements in the availability of education, which in 1914 covered nine per cent of school-age children, a ratio not achieved by Senegal, for example, until 1938. By 1990 seventy-two per cent of children attended primary school, with twenty-four per cent going on to secondary school.

Following the Anglo-French partition of the colony, Togo entered a period of stagnation, which was further aggravated by the global economic crash of the 1920s and 1930s. Average GDP growth during these years was 1.5 per cent per year and as late as 1949 Togo's volume of exports was much the same as during the German era. At the end of the Second World War the economy began to improve again, as a result of investments by the French FIDES programme, and in the mid-sixties new state funds became available as the country's phosphate industry came of age. In 1974 a temporary quadrupling of global prices of phosphates ushered in the country's third era of economic expansion, which due to misguided State spending led, however, to Togo's economic collapse in the 1980s.

Togo's main cash crops are cocoa and coffee (grown in the humid and hilly Kpalimé area near the Ghana border), palm nuts and cotton, the latter strongly expanding in the 1980s. These four crops have accounted for two-thirds of Togo's export earnings, with maize, millet, cassava (manioc), and sweet potatoes grown for local consumption.

Apart from revenues from tourism, which is the country's third-largest foreign exchange earner, and was particularly successful in the late 1970s, phosphate exports have been the key to much of the vibrance of the Togolese economy. With some of the richest deposits in the world, conveniently located near the coast, large exports of phosphate ore (especially after COTOMIB was nationalized in 1974) and by-products stabilized what would otherwise have been a weak agrarian economy. Although other mineral deposits abound, their relatively small quantities, or distant location from the coast, make their exploitation uneconomical. The Aveta limestone quarries are an exception.

Fuelled by the short-lived boom in global phosphate prices and heavy French and German largess in the 1970s, the Togolese economy underwent its most serious bout of expansion. Massive infrastructure building took place and dozens of parastatal plants, corporations, and ventures were set up, dramatically transforming Togo, and setting it apart from neighbouring Benin with which it had always invited comparison. A balanced development policy, which served the self-interests of the Kabre political elite, led for the first time to efforts to transform the neglected north, and to turn a blind eye to the highly lucrative smuggling activities of Lomé's marketwomen (a major political force in Togo) and other entrepreneurs, This, coupled with a liberal investment code, helped Togo to present the image of a stable, albeit military, polity, satisfying group demands while developmentally forging ahead.

However, what was referred to as the 'Togolese economic miracle' collapsed in the early 1980s. Massive corruption and administrative incompetence had crept in during the era of economic growth. Indeed, in the inevitable post-mortem of the deficitory State sector – set up largely in the 1970s and closed down (under lock and key), restructured or privatized at bargain-basement prices in the 1980s and 1990s – it was discovered that enterprises were at times authorized by cabinet members solely for the routine (ten per cent) kickback from contractors. Some senior officials were purged for corruption, but most, old Eyadema cronies, were simply shuffled to less sensitive posts where they continued their misdemeanours. The activities of the presidency, in any case, were not scrutinized until the remarkable revelations attending the attempt at democratization that came with the convening of the National Conference in 1991.

So long as the economy was booming, profligate and wasteful policies could continue, though at a heavy cost to the economy. The moment phosphate prices normalized, however, the parastatal sector became a major drag on the economy. Togo's imminent bankruptcy was recognized at the 1982 party congress of the *Rassemblement du Peuple Togolais* and the slow, costly and humiliating process of liquidating, restructuring or privatizing much of the State sector commenced. At the same time, both party and cabinet underwent certain changes, under global donor pressures (France and Germany), reluctant to provide additional aid under conditions in which large sums ended up in personal pockets. *The Guardian*'s issue of 21 August 1979 best summarized the ethos in Lomé: 'The whole administration has become so corrupt that it has fallen into anarchy; in the choice of investments profitability has ceased to matter. All that matters is the percentage rakeoff.'

Despite a decade of trimming the parastatal organizations the process is not yet complete, since in some areas buyers simply cannot be found, while in others the government will not accept the low bids tendered. Nevertheless, the stunning financial turnaround of several privatized enterprises (in two instances within one month) that commenced working without inflated labour forces (up to fifty per cent), layers of State sinecure administrators and consultants, and with a tight reign on expenses, suggests much of the State sector may yet be salvaged.

Fiscal austerity occurred because of the need to trim the bloated Togolese economy and civil service, and to control the staggering national debt, which at one time was the highest in the world on a per capita basis. This, coupled with the fact that Eyadema's military regime, always abrasive, now possessed few sources of patronage, destabilized the political system. This was accelerated by domestic pressures for democratization in the 1990s, and the continental 'winds of change' that began sweeping Africa. Within a decade one of West Africa's 'economic miracles' had become the region's 'sick man'. A country that in the early 1970s had even been referred to as 'the Switzerland of Africa' came to be equated with Zaire, the continental epitome of corruption, mismanagement, and dictatorial rule. Eyadema, like Mobutu, came to be referred to as one of Africa's 'dinosaurs' whose time of eclipse had long since gone.

The Eyadema era

Eyadema's years in power fall into several distinct phases: the period up until 1969 during which he was sensitive to his extra-legal status in a hostile Ewe environment, and strove to project an image of a societal 'honest broker'; followed by the period of 1969-1980, during which, aided by increased state revenues from booming phosphate exports and a generally improved economy, the regime felt secure enough to move toward a dialogue with allies within the newly-created single party, the *Rassemblement du Peuple Togolais*. Nevertheless, it was during this period that an ubiquitous Cult of Personality of grotesque proportions was developed – a continuation of earlier efforts to artificially orchestrate support for the regime.

Paradoxically, much of the relaxed style in Lomé in the 1970s and its stability at the time, can be attributed to Eyadema's early, surprisingly astute leadership of both the armed forces and the country. Civil-military stability was largely abetted by keeping the army's chain of command more-or-less intact through judicious promotions. Civilian criticism was kept to a minimum by constraints on the involvement of too many officers in political or civilian posts, and a low-key effort at keeping military self-aggrandizement within limited bounds.

Moreover, despite its later record and several brutal over-reactions, in its early years the regime was relatively 'forgiving' to opposition activity, and open to the infusion of new talent into the cabinet. Thus, what loyalty was denied Eyadema by virtue of his northern, military, and non-intellectual credentials, and his role in the murder of Olympio, he gained through a pragmatic easy-going political style, liberal economic policies, and the political cultivation of able Mina and Ewe technocrats. Benefiting from increased state revenues as Togo's phosphate industry, the fifth-largest in the world, came of age, the regime accelerated development in the south, commenced the first large-scale efforts at the socio-economic modernization of the north, and constructed major public works projects throughout the country, while keeping the civil service and armed forces happy with increased budgetary allocations. However, the short-lived 1974 spurt in phosphate royalties led the regime into a frenzy of public spending, the price for which was subsequent austerity at a time of rising expectations and multiple demands, and leading to the harshness of Eyadema's latter years.

The 1980s witnessed the regime's third 'era', as Eyadema claimed permanence to office: Togo obtained a constitution (1 January 1980), legislature and (single-party) elections, allegedly constitutionalizing and civilianizing Eyadema's rule. On the other hand, with the erosion of the Togolese economic dream Eyadema's early easy-going style came to an end. Not only had the ambitious and educated southern Togolese become too sophisticated to be swayed by the stifling personality cult and incredible political mythology that had been created to prop up the credentials of the unlettered *Le Guide* (who, allegedly even had aspirations to be nominated for a Nobel Peace Prize in the 1980s), but Eyadema became increasingly heavy-handed and authoritarian. His early astute appointments gave way to the nomination of sycophants, incompetents, personal friends, family members and individuals only interested in the benefits of public office.

Northerners and military officers gained in importance and privilege and officials caught embezzling State funds were simply shifted to less lucrative pastures in the public sector. Abuses of human rights increased, until Togo came to be judged as having Africa's worst human-rights record. By the early 1980s Togo was a country marked by repression, lack of civil zeal and public spirit, nepotism and chronic corruption. So bad was the regime's image abroad that in 1981 Eyadema hired a Washington-based public relations firm (one already existed in Paris) to whitewash his image overseas by commissioned articles and books, and by extending free holidays in Togo to public influentials.

The fourth period of Eyadema's rule emerges directly from the third in the mid-1980s, with the collapse of the economy due to its mismanagement and persistent, increasingly violent efforts, primarily by the Ewe (including Gilchrist Olympio, one of the Olympio sons) to permanently dislodge Eyadema from office. With development funds dried up and popular grievances building up, the social glue that had bound society together slowly dissolved, and political instability again became a fact of life. During this period most of the systematic and brutal abuses of human rights by the regime took place, such as arbitrary and mass arrests, imprisonment without trial, and torture and liquidation while in prison. The current era is characterized by the unstable period since 1990 when the economic crisis, global winds of change, and external donors forced Eyadema to convene a National Conference, which promptly declared itself sovereign. Although it originally seemed as if he had been pushed aside, Eyadema benefited from a paradoxical French *laissez-faire* policy, and used his loyalist, solidly northern army to terrorize society into submission, clawing his way back to power in 1993. Referring to this period, when one third of Lomé's population fled to Ghana during a paralysing eighteen-month strike, riots and social tumult in the south, the Economist Intelligence Unit noted (*Togo, Niger, Benin, Burkina: County Report*, no. 1, 1993, p. 10) that 'only the absence of weapons in the hands of the opposition is preventing a full-scale civil war . . . Eyadema's mainly Kabre army is operating as an army of occupation in the center and south of the country.'

Notwithstanding the resolutions of a euphoric National Conference, which stripped Eyadema of executive power, denied him the right to run for office, banned the RPT (even expelling it from its headquarters), and publicly revealed sordid details of brutal murder and crass corruption by Eyadema and his close associates, the dictator remained serene in the Presidential Palace. It was rather the interim Prime Minister Koffigoh (1991-1994) who was humiliated by troops which three times seized Lomé's radio station to lambast him and his interim government, mounted several attempted coups, stormed the National Assembly and finally kidnapped him for a confrontation with Eyadema. This led to a coalition of 'National Unity' with the RPT. In addition, it was members of the interim government who were murdered or intimidated right up to the flawed legislative and presidential elections of 1993-1994. Eyadema's prime nemesis and contender for the political throne, Gilchrist Olympio, was ambushed and shot by the military (led by Eyadema's son) while campaigning in central Togo, and later disqualified from the Presidential elections on a technicality.

The result of 'democratization' in Togo was Eyadema's re-election in August 1993 in a contest boycotted by all serious candidates. The populace turned out to vote primarily in the north, and most inter-national observers (including ex-President Carter) withdrew from monitoring the non-event. Olympio, back in self-imposed exile in Paris, redoubled his efforts to oust Eyadema by force, with armed assaults now reaching right into the Presidential House. The legislative elections of February 1994 were also marked by intimidation and violence by the army, though they were certified as fair. The RPT emerged as Togo's second-largest party, though now clearly a regionalist northern formation. With Gilchrist Olympio's party out of the race, the southern vote was split among several contenders, and Edem Kodjo, one minor Ewe leader from Kpalimé willing to cooperate with Eyadema was appointed by the latter on 22 April 1994 as Prime Minister of Togo, leading to the current parliamentary coalition between Kodjo's UTD and the RPT (as well as a few minor parties). The regime cannot be regarded as stable, however. One of the minor political forces in the country – the former Ewe PUT and their leader, Olympio – are disenfranchized; other large parties are in the opposition; and the Presidency was stolen by brute force by a minority (roughly thirty-five per cent) regional vote. Increasingly it seems that democracy will come from the barrel of the gun and not via the ballot box.

The implications are not too pleasant for either Eyadema, his cohorts or the Kabre in general. In neighbouring Benin, for example, where a similar northern military autocracy reigned supreme for seventeen years, General Kérékou accepted democratization, and his own eclipse ushered in Africa's fairest elections to date, to see his sins of omission and commission forgiven by a National Conference willing to put the past to rest and proceed with the reconstruction of an equally ravaged economy. In Benin there was subsequently no mass retribution, and the slow healing process commenced. Togo is probably not destined to follow this route. Far too much brutality has been committed since 1990 to allow a smooth political transition into Ewe hands when it finally takes place. The fact that as recently as May 1994 an editor could be sentenced to four years' imprisonment in Lomé for questioning the probity of African leaders including Eyadema, thus 'insulting the Head of State' (*West Africa*, 16 May 1994), is the best testimonial to how little has really changed in Togo.

The bibliography

Though Togo is, in terms of territory and demography, a relatively small country, and politically and socio-economically not very significant, a large amount of literature exists on it. Its early contact with European explorers, later merchants and slave traders; its original colonization and exploitation by Germany; conquest, partition and Trusteeship under France and England, and its subsequent evolution; the upward mobility of is southern populations; the socio-religious practices and/or beliefs of its ethnic groups; and the attraction to the country of a number of extremely prolific scholars, have all guaranteed Togo considerable academic attention. Since independence, moreover, a number of Togolese scholars have likewise produced valuable additional studies which enrich our knowledge in a variety of fields, from anthropology and history to religion and linguistics. Most of this material is found in the 'Bibliographies and Reference Works' section of this volume.

As could be expected, the bulk of the literature on Togo is in French, although there is not inconsiderable information available in German, both of historical origin and of an ongoing nature. This book reflects the preponderance of non English-language sources, especially since much of it is truly outstanding. However, although many French-language sources are seminal, and in some fields the material in French is overwhelmingly dominant, readers should be aware that by the mid-1990s considerable information had developed in the English language as well. This book specifically reviews such works where their value is significant, at other times only referring to this material within the context of a main entry in English or German.

Theses and Dissertations on Togo

Kao Abi. 'Les attitudes des Togolaises à l'égard de la polygenie' (Attitudes of the Togolese with regard to polygeny), PhD dissertation, University of Bordeaux, 1988.

Comlan R. Aboki. 'Essai de formulation d'une problematique de développement à partie de l'étude de développement sociale Kuma' (Essay on the formulation of a development problem, stemming from the study of Kuma social development), PhD dissertation, University of Paris, 1973.

Agbakenyo Jossi Adabra. 'L'action sanitaire au Togo' (Sanitary action in Togo.), PhD dissertation, University of Paris, 1979.

Samuel Suka Adabra. 'Les autorités traditionnelles et le pouvoir politique moderne au Togo' (Traditional authorities and modern political power in Togo), PhD dissertation, University of Paris, 1973.

M. Agier. 'Réseaux marchands, réseaux sociaux. Les commerçands soudanais du quartier zongo de Lomé' (Merchant networks, social networks. Sudanese business people in the Zongo quarter of Lomé), PhD dissertation, University of Paris, 1981.

Honorat Aguessy. 'Essai sur le myth de Legba' (Essay on the myth of Legba), PhD dissertation, University of Paris, 1973.

Sébastien Komi Ahado. 'Analyse de la relation entre l'education et quelques charactéristiques du talent managériel chez les propriétaires gestionnaires du secteur informel au Togo' (Analysis of the relationship between education and several characteristics of the managerial skills of managing directors in the informal sector in Togo), PhD dissertation, Laval University, 1992.

Pierre-Lawoetry Ajavon. 'Le mort chez les Guins du sud Togo' (Death among the Guin of south Togo), PhD dissertation, University of Bordeaux, 1980.

Pierre Alexandre. 'Political institutions of the Kotokoli, a tribe of northern Togo', PhD dissertation, University of London, 1959.

Iwuoha Edozie Aligwekwe. 'The Ewe and the Togoland problem: a case study in the paradoxes and problems of political transition in West Africa', PhD dissertation, University of Ohio, 1961.

Helmut K. Anheier. 'Private voluntary organizations, networks and development in Africa – Nigeria, Senegal and Togo', PhD dissertation, Yale University, 1986.

William Oscar Anku. 'Procedures in African drumming: a study of Akan/Ewe traditions and African drumming in Pittsburgh', PhD dissertation, University of Pittsburgh, 1988.

Dayoka Awissi. 'Contribution à l'étude de l'étiologie des gastro-enérites au Togo' (Contribution to the study of the etiology of gastro-enteritis in Togo), PhD dissertation, University of Quebec, 1981.

Karen Coffyn Biraimah. 'The impact of gender-differentiated education on Third World women's expectations: a Togolese case study', PhD dissertation, SUNY/Buffalo, 1982.

Suzanne Preston Blier. 'Architecture and the Tamberma', PhD dissertation, Columbia University, 1981.

E. Yao Bocco. 'Peuples et nationalisme, les partis ewe et l'église évangélique du Togo' (Peoples and nationalism, the Ewe groups and the evangelical church in Togo), PhD dissertation, University of Poitiers, 1982.

Florence M. Bouret. 'The Gold Coast and the British mandate of Togoland, 1919-1939', PhD dissertation, Stanford University, 1947.

Peter Buhler. 'The Volta region of Ghana: economic change in Togoland, 1850-1914', PhD dissertation, University of California at San Diego, 1975.

David Wayne Cheser. 'Effects of age, sex and cultural habitat on the development of Piagetian spatial concepts among rural and urban children from Togo', PhD dissertation, George Peabody College for Teachers, 1978.

Fogote Dipere. 'Le nouveau droit du mariage au Togo' (New marriage laws in Togo), PhD dissertation, University of Lille, 1989.

Lubin Kobla Doe. 'A simple macroeconomic model of Togo', PhD dissertation, University of Arizona, 1979.

M. K. Doku. 'Economics, foreign aid and foreign policy', PhD dissertation, Claremont College, 1972.

Samuel Ferjus. 'Le mise en valeur du Togo sous mandat français' (The development of Togo under French mandate), PhD dissertation, University of Paris, 1976.

David George Francis. 'Individual characteristics and structural effects as predicators of adoption of improved agricultural practices in Togo', PhD dissertation, Cornell University, 1971.

Amévi Gbedefé Gbégnon. 'Education and modernization in Togo since independence', PhD dissertation, University of Southern California, 1988.

Daté Fodio Gbikpi-Benissan. 'La chefferie dans la nation contemporaine: essaie de sociologie politique sur la chefferie en pays Bassari, Akposso et Mina' (Chiefdom in the contemporary nation: political sociology essay on chiefdom in Bassari, Akposso and Mina territory), PhD dissertation, University of Paris, 1976.

Candice L. Goucher. 'The iron industry of Bassar', PhD dissertation, University of California, Los Angeles, 1984.

Eugene Emil Grau. 'The Evangelical Presbyterian Church of Ghana and Togo', PhD dissertation, Hartford Seminary Foundation, 1964.

Sandra E. Greene. 'The Anlo-Ewe: their economy, society and external relations in the eighteenth century', PhD dissertation, Northwestern University, 1981.

Raymond Guillaneuf. 'La presse au Togo (1911-1966)' (The press in Togo [1911-1966]), PhD dissertation, University of Dakar, 1967.

Charles Théodore Hein. 'Adult literacy and adult language preference for the language of instruction and mass media in selected adult populations of southern Togo', PhD dissertation, University of Wisconsin, 1975.

Zokia Houndedoke. 'La femme ewe du sud du Togo' (Ewe women in the south of Togo), PhD dissertation, University of Limoges, 1989.

Gary Leighton Jones. 'Training leaders concerning spiritual issues for the growth of the church in Togo', DMin dissertation, Fuller Theological Seminary, 1993.

N. Kakaye. 'L'administration locale togolaise et ses problèmes' (Togolese local administration and its problems), PhD dissertation, University of Paris, 1978.

Arthur J. Knoll. 'Togo under German administration 1884-1910', PhD dissertation, Yale University, 1964.

Mensah Kodjo. 'Elements pour une sociologie politique de la vie togolaise' (Elements for a political sociology of Togolese life), PhD dissertation, University of Paris, 1967.

Akrima Eyadete Kogoe. 'Assessment of school effectiveness and professional needs of school administrators in the Republic of Togo', PhD dissertation, Southern Illinois University at Carbondale, 1981.

Ahlonko Komlan. 'Les politiques scolaires au Togo, 1884-1960' (School politics in Togo, 1884-1960), PhD dissertation, University of Geneva, 1982.

Ayi Foly Kouèvi. 'Effets de structures et de termes de l'echange sur le disequilibre du commerce extèrieure et la croissance intense du Togo 1921-1967. Etude complementaire sur l'évolution recente 1960-1967' (The effects of structure and of terms of exchange on the disequilibrium of foreign business and the intense growth of Togo, 1921-1967. Complementary study of the recent evolution, 1960-1967), PhD dissertation, University of Paris, 1969.

Corneille Kodjo Koulekey. 'Modèles mathematiques de précipitation: application à l'étude régionale de la pluviométrie au Togo' (Mathematical models of rainfall: application to the regional study of rainfall in Togo), PhD dissertation, University of Laval, 1978.

T. Koulon. 'Agriculture et aménagement rural au Togo: le Kabyé du Nord-Togo' (Agriculture and rural management in Togo: the Kabre of north Togo), PhD dissertation, University of Clermont-Ferrand, 1985.

Paul Robert Kozelka. 'The development of national languages: a case study of language planning in Togo', PhD dissertation, Stanford University, 1984.

Adjoa Hélène Kpeglo-Womas. 'Evaluation des besoins en formation des travailleurs sociaux de la région africaine: le cas du Togo' (Evaluation of the training needs of social workers in the African area: the case of Togo), PhD dissertation, University of Laval, 1981.

Kangni-Simon Kpodar. 'La lepre au Togo' (Leprosy in Togo), PhD dissertation, University of Paris, 1950.

Christine Mullen Kreamer. 'The art and ritual of the Moba of northern Togo', PhD dissertation, Indiana University, 1986.

Ayenam Kwobie. 'An economic analysis of the farmer resettlement project in northern Togo', PhD dissertation, University of West Virginia, 1982.

Antoine Lawrence. 'De l'assistance technique des Nations-Unies et les objectifs des plans de développement des pays africains: Togo, R.C.A.' (On the technical assistance of the United Nations and the aims of development plans in African countries: Togo, RCA), PhD dissertation, University of Paris, 1977.

Jacques Le Cornec. 'Le statut du Togo' (Togo law), PhD dissertation, University of Paris, 1957.

Marshall Lewis. 'Verb serialization in Gen and the structure of events', PhD dissertation, Indiana University, 1993.

David Lawrence Locke. 'The music of the Atsiagbeko', PhD dissertation, Wesleyen University, 1979.

Samba Mademba. 'Les institutions municipales en Afrique occidentales française au Togo et au Cameroun' (French West African municipal institutions in Togo and Cameroon), PhD dissertation, University of Paris, 1957.

Raphaela-Maria Marx. 'Sprachpraxis und Diskurs über Sprache: Französisch und Ewe im sudlichen Togo' (Linguistic practice and discourse on speech: French and Ewe in south Togo), PhD dissertation, University of Vienna, 1990.

Martin Meyer. 'Die Entwicklung des Medizinalwasser in der Republik Togo' (The development of medicinal waters in the Republic of Togo), MD dissertation, Wurtzburg University, 1987.

Douti Nalouara. 'Le système coopératif, un instrument de développement économique et social pour le monde rural togolais' (The co-operative system, an instrument of economic and social development for the Togolese rural world), PhD dissertation, University of Sherbrooke, 1985.

Germaine Niqueux. 'La situation alimentaire au Togo' (The nutritional situation in Togo), PhD dissertation, University of Paris, 1984.

Louis P. O'Brien. 'The Togo rural water sanitation development project in the context of community hand-pump maintenance', PhD dissertation, University of California/Los Angeles, 1986.

Honoré K. Patokideou. 'Les civilisations patriarcales des Kabré face aux programmes modernes de développement économique et social' (Patriarchal civilizations of the Kabre faced with modern economic and social development programmes), PhD dissertation, University of Paris, 1970.

Charles Piot. 'Production, exchange and symbolic forms among the Kabre', PhD dissertation, University of Virginia, 1986.

Diana Rey-Hulman. 'Les bilingualismes littéraires, signification sociale de la littérature orale chez les Tyokossi' (Literary bilingualism, the social significance of the oral literature of the Chokossi), PhD dissertation, Sorbonne University, 1976.

Sabit A. Salami. 'A l'héritage de la technique du conte africain dans l'oeuvre de Félix Couchoro' (On the heritage of the technique of African story-telling in the work of Félix Conchoro), PhD dissertation, University of Sherbrooke, 1979.

Seth Sewonou. 'Le sacrifice dans la croyance traditionnelle des Ewe' (Sacrifice in the traditional beliefs of the Ewe), PhD dissertation, University of Paris, 1967.

Dadja Halla-Kawa Simtaro. 'Le Togo "Musterkolonie", souvenir de l'Allemagne dans la société togolaise' (Togo, 'Musterkolonie', the memory of Germany in Togolese society), PhD dissertation, Aix-en-Provence, 1982.

David George Stillman. 'Population-related policy: a framework for analysis with examination of two cases: Ghana and Togo', PhD dissertation, Duke University, 1974.

Albert Surgy. 'La divination par Afa chez les Evhe du littoral' (Afa divination among the coastal Ewe), PhD dissertation, University of Paris, 1976.

Thiou Tchamié. 'Contribution à l'étude des savanes du Togo centrale' (Contribution to the study of the prairies of central Togo), PhD dissertation, University of Bordeaux, 1988.

Daké Trimua-Ekom. 'Naissance et développement de l'église évangélique au Togo, 1847-1980' (Birth and development of the evangelical church in Togo, 1847-1980), PhD dissertation, University of Strasbourg, 1983.

C. Van Dyck. 'An analytic study of folk-tales of selected peoples of West Africa', PhD dissertation, Oxford University, 1967.

Jean Verdier. 'Structure et imaginaire dans le conte togolais' (Structure and imagination in Togolese folk-tales), PhD dissertation, University of Grenoble, 1970.

Marcel Voule-Fritz. 'La fonction publique du Togo. Origine, évolution, perspectives' (Public office in Togo. Origins, evolution, prospects), PhD dissertation, University of Paris, 1966.

Ella Ozier Yu. 'Theoretical aspects of noun classes in Lama, Togo', PhD dissertation, University of Illinois, Urbana-Champaign, 1991.

Senouvo Zinsou. 'Le théâtre et la Bible: la Katata togolaise et le syncretisme culturel' (Theatre and the Bible: the Katata of Togo and cultural syncretism), PhD dissertation, University of Bordeaux, 1989.

The Country and Its People

1 **Connaissance du Togo.**
Boulogne, France: Editions Delroisse, 1970. 188p.
This is a profusely illustrated book that captures the essence and beauty of Togo. It is part of a series on the various countries of the world.

2 **Letters from Togo.**
Susan Blake. Iowa City, Iowa: University of Iowa Press, 1991. 179p.
In this book Blake presents her reminiscences of Togo and recounts her experiences as a Fulbright scholar and teacher in the country. She describes her 'settling-in' problems, and how she learned to behave and think in a different way in the context of her new environment. The author was based primarily in the Lomé region, and writes the book in the form of chronologically-arranged momentos of key events.

3 **Paysans africains: des Africains s'unisssent pour améliorer leur village au Togo.** (African peasants: Africans unite to ameliorate their village in Togo.)
Rémi Mangeart. Paris: Harmattan, 1984. 301p.
This is an eminently readable and graphic account, accompanied by pictures, of the daily lives of common farmers in twelve Kabre villages in an area south of Kara, and how they were trying to uplift themselves. The book describes their lives from birth to death, what they eat and where they live, how they cultivate their plots of land and what measures they were undertaking, at the time, to develop their region.

4 **Le Togo: des origines à nos jours.** (Togo: from its origins to the present day.)
Robert Cornevin. Paris: Académie des Sciences d'Outre-mer, 1988. 556p. bibliog. illust.
By far the best and most comprehensive single volume on Togo, this is now in its third edition, the first having appeared in 1959 as *Histoire du Togo* (Paris:

Berger-Levrault). It is a scholarly work written by the prolific and well-known colonial 'administrator-turned-academic', and is a masterful, thorough and encyclopaedic study of all aspects of Togo. The book covers the geography of the country, outlines its prehistory, and is especially strong on the history and ethnography of Togo's various peoples. Further smaller sections consider virtually every other aspect of Togo and the Togolese. The work is supported by fifty-three plates, numerous sketches, diagrams, tables and maps, and concludes with a comprehensive seventy-three-page bibliography. The latter largely ignores anglophone literature and is printed in running style that saves much space but is difficult to refer to. The book's weakness lies in its political timidity: the post-independence era merits only a cursory summary, and few of the harsher authoritarian features of the régime of General Eyadema surface in the brief section devoted to the latter's twenty-two years (at the time of publication) of misrule in Togo.

5 Le Togo.
Yvonne François.   Paris: Karthala, 1993. 189p. maps. plates.

A comprehensive, up-to-date work which surveys, with great insight, the country, its economy and its social and religious life, and which also contains chapters on the daily life of its different peoples. Included in the text is information on music, literature, health and education, as well as a lengthy chapter for prospective visitors, which provides details on tourist circuits and hotels. This is one of the best general monographs on Togo.

6 Togo: portrait of a West African francophone republic.
A. A. Curkeet.   Jefferson, North Carolina: McFarland, 1993. 216p.

A perceptive description of a summer spent in Togo by a Quebecois environmental consultant who was a guest of a Peace Corps volunteer in the country. Though the visit took place in 1983, Curkeet has updated her narrative to include references to the massive popular opposition to General Eyadema's régime. Although conversational in tone, this is much more than the recollections of a trip to Togo and is based on lengthy and careful research.

7 The village of waiting.
George Packer.   New York: Random House, 1984. 316p. map.

This book is a readable, sympathetic account of the life and tribulations of an American English-language teacher who served in a Togolese village with the Peace Corps between 1982 and 1983.

Togo.
See item no. 557.

Togo.
See item no. 562.

Travel and Tourism

8 **Lomé: capitale du Togo.** (Lomé: capital of Togo.)
   Bernard Gerard , et al.   Boulogne, France: Editions Delroisse, 1975.
   128p.

This largely pictorial book on Lomé and its urban population is part of the Delroisse series on Africa. Although, since the book's publication, the city has changed a lot through the urban renewal programmes of the late 1970s, this is a pleasant reminder of the provincial tranquility of the past. The book contains many beautiful pictures and most photographs are in colour. Possibly also of interest are the eight pages of colour photographs from Togo in the slim volume *Beautés du monde: l'Afrique Occidentale* (Beauties of the world: West Africa). Paris: Larousse, 1980, p. 1-8.

9 **The People's Republic of Benin and the Republic of Togo.**
   British Overseas Trade Board.   London: British Overseas Trade Board,
   1976. 63p.

This is a businessman's guide to the two countries. Besides some brief standard tourist information, including a map of Lomé, this manual includes useful material on the methods of 'doing business' in Togo.

10 **Togo.**
   Paris: Group J.A., 1977. 64p.

Part of a series on African markets, this is a manual intended for businessmen. It includes overviews of the economy, information on imports and exports and the code of investment, an outline of Togo's internal road transport, and concludes with practical tourist information for business visitors.

3

11 **Togo.**

Sylvia Ardyne Boone. In: *West African travels: a guide to people and places.* New York: Random House, 1974, p. 289-308.

Though dated, this is still a useful survey of the tourist possibilities of Togo, with brief details on sites of interest. See also: Latour B. Benot, 'Le "village du Bénin": une création originale à vacations multiples' ('Benin village': an original creation for various vacations). *Afrique Littéraire et Artistique,* vol. 30 (Nov. 1973), p. 43-46; R. Harrington, 'The Republic of Togo, West Africa'. *Travel,* 3 June 1970, p. 71-73; Kohou Nassou, 'Le Togo mise en valeur sur le tourisme' (Togo develops tourism). *Europe-Outre-mer,* no. 594 (July 1979), p. 21-25; 'La politique touristique' (Tourist policy). *Europe-Outre-mer,* no. 587 (March-April 1978), p. 53-56; Robert S. Kane, 'Togo'. In: *Africa from A to Z* . Garden City, New York: Doubleday, 1961.

12 **Togo.**

Geoff Crowther. In: *Africa on a shoestring.* Berkeley, California: Lonely Planet Publishers, 1992, p. 629-37.

Periodically updated, this book puts its emphasis on budget travel, and contains some valuable information that other guidebooks do not provide. This includes details on border crossings and internal travel. The chapter on Togo is somewhat leaner than those on other countries of comparable tourist interest, but is nonetheless very valuable. For an earlier, but similar guide see: Susan Blumenthal, 'Togo'. In: *Bright Continent. A shoestring guide to subsaharan Africa.* New York: Anchor Books, 1974, p. 242-60.

13 **Togo.**

In: *Guide de voyageur, Afrique de l'Ouest* (Travellers' guide, West Africa.) Paris: Ediafric, 1984, p. 261-70.

Condensed information for the tourist visiting Togo is provided in this section. See also: Arlette Eyraud, *Cote d'Ivoire, Haute Volta, Bénin, Togo* (Ivory Coast, Upper Volta, Benin, Togo). Paris: Hatier, 1976, p. 186-202.

14 **Togo.**

David Else. In: *Backpacker's Africa: a guide to West and Central Africa for walkers and overland travellers.* Chalfont St. Peter, England: Bradt Publishers, 1990, p. 212-30.

Designed primarily for the backpacker and other budget travellers, this book contains information on Togo which is not normally found in other travel guides. It includes basic data on the country, its entry and exit regulations, information on securing third-country visas in Lomé, and a town-by-town outline of points of interest.

15 **Togo.**

In: *Travellers guide to West Africa.* Edited by Alan Rake. London: IC Publications, 1988, 7th ed., p. 263-71.

This periodically updated travel guide contains information on the entire region of West Africa, including thumbnail details on Togo. For an additional, though dated source, see: Philip M. Allen, Aaron Segal, 'Togo'. In: *The traveler's Africa: a guide to the entire continent.* New York: Hopkinson & Blake, 1973, p. 661-70.

16 **Togo.**
Jim Hudgens, Richard Trillo. In: *West Africa: the rough guide.*
London: Harrap-Columbus, 1990, 2nd ed., p. 834-61.

A useful introductory section (p. 1-72) is provided in this guide to West Africa, followed by sections on the different countries, including Togo. These offer brief histories on each country and tourist information about the various parts of the country, as well as a directory of budget accommodation and restaurants, and an array of travel tips.

17 **Togo.**
Sherry A. Shuttles, Billye Shuttles-Graham. In: *Fielding's Africa south of the Sahara.* New York: Fielding Travel Books, 1986, p. 156-84.

This chapter provides comprehensive tourist information on Togo, which includes: hotels; restaurants; travel tips; data on each of the larger towns; and sites of interest to the tourist, the most unusual of which is a list of various fetish centres, something that is not available in any other guide. There are concise summaries of Togo's history and economy, and a brief section of key words in the Ewe language of the south.

18 **Le Togo aujourd'hui.** (Togo today.)
Maurice Piraux. Paris: Editions Jeune Afrique, 1977. 230p. bibliog.

In spite of its date, this is one of the best tourist books on Togo, and certainly the most colourful. Containing ninety-six colour photographs and sixteen itinerary-maps, this work provides information on all aspects of the country, such as: hotels; restaurants; shopping; tourist sights; as well as historical and cultural background material.

19 **Togo. Les hommes et leur milieu.** (Togo. The people and their setting.)
Bernard Passot. Paris: Harmattan, 1988. 193p.

This work is a comprehensive and extremely detailed guide to all aspects of Togo. It will be of great use to both the casual traveller and to the longer-term visitor, since it contains a detailed section on commerce; trade; industry; details on the daily life of the Togolese; and the problems of expatriates in the country. There is also detailed coverage, interspersed with photographs, of every region, town and village in Togo and information about hotels, tourist sights, restaurants and local customs. The book is written by an author with a wealth and depth of knowledge of the country, contains a great deal of material not available in any other source, and is currently the best single volume for anyone contemplating a serious visit to Togo.

20 **Togo.**
Alex Newton. In: *West Africa, a travel survival kit.* Berkeley, California: Lonely Planet Publications, 1992, p. 349-428.

Now in its second edition, this travel guide includes a chapter on Togo, which provides an introduction to the country for visitors, a concise account of its history, and a number of good maps. Extensive information about accommodation, restaurants, shopping and sights in Lomé and upcountry, is also presented, all with prices and, when applicable, telephone numbers.

21   **UTA Africa travel guide.**
     Paris: UTA Airlines, 1989. 396p.

The French UTA airline, which had the largest number of flights in Africa, issued and periodically updated this glossy guidebook which seems to be primarily aimed at travel agents and tourist bureaus. The book is well organized by country, with the sections on Togo usually filling around eighteen pages. Including many photographs, especially of hotels, the section on each country presents concise information on its geography, economy, and people, followed by valuable details on: its airports and internal air-links; transport options in Lomé; banks, hotels, and restaurants and their services, addresses and prices; as well as some information about the country's attractions. Early editions (dating from the 1970s) tended to stress overwhelmingly (with individual photographs and very detailed entries) each country's hotels, something that travel agents, and first-time visitors to Africa, found of great value. More recently, however, this section had been de-emphasized in favour of expanded coverage of tourist sights.

Le Togo. (Togo.)
See item no. 5.

Domaine reservée. (Reserved areas.)
See item no. 46.

Geography and Geology

22 **Africa: geography and development.**
   Alan B. Mountjoy, David Hilling.   Totowa, New Jersey: Barnes &
   Noble, 1988. 298p. bibliog.

This is a standard textbook, covering both human and physical geography, and
profusely illustrated with maps, photographs, diagrams and statistical data. The
various African states are dealt with in chapters which group contiguous countries.
For another good general volume, stressing economic geography see: Michael Hodd,
*The economies of Africa: geography, population, stability, structure, economic
performance.* Aldershot, England: Darmouth, 1991. 363p. bibliog.

23 **Annales hydrologiques du Togo de l'année 1971 à l'année 1979.**
   (Hydrological annals of Togo from 1971 to 1979.)
   ORSTOM.   Paris: ORSTOM, 1983. 188p.

The years 1971-79 are covered in this comprehensive statistical compilation of
waterflow data for Togo's various water-basins. The technical data is organized in
tables.

24 **Caractéristiques physico-chimiques des fluvisols inventoriés dans la
   moyenne vallée de l'Oti.** (Physical and chemical characteristics of
   fluvial soils inventoried in the middle valley of the Oti.)
   K. L. Allagle.   In: *Fourth meeting of the West African Sub-committee
   for soil correlation and land evaluation.*   Rome: Food and Agriculture
   Organization, 1981, p. 24-58. bibliog.

This technical article is an analysis of the geomorphology of the Oti River valley and
a breakdown and classification of the fluvial soils in its middle courses.

25 **Climatology of West Africa.**
Derek F. Hayward, Julius S. Oguntoyinbo. London: Hutchinson,
1987. 271p. bibliog.

A comprehensive study of the climate of West Africa, which includes the effect of the
climate on water resources, agriculture, health, population patterns and transport.
There are a large number of charts and statistical tables, as well as an extensive
bibliography. For a similar earlier text see Oyediran Ojo, *The climate of West Africa*.
London; Ibadan, Nigeria: Heinemann Educational Books, 1977. 219p. bibliog.

26 **Contribution à l'étude géologique du bassin sedimentaire côtier du
Dahomey et du Togo.** (Contribution to a study of the coastal
sedimentary basin of Dahomey and Togo.)
Maurice Slansky.   Paris: Editions Technip, 1962. 270p. bibliog.

This constitutes a thorough geological study of the coastal areas of Benin and Togo.
The survey, which is replete with plates, maps and diagrams, involved stratigraphic
and petrographic analysis aimed at identifying sedimentary rocks, and detecting
phosphates and other resources. For a more recent geological survey see H. Cappetta,
M. Traverse 'Une riche faune dans le bassin à phosphate de Kpogame-Hahotoe' (A
rich fauna in the phosphate basin of Kpogame-Hahotoe). *Geobios* (Lyon), vol. 21,
no. 3 (1988), p. 359-65.

27 **Etude géologique et structurale du nord-ouest Dahomey, du nord
Togo et du sud-est de la Haute Volta.** (Geological and structural
study of north-west Dahomey, north Togo and south-east Upper Volta.)
Pascal Affaton.   Saint Jérôme, Canada: Laboratoires des Sciences de
la Terre, 1975. 203p. bibliog. maps.

Part of a regional study, this work includes a geological survey of northern Togo. See
also: R. Poss, G. Rossi, 'Systèmes de versants et évolution morphopédologique au
nord Togo' (Hilly systems and the morphopedology of north Togo). *Zeitschrift für
Geomorphologie*, vol. 31, no. 1 (1987), p. 21-43.

28 **Etudes pédohydrologiques au Togo: contribution aux études pour
la mise en valeur des régions sud et nord.** (Pedohydrological studies
in Togo: a contribution to studies for the exploitation of the northern
and southern regions.)
Food and Agriculture Organization.   Rome: FAO, 1967. 3 vols. bibliog.

This three-volume study on Togo is accompanied by numerous maps and diagrams
and represents a comprehensive soil and hydrological survey of the entire country.
Assisted by the United Nations development programme and conducted by France's
ORSTOM, the study was aimed at pinpointing resources that might open up new
areas to development. For a soil analysis of the region of Bassar see A. Le Cocq,
Carte pédologique et carte des capacités agronomiques des sols: région de Bassar
(Pedological map, and map of the agronomic capacity of soils: the region of Bassar).
Paris: ORSTOM, 1986. 48p. In addition, a geological survey and study of soils and
soil-erosion in central Togo, can be found in: Jurgen Runge, 'Geomorphological
depressions and present-day erosion processes on the plantation surface of Central
Togo'. *Erkunde* (Bonn), vol. 45, no. 1 (1991), p. 52-65.

29 **L'évolution bioclimatique actuelle de la région des plateaux, sud-est du Togo.** (The bioclimatic evolution of the plateaux region, south-east Togo.)
G. Rossi. *Revue de Géomorphologie Dynamique* (Paris), vol. 33, no. 2 (1984), p. 57-72. maps. English summary.
In this important article, Rossi sums up research which was conducted in South-east Togo under the auspices of the French Ministry of Cooperation. Bio-climatic research revealed an irregular but gradual 'sensitive drying up process of the climate' (p.57) which was affecting this lush region of cocoa and coffee groves. Although there has not been an appreciable decline in precipitation the result has been a shift from an equatorial climate (with four seasons) to a South Guinean climate with two seasons and a longer period of high intensity harmattan winds. Climatological data for the 1950s (comprising tables with no text) from various meteorological stations in French West Africa, including Togo, can be found in: *Extraits des annales des services meteorologiques de la France d'outre-mer* (Extracts of the records of the meteorological services of Overseas France). Paris: Service Central de la Meteorologie de la France d'Outre-mer, 1963. 205p.

30 **Les forêts du Togo et du Dahomey.** (The forests of Togo and Dahomey.)
A. Aubreville. *Bulletin du Comité d'Etudes Historiques et Scientifiques de l'AOF* (Dakar), vol. 20, no. 1/2 (Jan.-June 1937), p. 1-112.
This early work on the forest regions of Togo and Dahomey (Benin), which have been much depleted since publication, still remains the definitive, and much-cited, classic on the subject.

31 **Geology and mineral resources of West Africa.**
Edited by J. B. Wright. London: George Allen & Unwin, 1985. 187p. bibliog.
This is an advanced geological textbook that provides thumbnail portraits of the geology and mineral resources of each country in West Africa, including Togo. The book includes a comprehensive glossary of terms and indices.

32 **Geomorphological depressions (bas-fonds) and present-day erosion processes on the plantation surface of Central Togo, West Africa.**
Jurgen Runge. *Erkunde* (Bonn), vol. 45, no. 1 (1991), p. 52-65. bibliog.
A large number of maps, diagrams, photographs and plans are included in this geological analysis of the depressions (called *bas-fonds* in French) found in part of the Central region in Togo.

33   **Ground water in North and West Africa.**
Economic Commission for Africa.   New York: United Nations, 1988.
405p. bibliog.

This is the first of two volumes on ground water covering the whole of Africa. It is organized in the form of two sections, a short one that provides a general overview of the region, followed by the bulk of the text (p. 19-396) which deals with specific countries. The material presented includes an inventory of ground water and its exploitation, as well as a general geological survey of each country.

34   **Hydrologie et hydrochimie d'un milieu lagunaire tropical.**
(Hydrology and hydrochemistry of a tropical lagoon area.)
Bertrand Millet.   Paris: ORSTOM, 1986. 228p. bibliog.

Originally presented as a PhD dissertation at the University of Paris, this is the first comprehensive and detailed study of the water chemistry and geology of the coastal Lake Togo, which is situated east of Lomé and near Togo's phosphate mines. The author first discusses the etiology of lagoons in general, and then undertakes a geological, geomorphological and oceanographic analysis of Lake Togo itself. He concludes with an extensive bibliography (p. 215-24).

35   **Pedogenese sur le socle granito-gneissique du Togo: differentiation des sols et remaniements superficiels.** (Origins of the granite bedplate of Togo: soil differentiation and superficial modifications.)
André Leveque.   Paris: ORSTOM, 1979. 224p. bibliog. plates.

Leveque has produced a wide-ranging study of the granite bedplate, soil formation, and soil mineralogy of four selected sites in Togo.

36   **Synthèse lithostratigraphique du precambrien supérieur infratillitique du bassin des Volta au Nord Togo.** (Lithostratigraphic synthesis of the infratillitic Upper Precambrian of the Volta basin in northern Togo.)
J. J. Drouet, et al.   In: *Géologie africaine: volume en hommage à L. Cahen.*   Edited by J. Klerkx, J. Michot.   Tervuren, Belgium: Musée Royal de l'Afrique Centrale, 1984. p. 217-25. bibliog.

This is a basic geological study of a long and complex sedimentary cycle that formed part of the Upper Volta basin in northern Togo.

37   **Les sols de la Kara.** (The soils of La Kara.)
Paul Faure, A. Forget.   Paris: ORSTOM, 1985. 281p. bibliog.

The authors provide a detailed analysis in this work of the soils in the La Kara region. It is a heavily populated area and suffers from acute soil degradation.

38 **Togo: diversity in miniature.**
R. J. Harrison Church. In: *West Africa: a study of the environment and of man's use of it.* London: Longman, 1980, 8th ed., p. 396-405. maps. plates.

A brief overview of Togo's geology, geography and relief is contained in this classic English-language geography text on West Africa.

39 **Togo: official standard names approved by the United States Board on Geographic names.**
Washington, DC: Board on Geographic Names, 1966. 100p.

An alphabetically-organized directory of 7,000 entries of places and features in Togo, as approved by the Board for cartography purposes. It should be noted, however, that this gazetteer was published before the various changes in town-names in Togo of the early 1970s.

Le Togo: des origines à nos jours. (Togo: from its origins to the present day.)
See item no. 4.

Le Togo. (Togo.)
See item no. 5.

Togo. Les hommes et leur milieu. (Togo. The people and their setting.)
See item no. 19.

Ecology

40 **La secheresse de 1982-83 et ses conséquences sur l'approvisionnement en eau potable de la ville d'Atakpamé.** (The 1982-83 drought and its effect on the supply of drinking water to the town of Atakpamé.)
G. Kwami Nyassogbo. Lomé: Université du Bénin, Département de Géographie, 1985. 57p.

The 1982-83 drought was the most serious to occur in Togo in thirty-three years. This is a report on its effect on the supply of drinking water to residents of Atakpamé and their reactions to it. The account is partly based on a 154-item questionnaire which was administered to long-term residents of the town. It includes a historical overview of droughts in the region, basic rainfall data and an analysis of the dimensions of the water crisis. In addition, the effect of the drought on the town's citizens is analysed, along with the ways in which they perceived, and tried to cope with it, including the use of religious and magic ceremonies. Some suggestions on how similar future crises can be averted are proposed.

41 **The impact of German colonial rule on the forests of Togo.**
Candice L. Goucher. In: *World deforestation in the twentieth century.* Edited by J. F. Richards, R. P. Tucker. Durham, North Carolina: Duke University Press, 1988. p. 56-69.

This article examines the degree to which even the short German colonial era depleted forest reserves in Togo, especially along the coast.

Les sols de la Kara. (The soils of La Kara.)
See item no. 37.

12

Flora and Fauna

42   **The bats of West Africa.**
D. R. Rosevear.   London: British Museum, 1965. 418p. bibliog.
Rosevear has compiled a comprehensive guide to the ninety-seven species of bats in West Africa, illustrated with 232 line drawings and preceded by a general introduction.

43   **Birds of West Central and Western Africa.**
C. W. Macwirth-Praed, C. H. B. Grant.   London: Longman, 1970, 1973. 2 vols.
Some 1,371 birds found in West Africa are included in this substantial inventory, which is illustrated with numerous colour plates and drawings. Small maps next to each entry pinpoint the areas where the birds are normally found.

44   **The carnivores of West Africa.**
D. R. Rosevear.   London: British Museum, 1974. 548p. bibliog.
This wide-ranging work catalogues each of the carnivores found in West Africa, providing details about their skull structure, habits, normal habitats and taxonomy. There are eleven colour photographs, 172 drawings and an extensive bibliography and index.

45   **Contribution aux études éthnobotaniques et floristiques au Togo.**
(Contribution to ethno-botanical and flower studies in Togo.)
Agence de Cooperation Culturelle et Technique.   Paris: Agence de Cooperation Culturelle et Technique, 1987. 671p. bibliog.
This lengthy volume resulted from the efforts of a large research team, led by Professor Adjanohoun, on a number of extensive field studies, on behalf of the ACCT 'Médecine traditionnelle et pharmacopée' series. It includes a large number of sketches and maps in what is the most comprehensive identification, enumeration and

classification imaginable of the country's flora and medicinal plants. There are also substantial indices, in Latin and in vernacular languages, of the plants that are used locally for medicinal purposes, and lists of individuals in the country with ethnobotanical experience. In 1988 Adjanohoun's more specific study, of plants used for traditional medicinal purposes, was published: *Médecine traditionnelle et pharmacopée* (Traditional medicine and pharmacopoeia). Paris: Agence de Cooperation Culturelle et Technique, 1986).

46 **Domaine reservée: la protection de la faune.** (Reserved areas: the protection of fauna.)
Louis Merlet. *Politique Africaine*, no. 27 (Sept.-Oct. 1987), p. 55-66. English summary.

A study of wildlife and nature reserves in Togo in which the author describes how the country's policy of conserving its remaining wildlife has been very enlightened and is a priority concern even to the detriment, if necessary, of rural development. There is, however, an atmosphere of secrecy about the whole issue that the author deplores. He continues with a detailed listing of all forest reserves and national parks, their wildlife, and relevant problems.

47 **A field guide to the birds of West Africa.**
William Serle, Gérard Morel. London: Collins, 1977. 351p.

This guide covers 1,097 species of birds, some of which are only mentioned briefly, and 515 of which are accompanied by illustrations (half in colour) and plates. The guide includes Latin as well as European names.

48 **Flore analytique du Togo.** (Analysis of Togo's flora.)
J. F. Brunel, P. Hiepko, H. Scholz. Berlin: Botanischer Garten und Botanisches Museums Berlin-Dahlem, 1984. 751p. bibliog.

This massive and definitive botanical tome is the product of ten years of research, although it still leaves some fifteen per cent of Togo's flora unidentified. The work comprises of a detailed catalogue, divided into fifteen large family groups, of Togo's vegetation, and concludes with a thirty-page bibliography.

49 **Forest elephants of Togo.**
African Wildlife (Cape Town), vol. 46, no. 2 (March-April 1993), p. 71-75. plates.

Contains a brief description, accompanied by photographs, of the dwindling herds of elephants in Togo.

50 **The grasshopper faunas of the savannas of Mali, Niger, Benin and Togo.**
L. D. C. Fishpool, G. B. Popov. *Bulletin d'IFAN*, vol. 43, no. 3/4 (July-Oct. 1981), p. 275-410.

Presents a wide-ranging survey of the acridoid fauna of the region, of which 214 are identified and decribed, together with their basic ecological survival strategies.

51   **Médecine et 'remèdes miracles' des plantes chez nous.** (Medicines
and 'miracle cures' of plants among us.)
They Ahaligah Komi Ayissi.   Lomé: self-published, 1989. 2 vols.

This is a remarkable inventory of medicinal plants found in Togo, which were used
historically, and to some extent to this day, as miracle cures for various maladies. The
volumes include the plant names in Latin, French, Ewe, Kabre and other African
languages, together with an indication of their use. The author, maintaining that these
are distinct from fetish cures, had the knowledge passed down to him by his grand-
father, who was a traditional healer.

52   **Medicinal plants in tropical West Africa.**
Bep Oliver-Bever.   Cambridge, England: Cambridge University Press,
1986. 375p. bibliog.

This is a seminal work, and an expansion of the author's previous monograph on
Nigerian plants. The book includes an introduction on the use of local plants for
medicinal purposes by traditional healers, followed by a comprehensive inventory of
the specific plants found in West Africa, their medical uses and their pharmacological
effects. The study is illustrated throughout with watercolours, and thoroughly
indexed.

53   **The rodents of West Africa.**
D. R. Rosevear.   London: British Museum, 1969. 604p. bibliog.

Rosevear has prepared an exhaustive catalogue of the rodents of West Africa, which
constitute the largest group of mammals in the region. The detailed descriptions of
each animal are supplemented with several colour plates and 248 line drawings.

54   **West African butterflies and moths.**
John Boorman.   London: Longman, 1970. 79p. bibliog.

In this inventory, which is illustrated with colour photographs and drawings, some
225 varieties of butterflies and moths are listed, grouped by family category.

55   **West African snakes.**
George S. Cansdale.   London: Longman, 1961. 74p.

A number of colour illustrations accompany this inventory of forty-three of the most
common snakes in West Africa. There is also information about the treatment of
snake bites.

56   **West African trees.**
D. Gledhill.   London: Longman, 1972. 72p.

This is a compact introduction to sixty-four of the most common trees in West Africa.
Grouped under six categories, they are illustrated by 121 colour and line drawings.

History

57 **Actes du colloque international sur les civilisations Aja-Ewe.**
(Proceedings of the international colloquium on the Adja-Ewe
civilizations.)
Cotonou, Benin: National University of Benin, 1978. 350p.

The twenty papers collected in this volume, most of which were written by leading
scholars, were presented at a December 1977 conference on the origins and history of
the Adja people, whose various different branches are spread out across a large
geographical area between Nigeria and Ghana. Among the papers, many of which are
in English, are those of: Roberto Pazzi, who discusses the early migrations of the
ancient Adja who eventually settled in Tado, in Togo; Nicoué L. Gayibor, who
focuses on Agokoli, the Adja king under whose oppressive reign the Adja dispersal
took place, with many clans deserting him and some settling in neighbouring Benin
where they originated; and Simon Amegbleame, who discusses Ewe theatre and
literature. Some papers examine Adja groups in either Benin or Ghana, while others
deal with broad cultural, literary, or linguistic matters. The contributions in English
include: Albert Van Danzig, 'Some late seventeenth century British views on the
Slave Coast', p. 85-104; A. S. Asiwaju, 'The Aja-speaking peoples in Nigeria: a note
on their origins, settlement, and cultural adaptation to 1945', p. 105-33; M. A.
Kwamena Poh, 'Traditions of origin of a goun-speaking group in modern Ghana',
p. 195-205; F. Agbodeka, 'The origin of the Republic idea in Eweland', p. 206-12; E.
K. Amenumey, 'The problem of dating the accession of the Ewe people to their
present habitat', p. 213-16; Houkpati Capo, 'Elements of Ewe-gen-Aja-Fon
dialectology', p. 217-41; Kofi Anyidoh, 'The Anlo dirge poet: his life as subject of
his songs', p. 270-80; E. Y. Egbewogbe, 'Personal names as a parameter for the study
of culture: the case of Ghanaian Ewes', p. 281-99; and D. Fiawoo, 'Some reflections
on Ewe social organisation', p. 300-11. The book is important for any study of the
Ghana-Benin coastal areas.

58 **Adjigovi.**
Messan Koffi Kponton Quam-Dessou, Amouzouvi Akakpo. Lomé:
Université du Bénin, Centre d'Etudes et de Recherches de la Tradition
Orale, 1983. 143p.

This work is a fascinating record of the oral history of the foundation of the town of
Aného and the dynasty of Adjigo. Some of the material included, such as the account
of the origins of the Lawsons and other families, is also covered in Fio Agbano's
Histoire de Petit Popo (q.v.), but it is viewed from a different perspective. This is due
to a major historical split and tug-of-war about the primacy of the clans and of the
families of that area. The book reproduces the text of a 1933 booklet, which details
some of these cleavages, as well as various accolades honouring Kponton Quam-
Dessou who died in 1981. Apart from being the head of the Adjigo clan, he was a
famous and multifaceted artist, musician, inventor and curator.

59 **Les Aja-Ewe, essai de reconstitution historique des origines à 1884.**
(The Aja-Ewe, a historical reconstitution from their origins to 1884.)
Nicoué Lodjou Gayibor. Lomé: Université du Bénin, Institut National
des Sciences de l'Education, 1984. 120p.

This is a comprehensive historical survey of the various coastal kingdoms in the
Ghana-Nigeria region. It covers their common origins in Ile-Ife in Nigeria, their trek
to Tado in Togo, and later dispersal to found the kingdoms of Allada, Savi, Abomey,
and Porto Novo (in Benin), and discusses the Ga and Fanti migrations that led to the
creation of the kingdoms of Glidji and Aného in Togo. A somewhat shorter version
exists in the author's more accessible *En savoir plus sur – les peuples et royaumes du
golfe du Bénin* (To better know – the peoples and kingdoms of the Gulf of Guinea).
Lomé: Université du Bénin, Institute National des Sciences de l'Education, 1986.
75p. bibliog.

60 **Atakora mountain refugees. Systems of exploitation in northern
Togo.**
Edward Graham Norris. *Anthropos*, vol. 81, no. 1-3 (1986), p. 109-36.
bibliog.

An overview of the arrival and settlement in the north of Togo of an aggressive 'band
of mercenaries and freebooters' (p. 135) from Côte d'Ivoire in the second half of the
18th century. Settling in the vicinity of Sansanné-Mango, the Anufom (generally
known as the Chokossi, or Tyokossi in French) originally raided their neighbours for
slaves, and, later levied a tribute from them. The author examines the history of the
Chokossi and their social organization, both from their own perspective, and from the
vantage point of the peoples they subjugated. See also: the author's earlier
contribution, 'Genealogical manipulation and social identity in Sansanné-mango,
northern Togo. An Imam-list'. *Bulletin of the School of Oriental and African Studies*,
vol. 45, no. 1 (1982), p. 118-37; and Robert Cornevin, 'Dynasties tyokossi de
Sansanné Mango' (Chokossi dynasties of Sansanné-Mango). *Annales de l'Ecole des
Lettres* (Lomé), vol. 1 (1972), p. 9-24.

61   **Autobiographies d'Africaines.** (African autobiographies.)
      Diedrich Westermann.   Paris: Payot, 1943. 338p.
Westermann, the famous historian and linguist of this part of West Africa wrote this
historical classic, which includes eleven fascinating autobiographies of various
Africans. The texts vary in length, with those on Togo (of Boniface Foli of Glidji
[p. 25-101] and Martin Akou [p. 282-336], who was shortly to become Togo's first
deputy to the French National Assembly) among the longest. Through the verbatim
narrative the author reveals the state of Togo in the 1930s.

62   **Bassar: a quantified, chronologically controlled regional approach
      to a traditional iron production centre in West Africa.**
      Philip de Barros.   *Africa*, vol. 56, no. 2 (1986), p. 148-74. bibliog.
This article, which is accompanied by maps, diagrams and photographs, is an
important, comprehensive study of the historical Bassari iron industry in northern
Togo, which was supplying neighbouring populations with iron implements as early
as the 14th century. De Barros pinpoints sites where smelting took place, based on
archaeological evidence and more contemporary records. He studies Bassari
production methods, assessing their average annual iron output (between seven and
twenty tons, or enough for the needs of some 50,000 people) and effect on the trading
relationships that developed in the region. De Barros also briefly compares the
Bassari sites with other major iron smelting centres in Africa, and with some Roman
sites in Europe. Since iron production continued until the first decades of colonial
rule, when imports from Europe made the local industry obsolete, de Barros argues
for more urgent research on this aspect of African economic history 'if we are to
capture the remaining invaluable ethnographic knowledge still available from those
who actually participated in the indigenous African Iron Age.' (p. 171). See also: the
author's 'Societal repercussions of the rise of large-scale traditional iron production:
a West African example'. *African Archaeological Review* (Cambridge), vol. 6 (1988),
p. 91-113; and 'L'archéologie et préhistoire togolaise' (Archaeology and Togolese
pre-history). *Etudes Togolaises*, no. 23/26 (1983), p. 1-13.

63   **La chefferie dans la nation contemporaine: essai de sociologie
      politique sur la chefferie en pays Bassari, Akposso et Mina.**
      (Chiefdom in the contemporary nation: essay on the political sociology
      of chiefdom among the Bassari, Akposso and Mina.)
      Daté Fodio Gbikpi-Benissan.   Lomé: Service de Reprographie de la
      Bibliothèque Universitaire, 1985. 465p. bibliog.
Originally the author's 1976 PhD dissertation for the Réné Déscartes University in
Paris, this work is a sweeping study of the pre-colonial role of chiefs among the
Bassar, Akposso and Mina peoples. It considers the differential manner in which the
arrival of the French affected the structure of chiefdom and the individuals in power
at that time, and the evolution of the three societies and their chiefs during the
colonial and post-colonial eras. The work, which has several indices and an extensive
bibliography (p. 412-27), synthesizes a great deal of material not easily available
elsewhere. For a micro-study see: A. Othily, *Jéta, un village Mina du sud-est du Togo*
(Jeta, a Mina village in south-east Togo). Lomé: ORSTOM, 1968. 261p.

64 **Colonial distortion of the Volta river salt trade.**
D. J. E. Maier. *African Economic History*, vol. 15 (1986), p. 13-37.
This article reviews the pre-colonial caravan trade-routes in the Volta river region, some of which dissected Togo, and considers their economic underpinnings, and the changes occasioned by the colonial implantation in West Africa. See also: Jack Goody, T. M. Moustapha, 'The caravan trade from Kano to Salaga'. *Journal of the Historical Society of Nigeria*, vol. 3, no. 4 (June 1967), p. 611-16.

65 **Contribution à l'histoire du peuplement: traditions, histoire et organisation de la cité chez les Akposso.** (Contribution to the history of population: traditions, history and the organization of the city among the Akposso.)
André Dovi Akposso. Lomé: Institut National de la Recherche Scientifique, 1970. 63p.
This is a study of the history and settlement patterns of the Akposso people, who were chased out of what was to become Ghana into hilly border regions in Togo, where they reside at a certain distance from their farms, only descending to cultivate them.

66 **Dream of unity. Pan-Africanism and political unification in West Africa.**
Claude E. Welch, Jr. Ithaca, New York: Cornell University Press, 1966. 396p. bibliog.
In this book one of America's best-known Africanists surveys a number of unificationist movements in Africa, including the one that took root among the Ewe. The material on Togo is found especially in chapters two and three ('The birth and growth of Ewe nationalism' and 'Conflict over self-determination in Togoland') in which the author examines the evolution of the Ewe national consciousness and the efforts, which were ultimately fruitless, to unify all the Ewe people under one state.

67 **El-Hadj Bukari dit "Modjolobo", ou, La guerre des fétiches à Sokodé.** (El Hadj Bukari "Modjolobo", or , The fetish war in Sokode.)
Jean-Claude Barbier. *Islam et Sociétés au Sud du Sahara* (Paris), vol. 5 (1991), p. 73-101. bibliog.
This article constitutes a study of the early history of Islam in Togo, and its rivalry with animist leaders in the Sokode area of northern Togo.

68 **Elements de polemologie en pays ewe.** (Elements of polemology among the Ewe.)
Nicoué Lodjou Gayibor. *Cultures et Développement*, no. 3/4 (1984), p. 511-36. bibliog.
A review of warfare and military organization among the pre-colonial Ewe who, with the exception of the Anlo in Ghana, had historically not created any centralized political systems. The author concludes that although they had to fight various enemies, the Ewe had no warrior or military tradition, nor glorified warfare as did some of their neighbours to the east and west.

69 **Entretiens en pays bassar.** (Conversations in Bassar country.)
D. Gbikpi-Benissan. Lomé: Institut National des Sciences de
l'Education, 1978-79. 2 vols.

Many of the studies of the Bassari peoples in northern Togo have focused on their
iron-smelting activities and role in regional trade. Gbikpi-Benissan's first volume
provides a detailed analysis of Bassari origins and migrations, the foundations of their
villages, and their various armed conflicts with neighbouring peoples. The second
volume focuses on their social stratification, political organization, and evolution
during the colonial era.

70 **Ertzberger and the German colonial scandals, 1905-1910.**
Klaus Epstein. *English Historical Review*, vol. 74, no. 293
(Oct. 1959), p. 637-63.

This is an account of the exposure of colonial scandals in German Africa, including
the colony of Togo, by the Zentrum deputy Matthias Ertzberger, which led to the
1907 dissolution of the Reichstag.

71 **The Eves of West Africa: the Anlo-Eves and their immediate
neighbours.**
Charles M. K. Mamattah. Accra: Volta Research Publications, 1978.
768p. bibliog.

This massive and most unusual book, partly written in Evegbe, is a painstaking
reconstitution of the whole of Ewe history, especially of the Anlo clan in Ghana. The
narrative is based on a vast amount of oral history collected by the author, and
contains a chronology starting in 1364, a fifty-nine-page bibliography, and scores of
photographs.

72 **The Ewe in pre-colonial times: a political history with special
emphasis on the Anlo, Ge and Krepi.**
D. E. K. Amenumey. Accra: Sedco Publishing, 1986. 122p.
bibliog.

Originally written in 1976 by one of Ghana's foremost Ewe scholars, a historian at
the University of Cape Coast, this book surveys the origins, migration patterns,
history and structural organization of the Ewe, especially the Anlo branch in Ghana.
The work contains maps, and an appendix with multiple king-lists suggested by a
number of scholars for the various chiefdoms. This is useful, since there is
considerable controversy about some, especially that of Aného. The book includes a
lengthy bibliography (p. 111-22). See also: Sandra Greene, 'Social change in
eighteenth century Anlo: the role of technology, markets and military conflict'.
Africa, vol. 58, no. 1 (1988), p. 70-86, bibliog. Another important article is R. A. Kea,
'Akwamu-Anlo relations c. 1750-1813'. *Transactions of the Historical Society of
Ghana* (Legon), vol. 10 (1969), p. 29-63.

73 **The Ewe-speaking peoples of the Slave Coast of West Africa.**
Alfred B. Ellis. Chicago: Benin Press, 1965. 331p.

A reprint of the 1890 text, this book is an early account of the Slave Coast (which
included the Togo littoral) written by a former major in the First Battalion of the West

India Regiment, who also wrote a book about Yoruba-speakers in Nigeria. Rather more specific attention is paid to the Fon Kingdom in neighbouring Dahomey, and its rites, rituals and military system, although the work is also of value to those interested in Togo. For several other reprints of interesting early descriptions of the region see: William Snelgrave, *A new account of some parts of Guinea and the slave trade.* London: Frank Cass, 1971. 288p.; Thomas Birch Freeman, *Journal of various visits to the kingdoms of Ashanti, Aku and Dahomi in western Africa.* London: Cass, 1968.; John Adams, *Remarks on the country extending from Cape Palmas to the River Congo.* London: Cass, 1966.; and Qilliam Bosman, *A new and accurate description of the coast of Guinea.* New York: Barnes & Noble, 1967. 577p.

74 **The Ewe unification movement.**
D. E. K. Amenumey.   Accra: Ghana Universities Press, 1989. 374p. bibliog.

This book, a revision of the author's PhD thesis at Manchester University, is a masterful and far-reaching study of what many scholars regard as Africa's first nationalist movement. Amenumey outlines the origins of the movement to unify all Ewe under one authority, which was somewhat paradoxical since the Ewe had never been united, even in pre-colonial days. He discusses the emergence of the *Bund der Deutschen Togolander* (a pre-cursor of Olympio's CUT), the subsequent reactions of British and French colonial officials, and the emergence of various political parties in French Togoland. The petitions to the United Nations, and the plebiscite that definitively partitioned the Ewe between the future Ghana and Togo are also covered. The author provides a distillation of this book for the pre-1947 period in the earlier article, 'The pre-1947 background to the Ewe unification question: a preliminary sketch'. *Transactions of the Historical Society of Ghana* (Legon), vol. 10 (1969), p. 65-85.

75 **The first shots of the Great War: the Anglo-French conquest of Togo, 1914.**
Eric J. Grove.   *Army Quarterly and Defence Journal* (London), vol. 106, no. 3 (1976), p. 308-23.

Among Togo's distinguishing historical events is the conquest by Anglo-French troops of German Togo, which was the first Allied victory in the First World War. This article describes the campaign and the efforts of the local German administration to avoid intra-European military conflict in Africa. Another article discusses the German withdrawal from Sokode on their military defeat in Togo. See: Jean-Claude Barbier, 'L'histoire veçue; Sokodé, 1914. Les Allemands évacuent le Nord-Togo' (Real-life history; Sokode, 1914. The Germans evacuate north Togo). *Revue Française d'Histoire d'Outre Mer*, vol. 75, no. 1 (1988), p. 79-88.

76 **Foli Bébé, ou, l'epopée des Ga du Togo.** (Foli Bebe, or , the epic of the Ga of Togo.)
Nicoué Lodjou Gayibor, Françoise Ligier.   Dakar, Senegal: Nouvelles Editions Africaines, 1983. 138p. bibliog.

This is a somewhat popularized biography of Foli Bebe, the legendary founder of the Glidji kingdom near Aného, and the evolution of that kingdom. Gayibor sets in perspective the two migrations of peoples from what is today Ghana: the Ga from Accra (1677-83) who founded Glidji; and the Fanti from Elmina who founded neighbouring Ané ho. He discusses the historical confusion as to whether Foli Bebe really was the first king of Glidji, or the founder of the dynasty. The controversy exists because, despite oral history and slave-trader references to his being the King of Glidji, there is no detailed information about him.

77   French West Africa.
Virginia Thompson, Richard Adloff.   London: George Allen & Unwin, 1958. 626p. bibliog.

This is a classic, meticulously-detailed, historical overview of the large French West African federation, and the various colonial components within it. Although Togo was not a colony, but rather a mandatary territory, it was for some time, and to a large extent, governed in a similar manner, from Cotonou in the neighbouring colony of Dahomey. Therefore, there are numerous references to Togo in this volume. See also: Jean Suret-Canale, *The colonial era in French West and Central Africa*. London: C. Hurst, 1970. For an account of the anti-French revolt in Lomé during the colonial era see: Messan Adimado Aduayom, 'Un prélude au nationalisme togolais: la révolte de Lomé' (A prelude to Togolese nationalism: the revolt in Lomé). *Cahiers d'Etudes Africaines*, vol. 24, no. 1 (1984), p. 39-50.

78   Les frontières togolaises: les modifications de 1927-1929. Etude et documents. (Togo's boundaries: the modifications of 1927-1929. A study and documentation.)
Amouzouvi Akakpo.   Lomé: Université du Bénin, Faculté des Lettres et Sciences Humaines, 1979. 227p. bibliog.

A detailed study of the Anglo-French border demarcation of 1927-29, how it was carried out in the field, the specific problems that were encountered, and the end result. The author includes documents relating to the demarcation.

79   German administration in southern Togo.
D. E. K. Amenumey.   *Journal of African History*, vol. 10, no. 4 (1969), p. 523-639.

This is an examination of German rule in Togo, aimed in part at assessing the validity of Nussbaum's argument that Togo was not the *musterkolonie* (showpiece colony) the Germans claimed it was, in the light of its status as the only colony to become self-sufficient. Amenumey notes that Togo escaped the worst abuses of concessionary company rule, that afflicted the other colonies, since it was ruled from the outset by Imperial officials. It also evaded settler colonialism, and inevitable land-alienation, because it was not suitable for European farming. Only because taxation was effective in Togo did the colony become self-sustaining. The same philosophy, however, animated colonial rule, the same rough insensitive and militaristic rule prevailed, and the same calibre of administrators were dispatched to Togo. Amenumey thus concludes that 'as far as the nature of the regime . . . the difference between Togo and the other German colonies was one of degree, not of kind' (p. 639). For a somewhat more pro-German view see: Marek Czaplinski, 'The German colonial civil service: image and reality'. *Africana Bulletin* (Warsaw), vol. 34 (1987), p. 107-19. The latter concludes (p. 119) that 'although the German civil servants were in some respects really worse than their counterparts in other colonies, the extremely negative opinion of them would be ungrounded'.

80 **Germany's model colony in Africa: Togo, 1884-1914.**
B. W. Hodder. London: University of London, Department of
Geography, 1980. 22p. bibliog.

In this Occasional Paper essay, Hodder considers the degree to which German rule in
Togo impacted on the landscape of the colony. It glosses over some of the brutalities
committed there, and focuses on the benefits of modernity which were introduced.
Hodder concludes that 'at least by the contemporary standards of European colonial
activity, the Germans could with some justification term Togo their model colony
(*Musterkolonie*)'.

81 **Le gouverneur Bonnécarrère au Togo.** (Governor Bonnécarrère in
Togo.)
Silivi Kokoe d'Almeida, Seti Yawo G. Gbedemah. Lomé: Nouvelles
Editions Africaines, 1982. 119p.

This is a study of Bonnécarrère's lengthy tenure as governor of Togo. The book,
which includes eight pages of plates, continues beyond Bonnécarrère's departure
from Lomé, and includes a list of some of the individuals elected to the Council of
Notables (that he created), which is difficult to obtain abroad.

82 **Les grandes compagnies Zarma au Dahomey et au Togo
(1875-1898). Régions de Djougou et de Sokodé.** (The large Djerma
groups in Dahomey and Togo [1875-1898]. The regions of Djougou
and Sokodé.)
Yves Person. *Le Mois en Afrique*, vol. 16, no. 203/204 (Dec. 1982-
Jan. 1983), p. 100-17; vol. 17 no. 205/206 (Feb.-March 1983), p. 127-44.

Written by one of France's foremost Africanists, this is a study of the arrival of
Djerma mercenaries from the north, to both Dahomey and Togo, in the last decades of
the 19th century. In the case of Togo their military might disturbed the delicate
balance-of-power which existed between the seven competitive Kotokoli villages, and
led one village to invite the intervention of a foreign military force. This ushered in
German colonial occupation.

83 **The Hausa kola trade through Togo, 1899-1912: some
quantifications.**
Edward Graham Norris. *Paideuma* (Frankfurt), vol. 30 (1984),
p. 161-84.

Prior to the arrival of colonial rule the land of Togo was criss-crossed by a number of
important east-west caravan routes. This article focuses on the trade in kola nuts,
largely controlled by Hausa merchants, and attempts to assess the quantities traded.
The subject of internal trade and commerce in the pre-colonial era is treated in depth
in Wolfgang Hetzel, *Studien zur Geographie des Handels in Togo und Dahomey*
(Studies in the geography of trade in Togo and Dahomey). Cologne: Geographisches
Institut der Universität zu Köln, 1974. 315p. bibliog.

84 **Histoire de Petit Popo et du royaume gen.** (History of Little Popo and
the Gen kingdom.)
Fio Agbano II. Lomé: Université du Bénin, Institut National des
Sciences de l'Education, 1984. 181p.

Prefaced, and with a commentary by Nicoué Lodjou Gayibor, this is a reprint of the
1934 classic history of the Gen, or Mina, people of Little Popo (Aného), which was
originally published with a slightly different title, and was written by their king,
Agbano II (1929-72). The work has two parts. The first recounts the history of the
founding of Glidji (near Aného) by immigrants arriving from the vicinity of Elmina
(hence their name) in the Gold Coast. It relies heavily on the 1895 historical work of
Carl Christian Reindorf, *The history of the Gold Coast and Asante*, sections of which
are copied verbatim. The second part (p. 103-42) is primarily the King's own
contribution, and is an account of Mina social life, customs, taboos and deities. This
fascinating book concludes with a lengthy section of footnotes by Gayibor, the well-
known Togolese historian, which is essentially a running commentary, and correction,
of Fio Agbano's text. See also: Nicoué Lodjou Gayibor, *Sources orales de la région
d'Aného* (Oral sources of the Aneho region). Niamey, Niger: Centre d'Etudes
Linguistiques et Historique par Tradition Orale, 1980. 82p.

85 **L'histoire presente, exemple du royaume Kotokoli au Togo.**
(Current history, the example of the Kotokoli kingdom in Togo.)
Jean-Claude Barbier. Talence, France: Centre d'Etudes d'Afrique
Noire, 1983. 72p. bibliog.

This is an eminently readable history of the foundation and evolution of the
chiefdoms of the Kotokoli in North Togo. Their history begins with the arrival of Gur
immigrants from Fada Ngurma (in contemporary Burkina Faso) who originally settled
in Tchaoudjo, and in the early 18th century expanded beyond their original seven
villages. The study examines in detail their inter-clan frictions, lineages, military
organization, economic resources, and the evolving role of their kings, and includes
lists of their kings, diagrams and maps. See also: Robert Cornevin, 'Contribution à
l'histoire de la chefferie cotokoli' (A contribution to the history of the Kotokoli
chiefs). *Cahiers d'Etudes Africaines*, vol. 4, no. 3 (1964), p. 456-60.

86 **Histoire traditionnelle des Kotokoli et des Bi-Tchambi du nord
Togo.** (Traditional history of the Kotokoli and Bi-Tchambi of north
Togo.)
Jean-Claude Froelich, Pierre Alexandre. *Bulletin d'IFAN* (Dakar),
vol. 22, no. 1-2 (1960), p. 211-74.

This is the seminal study of the history of the Sokode and Bassari peoples, written by
the two foremost scholars of the Kotokoli and Bassari peoples; both served in Togo in
the 1940s and 1950s as colonial administrators. The authors meticulously trace the
origins of the various groups in the two districts, and note their settlement patterns.
They then proceed to analyse the chiefdoms, including that of Tchaoudjo from which
the king of the Kotokoli comes. Numerous sketches and tables illustrate the
implements used by the population, and their scarifications.

87 **The independence of Togo.**
Marc Michel. In: *Decolonization and African independence: the transfers of power, 1960-1980*. Edited by Prosser Gifford, William Roger Louis. New Haven, Connecticut: Yale University Press, 1988, p. 295-320.

In this detailed study of the immediate pre-independence era in Togo, the author of this chapter focuses on the evolution of the pan-Ewe unification movement, and the reactions to it by the two mandatory powers (France and Great Britain) and the Trusteeship Council. He also considers the UN-supervised plebiscites, the eventual merger of British Togoland with Ghana and the separate independence of French Togoland. A more jaundiced view is expressed in Marc Michel, 'Le Togo dans les relations au lendemain de la guerre' (Togo in the international relations after the War). In: *Les chemins de la décolonisation de l'empire colonial Française*, edited by C. R. Ageron. Paris: CNRS, 1986, p. 95-107. See also: James S. Coleman, *Togoland*. New York: Carnegie Endowment for International Peace, 1956; and B. W. Hodder, 'The Ewe problem, a reassessment'. In: *Essays in political geography*, edited by C. A. Fisher. London: Methuen, 1968, p. 271-83.

88 **Introduction à l'histoire de l'aire culturelle ajatado.** (Introduction to the cultural region of the Adja peoples.)
Roberto Pazzi. Cotonou, Benin: University of Benin, 1979. 323p. bibliog.

Pazzi offers a very good general history of the Adja-speaking peoples who live along the coast, from Porto Novo in Benin (the Guin) to Lomé (the Ewe), and in the immediate hinterland, providing a unified approach to the understanding of regional events. It is an ambitious work, partly because of the extent of its geographical coverage (of nine distinct peoples and kingdoms), and partly because it touches upon several disciplines, although the thrust is primarily the history of the peoples.

89 **Naissance d'un état africain: le Togo, territoire pilot. Lumière et ombre, 1951-1958.** (Birth of an African state: Togo, pilot country. Light and shadow, 1951-1958.)
Robert Ajavon. Dakar, Senegal: Nouvelles Editions Africaines, 1989. 332p.

This is a remarkable book, if only for the fact that it was written fully twenty-five years after President Olympio's death. It constitutes a critical assessment of Olympio's role in the events leading up to the independence of Togo, written by one of his chief political supporters.

90 **Peuples du golfe du Bénin: Aja-ewe: colloque de Cotonou.** (People of the Gulf of Guinea: the Adja-Ewe: the colloquium of Cotonou.)
Edited by François de Medeiros. Paris: Karthala, 1984. 328p. bibliog.

This book comprises a collection of twenty-four papers, some of which are in English and a few overly short, which were presented at a major conference held in 1979 on the Adja-speaking peoples of the Ghana-Nigeria coastal littoral in Cotonou, Benin. Due to the lengthy interval between the congress and the publication of this volume, many of the papers have already appeared previously in print. Nevertheless the volume as a whole is very valuable and its papers provide useful insights into the history and culture of the Adja in Benin and Togo.

91 **Les peuples et royaumes du Golfe du Bénin.** (The people and kingdoms of the Gulf of Benin.)
Nicoué Lodjou Gayibor. Lomé: Université du Bénin, Institut National des Sciences de l'Education, 1986. 75p. bibliog.
Constitutes a good introduction to the several peoples and kingdoms which clustered along the Ghana-Nigeria littoral in the pre-colonial era. They include the kingdoms of Oyo, Benin, Porto Novo, Adja, Allada, Savi, Dahomey, Glidji, the Ewe and the Anlo.

92 **Les plantations allemandes du Mont Agou, 1884-1914.** (The German plantations in Mount Agou, 1884-1914.)
A. Ahadji. Lomé: Université du Bénin, Institut National des Sciences de l'Education, 1983. 114p. bibliog.
Written by a teacher of German at the local university, this is a pioneering study of the generally neglected area of settler plantations in Togo during the German colonial era. The monograph focuses on the 45,000 hectares acquired by the German company Hupfeld in the vicinity of Agou and Kpalimé, which were planted with cacao, sisal and kaoutchouk. The brevity of the German tenure in Togo, however, did not allow the plantation to attain viability. Ahadji's study concludes with twenty-two pages of hand-written records from the plantation.

93 **Prehistory and archaeology in Niger and Togo, Upper Volta, Dahomey and the Ivory Coast.**
Guy de Beauchene. *West African Archaeological Newsletter*, no. 5 (Nov. 1966), p. 6-8. bibliog.
This is an inventory of the archaeological sites and archaeological work performed in these countries up until the date of publication. For a record of some radio-carbon dates from various excavations see: B. M. Fage, 'Radiocarbon dates for sub-saharan Africa'. *Journal of African History*, vol. 8, no. 3 (1967), p. 513-27.

94 **Le referendum du Togo (28 octobre 1956): l'acte de naissance d'une république africaine autonome.** (The Togolese referendum of 28 October 1956: the birth of an autonomous African republic.)
Edmond Pierre Luce. Paris: Pedone, 1958. 243p.
Luce considers the crucial 1956 referendum in French Togoland, which set the course for an independent Togo, without its British Togoland component. See also: François Luchaire, 'Le Togo français de la tutelle à l'autonomie' (French Togo from tutelage to autonomy). *Revue Juridique et Politique*, vol. 20, no. 1 (Jan.-March 1957), p. 1-46; vol. 20, no. 3 (July-Sept. 1957), p.501-87; Marcel Merle, 'Les plebiscites organisés par les Nations Unies' (The plebiscites organized by the United Nations). *Annuaire Français de Droit International* (1961), p. 425-45; and D. Pepy, 'La république autonome du Togo devant les nations unies' (The autonomous republic of Togo before the United Nations). *Politique Etrangère*, vol. 22, no. 6 (1958), p. 671-90.

95 **Rélations commerciales entre l'Allemagne et le Togo, 1680-1914.**
(Commercial relations between Germany and Togo, 1680-1914.)
A. Ahadji. Lomé: Université du Bénin, 1984. 71p. bibliog.

In this work the author provides a history of trade between Germany and Togo. He begins with the period of commercial relations which existed before colonial rule was established (1680-1884), noting in particular the struggle for primacy between individual German traders (for example, J. K. Vietor) and concessionary companies in the area (such as Hupfeld). He then proceeds to discuss in detail levels of trade (imports and exports) during the colonial era. See also: A. Olurunfemi, 'Trade and politics and the German occupation of Togoland, 1882-1884'. *Africana Marburgensia*, no. 11 (1986), p. 48-70.

96 **Le remodelage des traditions historiques: la légende d'Agokoli, roi de Notsé.** (The remodelling of historical traditions: the legend of Agokoli, king of Notsé.)
Nicoué Lodjou Gayibor. In: *Sources orales de l'histoire de l'Afrique* (Oral sources of African history). Edited by Claude-Hélène Perrot. Paris: CNRS, 1989. p. 209-14.

One of the most widespread Ewe oral traditions – which is still celebrated annually to this day – is the historic dispersal from Notsé of various Ewe clans due to the brutality of their king, Agokoli. In his article Gayibor assesses a number of historical facts about this episode which have been manipulated over the years. See also: Michel Verdon, 'Political sovereignty, village reproduction and legends of origin'. *Africa*, vol. 51, no. 1 (1981), p. 465-76.

97 **A la rencontre du . . . Togo.** (Meeting . . . Togo.)
Jean de Menthon. Paris: Harmattan, 1993. 271p.

This is a well-informed general survey of the evolution of Togo since the early years of German colonial rule. The author considers the country's partition by France and Britain, independence, and the eventual dictatorship of General Eyadema. Menthon lived in Togo between 1956 and 1961 as a bank administrator, and still revisits it every year. The narrative includes a discussion of Togo's economic and social evolution, and is supplemented by various tables and maps.

98 **Togo, eine Musterkolonie?** (Togo, a showpiece colony?)
Manfred Nussbaum. Berlin: Rutten & Loening, 1962. 138p.

Nussbaum has adopted a Marxist approach in this influential East German study. He challenges the idea that the Germans had the conscious benevolent policy of creating a model colony in Togo, arguing that the latter attained the distinction of being self-supporting because of its financial strength, which other German colonies did not possess. A more recent, massive study, which has a very lengthy bibliography (p. 687-767) and includes plates and maps, takes another look at this issue, which seems to completely rivet German scholarship. Written by Peter Sebald, it is *Togo 1884-1914: eine "Musterkolonie"?* (Togo 1884-1914: a "showpiece colony"?). Berlin: Akademie Verlag, 1988. 792p. bibliog. German nostalgia for Togo continues to this day, and is reflected by the close diplomatic relations between the two countries, the number of German tourists who visit Togo, and the considerable amount of economic aid granted by Germany.

99 **Le Togo, 20e anniversaire.** (Togo, 20th anniversary.)
Robert Cornevin. *Afrique Contemporaine*, no. 142 (1987), p. 41-60.

A review of Togo's social, economic and political evolution, from Germany's colonial occupation up until 1987, on the occasion of the twentieth anniversary of General Eyadema's rise to power. Written by one of France's top historians, the work is marred, however, by a curiously misplaced optimism of Togo under Eyadema ('the richest in promises', p. 41), at a time when major revisionist studies were appearing and a few years before the demonstrations that would lead to Eyadema's partial eclipse.

100 **Le Togo au début de notre siècle.** (Togo at the beginning of our century.)
Achim Kratz. *Le Mois en Afrique*, no. 211/212 (Aug.-Sept. 1983), p. 144-65; no. 213/214 (Oct.-Nov. 1983), p. 124-42; no. 217/218 (Feb.-March 1984), p. 153-72.

The German conquest of Togo, and the opening of its economy for exploitation is considered in this comprehensive and detailed review. The author, an engineer with a university in Berlin, was at the time EEC representative to Togo.

101 **Le Togo de Congrès de Berlin à la Conference de Brazzaville.** (Togo from the Congress of Berlin to the Brazzaville Conference.)
Hermann Attignon. *Revue Française d'Etudes Politiques Africaines*, no. 81 (Oct. 1972), p. 28-58.

This is an overview of Togo's history from its allocation to German over-rule by the Congress of Berlin, until the 1944 Brazzaville Conference that signalled the liberalization of French colonial rule.

102 **Le Togo en 1884 selon Hugo Zoller.** (Togo in 1884 according to Hugo Zoller.)
Yves Marguerat, translated from the German by K. Amegan, A. Ahadji. Lomé: Editions Haho, 1990. 216p.

Two professors of German at the University of Benin prepared this French translation of the book by Zoller, entitled *Die Deutschen Besitzungen an der Westafrikanischen Kuste* (Berlin: W. Spemann, 1885). Zoller was a German arch-nationalist journalist, who ardently believed in his country's superiority and its need to expand its dominions globally. His imagination was fired by Germany's entry into Togo, and he travelled there to describe the colony to his readers. He stayed in Togo for a few weeks, and, although not a scientist, described everything he saw, including the vegetation, altitudes, temperature variations, and the customs of the people. Strongly racist, he was nevertheless forced to concede how graciously and politely he was treated by all the local people he met. The work, which is extremely interesting, was very influential in Germany at the time, and is also the first detailed first-hand European description of conditions along the coast and its immediate hinterland, since traders at this time did not venture much out of their trading enclaves.

103 **Togo under imperial Germany 1884-1914.**
Arthur J. Knoll. Stanford, California: The Hoover Institution Press,
1978. 224p. bibliog.

This important book on Togo's early colonial history is a revision of the author's PhD dissertation, and includes an important bibliography (p. 199-218), plates and diagrams. It is a tightly written overview of Togo's experience under German colonial rule, during which time an effort was made to transform it into an examplary 'Musterkolonie'. The core of the material is presented in seven succinct chapters: German imperialism; Missionaries and merchants; Early officials and explorers; The rulers; Some tasks of government; The mission factor in Togo; and Economic change under German rule. For several additional good studies of Germany's role in Africa see: L. H. Gann, P. Duignan, *The rule of German Africa, 1884-1914*. Stanford: Stanford University Press, 1977. 286p.; A. J. Knoll, L. H. Gann, *Germans in the Tropics*. New York: Greenwood, 1987; *Britain and Germany in Africa*, edited by Prosser Gifford, William Roger Louis. New Haven: Yale University Press, 1967. 825p.; and *German imperialism in Africa*, edited by H. Stoecker. London: C. Hurst, 1986.

104 **Togo unter deutscher Flagge.** (Togo under the German flag.)
Heinrich Klose. Berlin: D. Reimer, 1899. 561p.

Klose, a Lieutenant on a scientific expedition in Togo, found himself in Bassari at the time of the 1897 Konkomba rebellions, and stayed there for a few months writing about everything he observed. This included such topics as slavery, attitudes towards adultery in the region, and the ongoing German competition with Britain to secure the important trade entrepôt Salaga (now in Ghana). Klose also wrote about his personal travails, and the difficulties he encountered in setting up a darkroom to develop his photographs, a large number of which appear in this book. Klose was subsequently to write many other articles on Togo, especially for the periodical *Globus* between 1903 and 1904. The section of his book (p. 285-544) that contains his observations on what is now Ghana has been translated into English. See: *Klose's journey to northern Ghana*, translated by Inge Killick. Legon, Ghana: University of Ghana, Institute of African Studies, 1964. 210p. Needless to say, both Klose's book and most German writings present German rule in its best light. Indeed, the corpus of literature on Togo is cluttered with a large amount of publications by German writers, idealizing their German empire in Africa, surprising in light of its brief duration, and reinterpreting the German colonial era after its loss.

105 **Togoland under the Germans: thirty years of economic development.**
M. B. K. Darkoh. *Nigerian Geographical Journal*, vol. 10 (Dec. 1967), p. 107-22; vol. 11 (Dec. 1968), p. 153-68.

This article constitutes an overview of German colonial rule in Togo. The author reaches the conclusion that 'In spite of the snags of German rule, in spite of what the critics say, Togoland may be said to have seen one of the most remarkable phases of progress in the history of colonial rule' (p. 165).

106 The western Slave Coast and its rulers.
C. W. Newbury. Oxford: Clarendon Press, 1961. 234p. bibliog.

This is one of the English-language classics on the history of the littoral from the Volta River in Ghana to the Niger River delta in Nigeria. It is an extremely well-written work of erudite scholarship, which condenses a wide array of data, and includes several helpful maps. The material on Togo is localized in chapter five 'French and German interests' (p. 97-121) although there are additional references to Togo throughout the text, and the 1884 German-Togolese Protectorate Treaty appears in the appendix as well as a list of governors. Some material relevant to Togo is also to be found in the seminal I. A. Akinjogbin, *Dahomey and its neighbours 1709-1818* . Cambridge, England: Cambridge University Press, 1967.

Le Togo: des origines à nos jours. (Togo: from its origins to the present day.)
See item no. 4.

The impact of German colonial rule on the forests of Togo.
See item no. 41.

Mission und Kolonialpolitik: die nordeutsche Missiongesellschaft an der Goldkuste und in Togo. (Missions and colonial policy: the work of the North German Missionary Society in the Gold Coast and Togo.)
See item no. 122.

Religious freedom under international mandate.
See item no. 127.

Metallurgistes Bassar. (Bassari metallurgists.)
See item no. 159.

Organisation politique des Kotokoli du nord Togo. (The political organization of the Kotokoli of north Togo.)
See item no. 164.

Lomé, les étapes de la croissance. (Lomé: the steps in its growth.)
See item no. 193.

Bildung und Kolonialismus in Togo. (Education and colonialism in Togo.)
See item no. 252.

Deutschland und Togo 1847-1987. (Germany and Togo 1847-1987.)
See item no. 348.

The Ghana-Togo boundary 1914-1982.
See item no. 350.

Historical dictionary of Togo.
See item no. 541.

Religion

107 **Les affaires du mort.** (Death affairs.)
Myriam Smadja. *Systèmes de Pensée en Afrique Noire*, vol. 11
(1991), p. 57-89.
This is a general discussion of matters relating to death and death rites, followed by specific illustrations of funerary rituals among the Tamberma of northern Togo.

108 **Agbé-yéyé.**
André Depeursinge. Lausanne: Editions du Soc, 1966. 48p. plates.
Agbé-yéyé means in Evegbe 'new life', which is also the name of the film produced by Depeursinge for the missionary department of the Protestant Church of Romansche in Switzerland. The book (with black-and-white plates, taken from the film) depicts the daily life of Ewe Christians, the problems they face in a largely animist environment, and how they cope with them.

109 **Les ancêtres et nous: analyse de la pensée religieuse des Bé de la commune de Lomé.** (The ancestors and us: the religious thought of the Be in the commune of Lomé.)
Komla Agbetiafa. Dakar, Senegal: Nouvelles Editions Africaines, 1985. 95p.
This is a compact study of the religious life, customs and ancestor worship of the Ewe Be clan who live on the outskirts of the city of Lomé. The author surveys their main and secondary divinities, their sacred animals and sites (the woods where ceremonies are held), and outlines their funerary rites and the ritual sacrifices practised. For another study that focuses on the Be see: M. Amouzou, 'La fonction sociale de la religion et la sociologie de la connaissance chez les dirigeants religieux – les Bé du Togo' (The social function of religion and the sociology of knowledge among religious leaders – the Be of Togo). *Etudes Togolaises*, no. 23/26 (1983), p. 33-61.

110 **Anthropologie religieuse des Evé du Togo.** (Religious anthropology of Togo's Ewe.)
Claude Rivière.   Paris: Nouvelles Editions Africaines, 1981. 215p. bibliog. plates.

Although Voodoo practices are normally associated with Haiti and Benin, they are equally an integral part of the religious life and cosmology of the Ewe. The Ewe, who live in southern Togo (as well as in neighbouring Ghana) believe that, between an essentially benevolent supreme God (Mawu) and the malevolent forces of sorcerers, an array of spirits are found, amongst which are ancestors and voodoo. These spirits can be supplicated for intercession in mortal affairs, and must be appeased through sacrifices. In turn, they communicate with mankind in a variety of ways, including through the medium of divination practices. In this book the author, a Sorbonne professor who formerly taught for four years at the University of Benin in Lomé, describes Ewe cosmology, their concepts of the material and spiritual world, and the role of spirits, sacrifices, divination, magic and initiation rites in their religion. See also: the author's, 'Dzo et la pratique magique chez les Ewe du Togo' (Dzo and the practice of magic among the Ewe of Togo). *Cultures et Développement*, vol. 11, no. 2 (1979), p. 193-218. bibliog. For a briefer analysis of Ewe cosmology and ancestor cults and their conception of Mawu, see: Edward Geoffrey Parrinder, 'Theistic beliefs of the Yoruba and Ewe peoples of West Africa'. In: *African ideas of God: a symposium*, edited by Edwin William Smith. London: Edinburgh House Press, 1950, p. 224-40; and Claude Rivière, 'Mawu, l'insurpassable chez les Ewe du Togo' (Mawu, the insurpassable, among the Ewe of Togo). *Anthropos*, vol. 74, no. 1/2 (1979), p. 25-39. For a more comprehensive, and comparative study see: Geoffrey Parrinder, *West African Religion: a study of the beliefs and practices of Akan, Ewe, Yoruba, Ibo and kindred peoples.* New York: Barnes & Noble, 1970. 2nd ed. 203p. bibliog.

111 **A church between colonial powers: a history of the church in Togo.**
Hans W. Debrunner.   London: Lutterworth Press, 1965. 368p. bibliog.

This is a study of the Evangelical Church of Togo, which developed from the work of the German Mission of Bremen, followed (after France had gained control of the colony) by the Paris Mission. The author traces the slow growth of Christianity in the country, and especially among the Ewe in the south, and the problems faced in a country still largely animist and with a strong Muslim minority.

112 **Essai sur la conception religieuse du peuple Mina.** (Essay on the religious conceptions of the Mina people.)
Roberto Pazzi.   *Bulletin de l'Enseignement Supèrieure du Bénin* (Lomé), vol. 7 (1968), p. 87-104.

This article is a succinct overview of the religious cosmology of the Mina people of southern Togo.

113 **Die Religion der Eweer in Sud-Togo.** (The religion of the Ewe in south Togo.)
Jacob Spieth. Göttingen, Germany: Vandemhoeck & Ruprecht, 1911. 316p.

Written by the famous missionary and linguist of the Norddeutschen Missions-gesellschaft, this is one of the first authoritative studies of the Ewe peoples and of their culture and religious cosmology.

114 **La divination par les huits cordelettes chez les Mwaba-Gurma (nord Togo).** (Divination by eight cords among the Moba-Gurma of north Togo.)
Albert de Surgy. Paris: Harmattan, 1983, 1986. 2 vols. bibliog.

This is a masterful and extremely detailed description and analysis of the religion and religious practices, cosmology, spiritual world, sacrifices and divination practices of the Moba and Gurma who live in the extreme north of Togo. Amongst them some elements are found of the original ancient populations of the region. With their ethnic capital at Dapaong, the two groups are segmented into clans, each sharing a specific common taboo, but with extended families living autonomously in quasi-autarky. The divination practices, which were adopted some 300 years ago, are described in great detail, and are seen by de Surgy as 'the veritable cement of the Moba-Gurma people.' (p. 13). For a shorter version of this material see the author's, 'Principes de la divination Mwaba-Gurma' (Principles of Moba-Gurma divination). *Revue de l'Histoire des Religions* (Paris), vol. 68, no. 1 (1981), p. 3-28.

115 **La géomancie à l'ancienne Côte d'Esclaves.** (Geomancy in the old Slave Coast.)
Bernard Maupoil. Paris: Institut d'Ethnologie, 1943. 690p. bibliog.

This is the classic study of divination among all coastal groups in this region, with particular reference to those in neighbouring Benin. Supplemented by colour illustrations and plates, this is an incredibly detailed and comprehensive study of the array of spirits and sorcery found along the Slave Coast, which stretches from Ghana to Nigeria. The work pinpoints and describes sites of divination, the accessories used, divination signs and their meanings and the process of initiation into sorcery.

116 **La géomancie et le culte d'Afa chez les Evhé du littoral.** (Geomancy and the cult of Afa of the littoral Ewe.)
Albert de Surgy. Paris: Publications Orientalistes de France, 1981. 444p. bibliog.

De Surgy is one of France's greatest Africanists and in this massive study, which contains sixteen pages of plates and numerous diagrams and sketches, he considers the topic of divination among the coastal Ewe. Commencing with a discussion of the origins of the Ewe people, from their dispersal point in Tado (Togo), the author discounts alternative arguments that there was an earlier migration to Tado from Nigeria, via Kétou in Benin. He then engages in a remarkably detailed analysis of the practice of consulting Afa diviners, the various ceremonies and sacrifices involved and their significance, and the initiation rites of Afa diviners themselves and their associates.

117 **Guinea corn harvest rituals among the Konkomba of northern Ghana.**
Henryk Zimon. *Anthropos*, vol. 84 (1989), p. 447-58. bibliog.

Based on fieldwork conducted between 1984 and 1985, the author describes the harvest rituals of the Konkomba, an ethnic group that resides on both sides of the Ghana/Togo border. The rituals and sacred activities which are performed – and through which the Konkomba establish contact with their supernatural beings – have economic, social and religious importance, signifying the power and social control of the elders over their people.

118 **Heviesso et le bon ordre du monde: approche d'une religion africaine.** (Heviesso and the well-ordered world: the approach of an African religion.)
Bruno Gilli. Lomé: Haho, 1987. 230p. bibliog.

This study of the religious life, customs and rites of ethnic groups in coastal Togo and Benin focuses on the widespread prevalence of Voodoo, and assesses the latter's cosmological roots. The book is illustrated with a number of plates, and includes a significant bibliography (p. 219-24).

119 **Histoire de l'eglise catholique au Togo.** (History of the Catholic Church in Togo.)
Karl Muller. Lomé: Editions Librairie Bon Pasteur, 1968. 251p.

Translated from the 1958 German original, this study constitutes a history of the Catholic Church and its missionary activity in Togo. It includes eight pages of plates. For the early origins of Methodist influences along the coast see: P. Ellingsworth, 'Methodism on the Slave Coast: 1842-1870'. *Society for African Church History Bulletin*, vol. 2, no. 3 (1967), p. 239-48.

120 **Kabiye fetish religion: a comparative study.**
Thomas J. Larson. *Anthropos* (Fribourg), vol. 79, no. 1/3 (1984), p. 39-46. plates.

In this eminently readable article, the Kabiye (Kabre) religious practices of northern Togo, which centre around Lama Kara, are compared with those of the Hambukushu of Botswana in southern Africa. The author, an anthropologist who conducted fieldwork among both societies, argues that 'Westerners associate fetish religion and the appeasement of ancestral spirits with pagan religions' while he wishes to place 'traditional religions in their proper context of monotheism and recognition of a High God'. He states that 'Though both the Kabiye and the Hambukushu recognize the same High God as Christians and Muslims, their approach to the higher deity is based upon their particular needs and experience' (p. 39). Larson describes Kabre cosmology, which recognizes no Hell, although only the good go to Heaven when they die. He considers their approach to a benevolent supreme creator (Esso) when asking for favours and assistance through sacrificial offerings (chickens) and also the supplications which are made to intermediaries (*siou*, fetish spirits, who have localized abodes), since Esso cannot be approached directly. The strong traditional values of the Kabre serve to powerfully integrate society and lend it its identity and internal unity.

121 **Mgr. Dosseh, archevêque de Lomé.** (Mgr. Dosseh, Archbishop of
Lomé.)
Comi M. Toulabor. *Politique Africaine*, no. 35 (Oct. 1989), p. 68-76.
A highly critical look at the activities of the Archbishop of Lomé by a noted Togolese
academic in self-imposed exile. Toulabor argues that Dosseh is an arch-authoritarian
in his diocese and rarely uses the funds he receives for the benefit of his priests. He
finds that instead, Dosseh channels them into diocese fetes or to cover the expenses of
his own extended family. In this way he tarnishes the prestige and status of the
Church in Togo.

122 **Mission und Kolonialpolitik: die Norddeutsche Missiongesellschaft
an der Goldkuste und in Togo.** (Missions and colonial policy: the
work of the North German Missionary Society in the Gold Coast and
Togo.)
Martin Pabst. Munich: Anarche, 1988. 645p. bibliog.
Togo experienced only thirty years of German colonial rule, and even then religious
proselytizing was largely restricted to its coastal areas, where indigenous religions
strenuously resisted the imported faiths. Nonetheless, the North German Missionary
Society played a major early role in forming the first Christian communities, and by
extention some of the country's future leaders. This voluminous work is a study of
the historical role and travails of the Mission in the coastal areas of the Gold Coast
and Togo, and is supplemented by many plates and an impressive bibliography
(p. 612-35) .

123 **Muslims in Mango.**
Emile A. B. van Rouveroy van Nieuwaal. Leiden, Netherlands:
African Studies Center, 1986. 66p. bibliog. (Research Report, no. 27).
This slim, illustrated volume is written by a prolific Dutch author, who has
specialized in studying the Chokossi ethnic group of northern Togo. They call
themselves Anufom and this is the name the author uses. He provides information
about their migration to Togo (from Côte d'Ivoire), the role of Islam among them,
magic and religious rites in their daily life, and the manner in which new Imams are
chosen. All this information forms part of the background notes he made for a film he
shot in Mango with his wife. See also: the author's *Ti Anufo: un coup d'oeil sur la
société Anufom au Nord-Togo* (The Anufo: a bird's eye view of the Anufo society in
north Togo). Hasselt, Netherlands: Hasselt, 1976, 123p. The latter includes extensive
textual material for three documentary films on the Chokossi (including the French
version of *Muslims in Mango*), photographs from the films shot and lineage tables of
the chiefly line. Since the Chokossi also reside in northern Ghana, another more
comprehensive book on their cosmology, shrines and divination is also useful. See:
Jon. P. Kirby, *Gods, shrines and problem-solving among the Anufo of northern
Ghana*. Berlin: D. Reimer, 1986, 368p. See also: David C. Davis, 'Strategies of
minority survival: the case of the Gambaga imams'. *Journal of the Institute of Muslim
Minority Affairs*, vol. 7, no. 1 (1986), p. 232-46.

124 **Les musulmans au Togo.** (The Muslims in Togo.)
Raymond Delval. Paris: Publications Orientalistes de France, 1980.
340p. bibliog.

In this comprehensive, definitive, invaluable, and eminently readable study, the author offers an encyclopaedic overview of all things relating to Togo's Muslim community. This includes information on: their numbers, origins, and composition; their ethnic and geographical concentrations; structural organizations, activities, and religious orders; leadership hierarchies; and internal splits. The book is liberally interspersed with maps, tables, diagrams and photographs, some of which are in colour and most of which cannot be found in any other source. It includes a discussion of the origins, and biographical sketches, of some religious leaders. Since records were seldom kept, and if so remain in local archives, this is the only comprehensive source of detailed information on this community. For a briefer article by the same author see: 'Les musulmans au Togo' (Muslims in Togo). *L'Afrique et l'Asie Moderne*, no. 100 (1974), p. 4-21. See also: Seti Sidza, 'Islam in Togo'. *Bulletin on Islam and Christian-Muslim relations in Africa* (Birmingham), vol. 7, no. 1 (1989), p. 1-12; vol. 7, no. 2 (1989) p. 1-26; B. G. Martin, 'Les Tidjanis et leurs adversaires: développements récents de l'Islam au Ghana et au Togo' (The Tidjani and their adversaries: recent developments in Islam in Ghana and Togo). In: *Les ordres mystiques dans l'Islam* (Mystic orders in Islam), edited by A. Popovic, G. Veinsein. Paris: Ecole des Hautes Etudes en Sciences Sociales, 1986. p. 283-91; Pierre Alexandre, 'Le facteur islamique dans l'histoire d'un état du moyen-Togo (Kotokoli)' (The Islamic factor in the history of a state in central Togo [Kotokoli]). *L'Afrique et l'Asie*, no. 65 (1964), p. 26-30.

125 **'Ouvrir la bouche de l'ancêtre': le processus d'ancestralisation à travers quelques séquences des rites funéraires chez les Bassar du Nord-Togo.** ('Opening the mouth of the ancestor': the process of ancestralization through several sequences of funerary rites among the Bassari of north Togo.)
Stéphan Dugast. *Systèmes de Pensée en Afrique Noire*, vol. 11 (1991), p. 131-80. bibliog. English summary.

This is a fascinating study, with a brief summary in English, of the northern Bassari cosmology, ancestor veneration, conceptualization of death, and funerary rites.

126 **La participation des institutions d'afa et du vodu dans les processus de la socialisation des enfants en milieu Ewe.** (The participation of the afa and vodu institutions in the socialization process of children in an Ewe context.)
Svetlana Koudolo. Lomé: DIFOP, 1991. 70p. bibliog. illust.

This is an original analysis by Koudolo, who in an earlier study (see Education) focused on traditional Ewe child socialization processes. In this study she analyses the role of the traditional religious practices, rites and ceremonies of afa and vodu, which are very prevalent in south Togo, in the formative years of Ewe children. This is a means of perpetuating indigenous religious beliefs from generation to generation. The work is supplemented with a number of illustrations.

127 **Religious freedom under international mandate: the case of French Togo Muslims. 1922 to World War II.**
R. O. Lasisi. *Journal of the Institute of Muslim Minority Affairs* (London), vol. 8, no. 1 (1987), p. 144-55.

In this somewhat contentious article, the author argues that during the mandatory era in Togo 'the French did not allow freedom of religion as the Muslims knew it to be . . . [and] their real "well-being and development" as envisaged by the mandate system, was not promoted' (p. 153).

128 **Le sacrifice à la lumière des conceptions mwaba-gurma et Evhé.**
(Sacrifice in light of Moba-Gurma and Ewe concepts.)
Albert de Surgy. *Anthropos* (Fribourg), vol. 84, no. 1/3 (1989), p. 63-80. bibliog. English summary.

This article, which is accompanied by a brief English summary, is a study of the practice of making sacrifices and other offerings to deities and ancestors of the autochtonous Moba in the extreme north of Togo, as well as the Ewe in the south. The author differentiates between various symbolic practices which: appease propensities of misfortune; which appease the powers that act on the thought and will-power of individuals; and which pay hommage to beings who send unexpected beneficial events to the world. Only the hommage can truly be seen as a 'sacrifice'. The author further elaborates on many of these themes in his seminal *De l'universalité d'une forme africaine de sacrifice* (On the universality of an African form of sacrifice). Paris: CNRS, 1988, 286p. bibliog.

129 **Scriptures of an African people: ritual utterances of the Anlo.**
Christian R. Gaba. New York: NOK Publishers, 1973. 154p.

According to Gaba 'Man in traditional Anlo milieu is a *homo religiosus*' (p. 1). This unusual book translates 105 utterances, some of which are very lengthy, and which are used on various occasions by the Ewe people of the Anlo clan. The author provides an index defining their precise usage and in what context or ritual they are said.

130 **La sorcellerie au Sud-Togo.** (Sorcery in south Togo.)
Claude Rivière. *Ethnopsychologie*, vol. 35, no. 4 (Oct. 1980), p. 63-84.

This is a study of the multi-faceted features of sorcery and witchcraft among the Ewe and Mina of southern Togo.

131 **La structure socio-politique et son articulation avec la pensée religieuse chez les Aja-Tado du Sud-Togo.** (The socio-political structure and its articulation within the religious thought of the Adja-Tado of south Togo.)
Komi E. Kossi. Stuttgart, Germany: Steiner, 1990. 324p. bibliog.

Tado, in Togo, is the common historical point of origin of most of the ethnic groups along the Togo-Benin littoral belt. Through oral tradition, these groups can actually trace their more distant point of origin to Kétou in Benin, and on to western Nigeria. In this work Kossi illustrates the deep intertwining of Ewe social and political structures with their traditional customs and religion.

132 **Le système religieux des Evhé.** (The religious system of the Ewe.)
Albert de Surgy. Paris: Harmattan, 1988. 334p. bibliog.

This is a comprehensive study of the spiritual world of the Ewe in several southern Togo localities. The author, who has written numerous books and articles on this topic, concentrates in this work on explaining Ewe conceptualizations of God (Mawu) and their own role on earth. He explores the nature of possession rites, and the role of ancestors, divinities and the other forces that live in the spiritual world, and analyses the meaning of life, death, the birth of twins (which in most societies is a momentous event of special significance) and the function of initiation rites, sacrifices and magic. For other contributions by de Surgy on ancestor worship and the role of fetish among the Ewe see: 'Le "cult des ancêtres" en pays evhe' (The 'cult of ancestors' in Ewe country). *Systèmes de Pensée en Afrique Noire*, no. 1 (1975), p. 105-28; 'Examen critique de la notion de fétiche à partir du cas Evhé' (A critical examination of the concept of fetish based on the Ewe case). *Systèmes de Pensée en Afrique Noire*, no. 8 (1985), p. 263-304. De Surgy also edited the annual issue of *Systèmes de Pensée en Afrique Noire* (no. 12, 1993), entitled *Fetiches II: puissance des objets, charme des mots* (Fetishism II: the power of objects, the charm of words), in which is found more material on fetish practices in Togo.

133 **Togo singt ein neues Lied.** (Togo sings a new song.)
Erich Viering. Erlangen: Verlag der Evangelisch-Lutherischen Mission, 1969. 269p. bibliog. plates.

This is a religious history and chronology of the missionary activity of the Lutheran Church in Togo. It includes photographs.

134 **Voodoo: Africa's secret power.**
Gert Chesi. Cape Town: C. Struik, 1980. 275p. maps. plates.

Although essentially a coffee-table book translated from the German original, in terms of structure, text and plates, this is the best graphic portrayal and compact English introduction to the widespread practice of Voodoo ceremonies in Togo. The book has a large-font text and over one hundred photographs, most of which are in colour.

135 **Le vodu en Afrique de l'Ouest: rites et traditions, le cas des sociétés Guen-Mina (Sud-Togo).** (Voodoo in West Africa: the case of Gouin and Mina societies in south Togo.)
Ines de La Torre. Paris: Harmattan, 1991. 175p. plates.

Written by an academic with impeccable credentials, this is a popular work on the divinities and religious practices of the Mina and Guin people of southern Togo, and especially the Epe-Ekpa new year festivities. See also: Edoh Adjakly, *Pratique de la tradition religieuse et réproduction sociale chez les Guin/Mina du sud-est du Togo* (Traditional religious practices and social reproduction among the Guin/Mina of south-east Togo). Geneva: Institut Universitaire d'Etudes du Développement, 1985.

Initiations africaines et pédagogie de la foi: le mariage chrétienne traditionnelle Kabiyé. (African initiations and the pedagogics of the faith: traditional Kabre Christian marriage.)
See item no. 153.

Origine et fonction humanisante de la mort selon les Mwaba. (The origins and humanizing function of death according to the Moba.)
See item no. 165.

The People

136   **L'anthropologie de la maladie.** (The anthropology of disease.)
M. Augé.   *L'Homme*, vol. 26, no. 1-2 (1986), p. 81-87. bibliog.

This is a study in medical anthropology, as exemplified by the Togolese experience. It outlines how the etiology of disease is often perceived as being rooted in spiritual forces and therefore requires a spiritual cure.

137   **Les Bassari du nord Togo.** (The Bassari of north Togo.)
Robert Cornevin.   Paris: Berger-Levrault, 1962. 156p. bibliog. plates.

The Bassari are a complex group of diverse ethnic origins living in the district of Bassar. In pre-colonial days, they were renowned and respected for their metallurgical skills, but these rapidly declined with the introduction of iron from Europe and the collapse of the caravan routes through their territory. Cornevin's study was the first to appear on this ethnic group since the pioneering work of the German authors, Zech, Klose and Frobenius. This monograph traces Bassari origins, social structures, patterns of habitation, development of metallurgy, religion and art. See also: Cornevin, 'Le centre urbain de Bassari' (The urban centre of Bassari). *Bulletin de l'IFAN* (1957), p. 81-84. For a discussion of the origins and migrations of the Bassari see: Monique Gessain, *Les migrations des Coniagui et Bassari* (The migrations of the Coniagui and Bassari). Paris: Société des Africanistes, 1967. Jacek Jan Pawlik covers Bassari funerary rites in *Expérience sociale de la mort: étude des rites funéraires des Bassar du nord Togo* (The social experience of death: funerary rites of the Bassar of north Togo). Fribourg: Editions Universitaires de Fribourg, 1990. For the original work of Klose on the Bassari see: H. Klose, 'Das Bassarivolk' (The Bassari people). *Globus*, vol. 33 (May 1903), p. 309-41.

138 **Les bilingualismes littéraires: signification de la littérature orale tyokossi.** (Literary bilingualisms: the social meaning of Chokossi oral literature.)
Diana Rey-Hulman. Paris: Société d'Etudes Linguistiques et Anthropologiques de France, 1981. 295p. bibliog. English summary.

This book consists of an anthropological and socio-linguistical study of the social life and customs of the Chokossi people, as seen from their folklore, oral traditions and language usage. Oral literature is perceived by the author as 'an act of communication among speakers'. In the case of the particularly complex Chokossi society 'there is no question of a written language/spoken language or a national language/regional language bilingualism, but rather of different forms of bilingualism expressing relationships among social groups: masters/underlings, dead/living, old/young, men/women etc.' (p. 295). The society's complexity gives the author scope to make constant reference to its history, economy, organization and evolution. The book contains a brief English summary. See also: the author's 'Pratiques lingnagières et formes littéraires'. *Journal of the Anthropological Society of Oxford*, vol. 13, no. 1 (1982), p. 1-13. For a specialized bibliography on the Chokossi see: 'Bibliographie Tchokossi' *Documents de Centre d'Etudes et de Recherches de Kara*. Togo: Kara, 1968.

139 **Les cérémonies de purifications des mauvaises prénataux chez les mwaba-gurma du Nord-Togo.** (Ceremonies of purification of prenatal problems among the Moba-Gur of north Togo.)
Albert de Surgy. *Systèmes de Pensée en Afrique Noire*, vol. 4 (1979), p. 9-75. bibliog.

The Moba are among Togo's earliest peoples, residing in the extreme north of the country. This lengthy article provides a comprehensive outline of their conceptions of life and death, predestination, fate and disease, and the role purification rites play in traditional Moba religious ceremonies. The specific measures the Moba undertake to guard against birth complications, in the light of their conception of life before birth, are the thrust of this article, and are described in detail. See also: M. Cartry, 'Le calebasse de l'éxcision en pays gourmantché' (The excision calabash in Gurmantche country). *Journal de la Société des Africanistes*, vol. 38, no. 2 (1968), p. 189-225.

140 **The dance of death: notes on the architecture and staging of Tamberma funeral performances.**
Suzanne Preston Blier. *Anthropology and Aesthetics*, vol. 2 (1987), p. 107-43.

Blier, who has also written an outstanding work on architecture among the Tamberma, studies here, in meticulous detail, the preparatory arrangements for funerals, and actual funerary rites. See also: Didier Boremanse, 'The Tamberma of Togo'. *Geographical Magazine*, vol. 51, no. 3 (1978), p. 196-200.

141 **Détermination économique versus fondements symboliques: la chefferie de Bassar.** (Economic determinants versus symbolic foundations: the Bassar chiefdom.)
Stéphan Dugast. *Cahiers d'Etudes Africaines*, vol. 28, no.2 (1988), p. 265-80. bibliog.

This is a study of the conditions that led to the emergence of chiefs among the Bassar people of central Togo. The development of metallurgy and the prosperity this brought with it consolidated Bassar society and gave chiefs the military means to impose transit taxes on the Hausa kola trade which passed through their region. The article also assesses the somewhat different conclusions on the issue arrived at by other scholars, such as De Barros and Martinelli.

142 **Le deuil du conjoint en pays evhé (Togo/Ghana).** (Ewe mourning rites [Togo/Ghana].)
Albert de Surgy. *Systèmes de Pensée en Afrique Noire*, vol. 9 (1986), p. 105-33. English summary.

This is an insightful study of the role played by mourning rites, which are performed independently of funeral ceremonies, among the Ewe of Ghana and Togo. The depth of the mourners' feelings towards the deceased is not relevant to the mourning rites, which have the function of assuaging the bereaved 'to prevent reactions of depressive self-accusation that one has not fulfilled duties' towards the deceased. At the same time they serve as an initiation of the deceased to his/her new status, which is regarded by the Ewe not as 'a definitive departure or annihilation, but a transformation of the way he is present' (p. 161). The article has a brief summary in English. For two additional interesting articles on this theme see: Claude Rivière, 'Deuil et veuvage chez les Eve du Togo' (Mourning and widowhood among the Ewe of Togo). *Anthropos*, vol. 77, no. 3-4 (1982), p. 461-74; and Lawoetey-Pierre Ajavon, 'Une certaine conception de la mort chez les Ge-Mina du sud-est Togo' (A certain conception of death among the Ge-Mina of south-east Togo). *Anthropos*, vol. 85, no. 1-3 (1992), p. 182-87. bibliog.

143 **Die Ewe-Stamme.** (The Ewe tribe.)
Jakob Spieth. Berlin: D. Riemer, 1906. 962p.

Written by the famous German scholar, Spieth, this is one of the classic texts about the Ewe ethnic group. Voluminous and detailed, it includes an encyclopaedic array of data on Ewe life at the turn of the century, their history, social and political organization, religious beliefs, and language.

144 **Die Glidji-Ewe in Togo.** (The Glidji-Ewe in Togo.)
Diedrich Westermann. Berlin: Gruyter, 1935. 332p.

This benchmark study by the famous linguist, Westermann, constitutes a study of the Ewe population in Glidji. For another case-study see: C. Litoux-Le Coq, *Contribution à la connaissance régionale du sud-est du Togo: sur peuplement et migrations; le village de Fiata* (Contribution to the regional knowledge of south-east Togo: on peoples and migrations; the village of Fiata). Lomé: ORSTOM, 1974. 131p.

145 **Diviners and alienists and annunciators among the Batammaliba of Togo.**
R. Blier.   In: *African divination systems: ways of knowledge.*   Edited by Philip M. Peek.   Bloomington: Indiana University Press, 1991. p. 82-93.

The Batammaliba, or Somba, of northern Togo (and neighbouring Benin) have attracted considerable scholarly attention due to their unique building styles and individual social groupings. This particular contribution outlines their world outlook, their conceptualization of the spiritual world, and the role of diviners within it.

146 **The Ewe of Ghana and Togo on the eve of colonialism: a contribution to the Marxist debate on pre-capitalist socio-economic formations.**
Ansa K. Asamoa.   Tema, Ghana: Ghana Publishing Corporation, 1986. 78p. bibliog.

Asamoa attempts to provide a cultural and economic anthropology of the Ewe people, both prior to and after colonialism. His aim is to break their social history down into periods, according to socio-economic formation, and thus offer readers 'a deeper historical, materialist insight into historical categories metaphysically simplified, if not vulgarized, by bourgeois historians.' (p. ix).

147 **The Ewe-speaking people of Togoland and the Gold Coast.**
Madeline Manoukian.   London: International African Institute, 1952. 63p.

Although now dated, this was, and indeed still is, one of the best summary introductions to the Ewe people, who were found divided at the turn of the century into some 120 independent political clans. In this work, Manoukian discusses their origins, tradition and history, physical environment, economy, social and political organization, and religious beliefs.

148 **Fathers and sons: domestic production, conflict, and social forms among the Kabre.**
Charles D. Piot.   *Research in Economic Anthropology* (Greenwich, Connecticut), vol. 10 (1988), p. 269-85.

This article is a critique of Fortes' influential developmental cycle of domestic groups, which was based on an examination of the practice among the Kabre of northern Togo. Piot argues that there is a central contradiction in the productive system of the Kabre that rests on the conflicting labour needs of father and son. This explains certain Kabre practices such as child fosterage, household fission, dispersal of settlements, out-migration of young men, and the Kabre's progressive expansion outwards into new lands during the past several decades.

149 **Féte traditionnelle akposso-akebou Avozou 1980 à Badou.** (The 1980 Ovozou traditional Akposso-Akebou festivities.)
E. Sédjroh Onuh Adjéodah. Lomé: Cercle d'Etudes Akposso, 1980. 28p.

Written in both French and Kposo, this is an analysis of the significance of male and female given names among the Akposso of central-south Togo, and the Avozou ceremonies that are central to Akposso life. The author provides a long list of names, and their traditional meaning in Akposso society.

150 **Du folklore à la culture national. Force pensée africaine: cas des Ewes-Akposso et Moba du Togo.** (From folklore to national culture: the power of African thought: the case of the Ewe-Akposso and the Moba of Togo.)
E. Sédjroh Onuh Adjéodah. Lomé: Institut National de la Recherche Scientifique, 1985. 31p. bibliog.

This is a survey of the Akposso and Ewe concepts of life and death, spirituality and incarnation, and the role and purposes of ritual sacrifices in these contexts. Special attention is paid to the cult of the Dambasu serpent divinity. The author compares these with Moba concepts and practices, since although the Moba are geographically distant, they have certain cosmologies which are remarkably similar. The material is gleaned from oral history and four Akpasso Dambasu practitioners.

151 **La grossesse chez les Evé du Togo.** (Size among the Ewe of Togo.)
Claude Rivière. *Le Mois en Afrique*, no. 227/228 (Dec. 1984-Jan. 1985), p. 120-32. bibliog.

Rivière presents an unusual analysis of the way physical size, and other personal attributes, are perceived by the Ewe in southern Togo.

152 **L'habitat et l'occupation de la terre chez les Somba.** (Habitat and land occupation among the Somba.)
Paul Mercier. *Bulletin d'IFAN* (1953), p. 798-817. bibliog.

This is a detailed study of the Somba of the Atakora mountains that rise up on both sides of the Togo-Benin border. It considers their social organization, land-use, and unique building style. More detail on the latter's castle-like appearance is provided by Mercier in, 'L'habitation à étage dans l'Atakora' (Living on floors in the Atakora). *Etudes Dahoméennes*, no. 11 (1951), p. 29-86; and A. Maurice 'Les chateaux Somba' (The Somba castles). *Tropiques*, vol. 55, no. 395 (May 1957), p. 59-66.

153 **Initiations africaines et pédagogie de la foi: le mariage chrétienne traditionnel Kabiyé à la lumière du Concile Vatican II.** (African initiations and the pedagogics of the faith: traditional Kabre Christian marriage in light of the Vatican Council II.)
Pidalani Pignan. Paris: Sogico, 1988. 178p. bibliog.

This work constitutes a detailed description of Kabre marriage customs and rites, their base in traditional cosmologies, and how they can be seen to correspond to the more liberal codiciles of the Vatican Council II. To this end the author, who is a local priest, provides an overview of how the Kabre regard marriage, the manner in which marriage partners are chosen, the role of parents, relatives and chiefs in the proceedings, the initiation and purification rites, the ceremony itself, and the rights and duties of both married partners.

154 Kinship and marriage among the Anlo Ewe.
G. K. Nukunya.   London: Athlone Press, 1969. 217p. bibliog.

The Anlo, who reside just across the Togolese border in Ghana, are the largest, and historically the only centralized clan of the 120 or so Ewe groups that exist between the Volta and the Mona rivers. This book, a former PhD thesis for London University, is a study of the patterns of marriage and divorce among the Anlo, set against the broader background of their kinship and household system. The author concludes his study by noting how social change is eroding traditional Ewe values. For two other articles on marriage among the Ewe see: Anani Ahianyo-Akakpo, 'Kososo, une forme de mariage traditionnel' (Kososo, a form of traditional marriage). *Etudes Togolaises* (Lomé), no. 1 (Jan.-March 1971), p. 75-85; and Claude Durand, 'Le mariage traditionnel au Togo' (Traditional marriage in Togo). *Annales de l'Université du Bénin* (Lomé), 1979. Special Issue, p. 5-23.

155 The Konkomba of northern Ghana.
David Tait.   London: Oxford University Press, 1961. 255p. bibliog. English summary.

The Konkomba are an ethnic group living along the Oti river (north and west of the Kotokoli and Bassari) on both sides of the Ghana-Togo boundary, and as such have been studied by anglophone scholars as well as French. This book, although dated (it is based on research carried out between 1950 and 1955), is recognized as the classic work on this ethnic group. In it Tait explores the Konkomba form of social and domestic organization, and documents the group's rituals, divination practices and sacrifices. His work, which includes diagrams and plates, was posthumously assembled and completed by Jack Goody, and consists in part of Tait's own PhD dissertation. See also: the additional articles by David Tait, 'The political system of the Konkomba'. *Africa*, vol. 23 (1953), 213-23; 'Konkomba friendship relations'. *African Studies*, vol. 13 (1954), p. 77-84; 'The place of libation in Konkomba ritual'. *Bulletin d'IFAN*, vol. 17 (1955), p. 168-72; and 'The family, household and minor lineage of the Konkomba'. *Africa*, vol. 26 (1956), p. 332-42. See also: Henryk Zimon, *Afrykanskie rytualy agrarne na przykladzie kudu Konkomba* (African agrarian rituals as illustrated by the Konkomba people). Warsaw: Verbinum, 1992. 156p. bibliog. It contains an extensive summary in English.

156 Land tenure and inheritance in Anloga.
G. K. Nukunya.   Legon, Ghana: University of Ghana, Institute of Statistical, Social and Economic Research, 1972. 34p.

This brief monograph deals with some of the more controversial aspects of Ewe social organization, exemplified by an analysis of the Anlo clan found just across the border in Ghana. Nukunya outlines the general principles governing traditional patterns of land tenure and inheritance, and the changes that have occurred as share cropping, tenancies, pledging and purchasing of land have developed to meet the demands of modern farmers.

157　**Malheur de l'homme et mise à mort rituelle de l'animal domestique dans la société Kabiyé.** (Man's misfortune and ritual killing of domestic animals in Kabre society.)
Raymond Verdier.　*Systèmes de Pensée en Afrique Noire*, no. 5 (1981), p. 155-73.

Verdier provides a detailed analysis of the ritual role, and manner of conducting animal sacrifices in Kabre society. Various restrictions are in force however. While everyone has a duty to sacrifice animals, not everyone can perform the function; for a variety of reasons, for example, women cannot. In addition, while only domestic animals can be sacrificed (wild ones 'belong' to other spirits), not all are acceptable. These are: cats; pigs; horses; and ducks, although non-Kabre or recent imports of the latter two are gaining acceptance.

158　**Die materielle Kultur der Bassar (nord Togo).** (The material culture of the Bassar [north Togo].)
Hans Peter Hahn.　Stuttgart: Franz Steiner Verlag, 1991. 237p. bibliog.

This work is a veritable *tour-de-force* on the material world of the Bassari people, as well as on their social life and customs. Meticulously detailed and profusely illustrated with diagrams, sketches, plates and maps, the book is a comprehensive inventory of all Bassari handicrafts, pottery, gourdes, weaponry, agricultural and personal implements, basketry and musical instruments. It concludes with by far the most comprehensive multi-language bibliography on this ethnic group.

159　**Metallurgistes Bassar.** (Bassari metallurgists.)
Bruno Martinelli.　Lomé: Université du Bénin, Institut National des Sciences de l'Education, 1982. 114p. bibliog.

The Bassari, residing near the border of Ghana to the west and north of Sokodé, have received considerable academic attention from the days of German colonial rule. More recently, however, a number of scholars have again focused on this ethnic group, whose prime uniqueness lies in their development of iron-smelting in the pre-colonial era. With their skills much sought-after by neighbouring peoples seeking iron agricultural tools and weaponry, pre-colonial caravan trails passed through their villages, providing the Bassari with a measure of trade, wealth and power they might not otherwise have had. Martinelli's book, which includes sketches, maps, diagrams and a useful bibliography, notes the diverse and complex ethnic origins of the Bassari people, whose metal-workers resided in distinct villages in the area. He illustrates and discusses their metallurgical processes, technology and the implements they created in detail. Bassari iron-smelting declined sharply with the onset of the colonial era when European iron imports began to arrive in large quantities, revived somewhat during the isolation from Europe during the First World War, and during the 1929 global recession. Smelting then disappeared completely, becoming totally uneconomical. See also: D. Kuevi, 'Le travail et le commerce du fer au Togo avant l'arrivée des Européens' (Work and commerce in iron in Togo before the arrival of the Europeans). *Etudes Togolaises*, vol. 11/12 (1975), p. 22-43.

160 **Mundliche Uberlieferungen zur Geschichte der Moba.** (Oral
traditions, history and family life of the Moba of Togo.)
Jurgen Zwernemann. *Afrika und Ubersee* (Berlin), vol. 60 (1977),
p. 86-116.

This is a study of the Moba, who are possibly the only autochtonous people in Togo,
and who live in the extreme north of the country but share certain similarities with the
coastal Ewe.

161 **La naissance chez le Evé du Togo.** (Birth among the Ewe of Togo.)
Claude Rivière. *Journal des Africanistes*, vol. 51, no. 1/2 (1981),
p. 71-95. bibliog.

In most African belief-systems, as among the Ewe, birth represents a particularly
difficult and dangerous passage from the world of the ancestors (from which people
come back to life) to the land of the living. Consequently various religious rites,
sacrifices, purification procedures, and magic practices are necessary to aid in the
survival of the newborn. Prayers are aimed at the ancestors, sacrifices appease the
gods of divination and lineage, while various prohibitions and rites imposed upon
mothers cleanse them of any moral impurity. The author discusses all aspects of the
process of childbirth, including the allocation of (several) given names to the
newborn and rites that confirm its entrance into the family.

162 **Note sur le canicide chez les Kabiyé du Nord-Togo.** (A note on
dog-killing among the Kabre of north Togo.)
Raymond Verdier. *Systèmes de Pensée en Afrique Noire*, no. 1
(1975), p. 129-136.

The fact that dogs are part of both the savage and the domestic worlds is the subject
of many myths and tales in oral literature, as well as in the initiation rites of the *afala*
age-class among the Kabre. There, the dog symbolizes the mortal nature of man, and
through its death by strangulation marks the rites of passage from childhood to
adolescence.

163 **L'objet du sacrifice Moba.** (The object of Moba sacrifice.)
Albert de Surgy. In: *Ethnologiques: hommages à Marcel Griaule*.
Edited by S. de Ganay, et al. Paris: Hermann, 1987. p. 391-413.
bibliog.

This is an analysis of the role sacrifices, which are usually chickens, play in Moba
society in north Togo. De Surgy describes in detail the ceremonies and rituals and
their meaning, and provides several alternative explanations for the continued
survival of the rites. See also: De Surgy, 'Les libations et le rôle de la presentatrice
d'eau enfarinée dans le sacrifice Mwaba-Gurma (Nord-Togo)' (Libations and the role
of the presenter of floury water in Moba-Gur sacrifices [north Togo]). *Systèmes de
Pensée en Afrique Noire*, no. 5 (1981), p. 127-54.

164 **Organisation politique des Kotokoli du nord Togo.** (The political organization of the Kotokoli in north Togo.)
Pierre Alexandre. *Cahiers d'Etudes Africaines*, vol. 4, no. 2 (1963), p. 228-74. bibliog.

This article, which includes maps, diagrams, and a number of tables, is a distillation of the author's 1959 University of London thesis, material from which was also used for his contribution to *Les populations du Nord-Togo* (q.v.). This article represents a comprehensive study of the origins, social and political organization, and history of the Kotokoli kingdom, that emerged south of the Kabre and Bassari territory in north Togo and stretched from Ghana to Benin. With 70,000 Kotokoli people living within Togo's borders, they inhabit two-thirds of the Sokodé region. Alexandre discusses in particular its feudal aspects, sources of social and regal power, and the lineage, ritual and religious bonds that tied its component parts together.

165 **Origine et fonction humanisante de la mort selon les Mwaba.** (The origins and humanizing function of death according to the Moba.)
Albert de Surgy. *Anthropos*, vol. 79, no. 1/3 (1984), p. 129-43. bibliog.

The author discusses the concept of death, and the myths surrounding its 'origins' in several African societies, including among the Moba. Just as those who are living interact with the spiritual world via ancestors, so people who die return to the world of the living after the first funeral ceremony, to remain near their offspring. A popular Moba tale about the dual continuation of the human soul that keeps one foot in the human world and one in the land of ancestors (for several generations) humanizes death and keeps society cohesive. Another article by de Surgy which may be of interest is: 'Par quelle voie et dans quelle mesure les Mwaba du Togo estiment-ils être mis en demeure d'exercer leur liberté' (By what means and to what measure do the Moba estimate themselves as capable of exercising their freedom). *Droit et Cultures* (Nanterre), vol. 5 (1983), p.71-86.

166 **Le pays Kabiyé: cité des dieux – cité des hommes.** (Kabre country: city of the gods – city of men.)
Raymond Verdier. Paris: Karthala, 1982. 215p. bibliog.

This is possibly the most important book to be written on the Kabre of northern Togo; it contains twenty-eight pages of plates, diagrams and numerous maps. Verdier dissects all aspects of Kabre society, belief-systems, customs, clan-structure, rites, sorcery, and daily life, as well as providing specific examples of the kinds of cases which come up for adjudication before chiefs. The work includes annexes containing concise data on such subjects as Kabre linguistics and artisanal work.

167 **Les paysans Kabré du Nord-Togo.** (The Kabre peasants of north Togo.)
Leo Frobenius. *Le Monde Non-Chretién*, no. 59-60 (July-Dec. 1961), p. 101-72.

This is one of the pioneering studies of the Kabre by the famous Frobenius, translated from the original German and republished.

168 **La pince et le soufflet: deux techniques de forge traditionnelles au Nord-Togo.** (The claw and the air-blower: two traditional smelting techniques in north Togo.)
Albert de Surgy. *Journal des Africanistes,* vol. 56, no. 2 (1986), p. 29-53. bibliog.

The author investigates the activities of the Bassari blacksmiths in northern Togo, and identifies two different, distinct and specialized groups, which are complementary in their activities. A detailed comparison follows, of their tools, work organization, techniques, and exchange relations in the booming trade that developed within their villages.

169 **Les populations du Nord-Togo.** (The populations of north Togo.)
Jean Claude Froelich, Pierre Alexandre, Robert Cornevin. Paris: Presses Universitaires de France, 1963. 199p. bibliog.

Authored by three of France's greatest anthropologists, with the collaboration of Pastor J. Delord, this is by far the best-known general study of the peoples of north Togo, and it is still an invaluable one. The work covers *inter alia* the Kabre and the Lamba, the Kotokoli and Bassari, the Konkomba and Moba, and in a much briefer form the Akebou and the Chokossi. Supplemented by maps and tables, the book also provides founding dates and notes on the historical origins of key northern villages. The chapters may appear short (for example, the Kotokoli and Bassari share only fifty-two pages) in the light of the comprehensive historical and anthropological treatment provided, but they masterfully synthesize a great deal of material, and as a broad background to the northern ethnic groups this book still has no match.

170 **Pratiques de maternage chez les Kotokoli du Togo et les Mossi de Haute Volta.** (Child-rearing practices among the Kotokoli of Togo and the Mossi of Upper Volta.)
Suzanne Lallemand. *Journal des Africanistes,* vol. 51, no. 1/2 (1981), p. 43-70.

This comparative analysis outlines the similarities and differences of the assumptions and objectives of two traditional rural societies with regard to infancy. Lallemand finds that different child-rearing practices, though reflecting a compromise between the values (including religious) and activities of adults, and the needs of children, in reality mirror a people's ethical concepts, and their choice between productive and reproductive roles for society.

171 **La production des outils agricoles en pays Basar.** (The manufacturing of agricultural implements in Bassari country.)
Bruno Martinelli. *Cahiers ORSTOM,* vol. 20, no. 3/4 (1984), p. 485-504. bibliog. English summary.

This article, which includes diagrams and a brief summary in English, focuses on the nature of the agricultural implements produced by the Bassari people from iron deposits in their area. These implements were used for domestic purposes as well as for trade with neighbouring peoples and the caravans that passed by to trade. Though the practice of iron-smelting has long since ended, it is still possible to distinguish the differing needs that various people at the time had for agricultural tools, from the current distribution of such implements.

172   **Les proverbes du peuple Gen (Mina) au littoral Togo-Bénin.**
(Proverbs of the Gen [Mina] people along the Togo-Benin littoral.)
Roberto Pazzi.   Lomé: Université du Bénin, Institut National des
Sciences de l'Education, 1985. 329p. bibliog.

In this study Pazzi undertakes a wide-ranging analysis of 1,340 Mina proverbs
gleaned from the peoples along the coast of Togo-Benin, in order to provide insights
about Mina values and cosmology. The proverbs are organized under twelve thematic
sections (such as animals, family and society, and natural elements) and each proverb
is accompanied by notes regarding its social and moral significance, and any
variations that might have been found from locality to locality. The book concludes
with a brief lexical analysis of the language.

173   **Proverbes et traditions des Bassars du nord Togo.** (Proverbs and
traditions of the Bassari of north Togo.)
Marian Szwark.   St. Augustin, Germany: Haus Volker und Kulturen,
1981. 137p. bibliog.

Written in French and Tobote, this work is a study of the history, social life, mores,
religion and customs of the Bassari people, as illustrated through their proverbs. With
this objective, the author examines 604 Bassari proverbs, dissecting them for their
insights on the Bassari cosmology. The primary aim of the study is to help
missionaries in Bassari districts to better understand the culture of the region, and
more effectively communicate with potential catechists.

174   **Quelques aspects des problèmes socio-culturels akposso-akébou:
fétes traditionnelles Ovazou, Amlame.** (Several aspects of
Akposso-Akebou socio-cultural problems: the Ovazou traditional
feasts at Amlame.)
E. S. Onuh Adjéodah.   Lomé: Cercle d'Etudes Akposso, 1979. 25p.

This is an overview of Akposso cosmology, and the significance of Ovazou, their
traditional festivity. The author details the preparations for, and activities in, this
three-day feast, and locates it within the social life and customs of the Akposso
people.

175   **La relation au conjoint idéal et la statut de l'imaginaire chez les
Evhé.** (The relationship with the ideal spouse and the status of the
imaginary among the Ewe.)
Albert de Surgy.   *Journal des Africanistes*, vol. 50, no. 2 (1980),
p. 73-108. bibliog.

This is a unique contribution on the Ewe concept of pre-natal social ties. The Ewe
join each individual, from the moment the embryo starts developing, with an invisible
ideal spouse in the spiritual world, which will affect one's personality from birth to
death. Very frequent consultations with soothsayers, and religious rites, aim at getting
in touch with this pre-natal link in order to better adapt to the ideal that it represents.
It is also believed that one chooses friends in the physical world who are
representatives of those with whom one has kept company before birth; maintaining
these ties contributes to the individual's mental well-being.

176 **Un rite agraire chez les Kotokoli du nord Togo: la féte Sinda.** (An agrarian rite among the Kotokoli of north Togo: the Sinda festival.) Suzanne Lallemand, H. Aboudou Issifou. *Journal de la Société des Africanistes*, vol. 37, no. 1 (1967), p. 73-85. bibliog.

The authors describe the nature, significance, and festivities connected with the Kotokoli Sinda agrarian rites.

177 **Sociologie des sociétés orales d'Afrique noire.** (Sociology of oral societies in Black Africa.) F. N'Sougan Agblemagnon. Paris: Silex, 1984. 216p. bibliog.

This book is a re-issue of the classic socio-linguistic study published in 1973 by Agblemagnon. It discusses, in connection with the Ewe, the role and significance of oral history, folklore, proverbs, given names, music and songs.

178 **La terre et le pouvoir chez les Guin du sud-est du Togo.** (Land and power among the Guin of south-east Togo.) Alain Mignot. Paris: Publications de la Sorbonne, 1985. 288p. bibliog.

The Guin, whose name is a corruption of Ga, originated from the vicinity of Accra, which now falls within the borders of Ghana, and arrived in their habitat in south-east Togo around the year 1660. One of their major centres is Glidji, which is near the coastal town of Aného. This book, with a preface written by Claude Rivière, who places Mignot's work in perspective, and aided by diagrams and maps, is a comprehensive study of the intertwining of traditional authority, kinship, clan, religion and land tenure among the Guin.

179 **Three ceremonies in Togo.** Gena Reisner. *The Drama Review* (New York), vol. 25, no. 4 (Winter 1981), p. 51-58.

This article uses photographs for a graphic portrayal of three folk ceremonies in Togo: an Ewe planting festival; a Kotokoli hunting ceremony; and a Mina funerary rite.

180 **Toi et le ciel, vous et la terre: contes paillards tem du Togo.** (Thou and the sky, you and the earth: bawdy Tem tales of Togo.) Zakari Tchagbale, Suzanne Lallemand. Paris: Société d'Etudes Linguistiques et Anthropologiques de France, 1982. 235p. bibliog.

The twenty-five Kotokoli folk-tales presented in this book are preceded by a compact but comprehensive twenty-page guide to the phonology and morpho-syntax of the Tem language, spoken by the Kotokoli ethnic group. Tchagbale and Lallemand also provide an anthropological background to these people of central Togo. Each of the tales included in the collection either focuses on the sexual act as its central theme, or has sexual organs as its heroes. The authors assess the moral content of these stories and their underlying images and fantasies, and place the Kotokoli examples within a wider African context where similar folk-tales exist. For a broader study of Kotokoli oral literature see: Mamah Fousseni Abby-Alphah Ouro-Djobo, *La culture traditionnelle et la littérature orale des Tem* (Traditional culture and Tem oral literature). Stuttgart: Franz Steiner Verlag, 1984. 336p. bibliog.

181 **La tribu Konkomba du nord Togo.** (The Konkomba tribe of north Togo.)
Jean Claude Froelich. Dakar, Senegal: IFAN, 1954. 253p. bibliog.

This book is the pioneering study of the Konkomba ethnic group by one of France's foremost anthropologists. The work, which contains plates, illustrations, diagrams and maps, discusses in compact thematic chapters: the history of the Konkomba and the diverse origins of their several clans; their social organization and economy; family life; religious and initiation/divination rites; concepts of life, illness, death and reincarnation; pre-colonial military alliances and warfare; and dress and material life.

Le Togo: des origines à nos jours. (Togo: from its origins to the present day.)
See item no. 4.

Le Togo. (Togo.)
See item no. 5.

Togo. Les hommes et leur milieu. (Togo. The people and their setting.)
See item no. 19.

Actes du colloque international sur les civilisations Ada-Ewe. (Proceedings of the international colloquium on the Adje-Ewe civilizations.)
See item no. 57.

Adjigovi.
See item no. 58.

Les Aja-Ewe. (The Adja-Ewe.)
See item no. 59.

Atakora mountain refugees.
See item no. 60.

La chefferie dans la nation contemporaine. (Chiefdom in the contemporary nation.)
See item no. 63.

Contribution à l'histoire du peuplement: traditions, histoire et organisation de la cité chez les Akposso. (Contribution to the history of population: traditions, history and the organization of the city among the Akposso.)
See item no. 65.

Dream of unity. Pan-Africanism and political unification in West Africa.
See item no. 66.

Elements de polemologie en pays ewe. (Elements of polemology among the Ewe.)
See item no. 68.

Entretiens en pays bassar. (Conversations in Bassar country.)
See item no. 69.

The Eves of West Africa: the Anlo-Eves and their immediate neighbours.
See item no. 71.

The Ewe in pre-colonial times.
See item no. 72.

The Ewe-speaking peoples of the Slave Coast of West Africa.
See item no. 73.

The Ewe unification movement.
See item no. 74.

Foli Bébé.
See item no. 76.

Histoire de Petit Popo et du royaume gen. (The history of Little Popo and the Gen kingdom.)
See item no. 84.

Histoire presente, exemple du royaume Kotokoli au Togo. (Current history, the example of the Kotokoli kingdom in Togo.)
See item no. 85.

Histoire traditionnelle des Kotokola et des Bi-Tchambi du nord Togo. (Traditional history of the Kotokoli and Bi-Tchambi of north Togo.)
See item no. 86.

Peuples du golfe du Bénin. (The people of the Gulf of Benin.)
See item no. 90.

Les peuples et royaumes du Golfe du Bénin. (The people and kingdoms of the Gulf of Benin.)
See item no. 91.

Anthropologie religieuse des Evé du Togo. (Religious anthropology of the Ewe of Togo.)
See item no. 110.

Essai sur la conception religieuse du peuple Mina. (Essay on the religious conceptions of the Mina people.)
See item no. 112.

Die Religion der Eweer in Sud-Togo. (The religion of the Ewe in south Togo.)
See item no. 113.

La géomancie à l'ancienne Côte d'Esclaves. (Geomancy in the old Slave Coast.)
See item no. 115.

La sorcellerie au Sud-Togo. (Sorcery in south Togo.)
See item no. 130.

La structure socio-politique et son articulation avec la pensée religieuse chez les Aja-Tado du Sud-Togo. (The socio-political structure and its articulation within the religious thought of the Adja-Ewe of south Togo.)
See item no. 131.

La système religieuse des Evhé. (The religious system of the Ewe.)
See item no. 132.

Die Glidji-Ewe in Togo. (The Glidji-Ewe in Togo.)
See item no. 144.

Enquête socio-démographique chez les Moba-Gurma. (Socio-demographic survey of the Moba-Gurma.)
See item no. 184.

Aménagement de l'espace et mouvements de population au Togo: l'exemple du pays Kabye. (Space management and migratory movements in Togo: the example of Kabre country.)
See item no. 211.

L'ancienne colonisation Kabre et ses possibilités d'expansion dans l'Est-Mono. (The former Kabre colonization and its possibility of expansion into eastern Mono.)
See item no. 212.

La colonisation des terres neuves du Centre-Togo par les Kabre et les Losso. (The colonization of new land in central Togo by the Kabre and the Losso.)
See item no. 213.

Les migrations rurales des Kabyé et des Losso. (The rural migrations of the Kabre and the Losso.)
See item no. 218.

Die rolle der Frau bei den Kabre in nord Togo. (The role of the woman among the Kabre in north Togo.)
See item no. 231.

Le divorce chez les Evé du Togo. (Divorce among the Ewe of Togo.)
See item no. 232.

Etude socio-démographique du mariage chez les Coniagui et Bassari. (Socio-demographic study of marriage among the Coniagui and Bassari.)
See item no. 234.

Le mariage traditionnel au Togo. (Traditional marriage in Togo.)
See item no. 240.

Mariage traditionnel dans les pays ewe. (Traditional marriage in Ewe country.)
See item no. 241.

A la recherche de la justice. (In search of justice.)
See item no. 292.

Loin de Mango. Les Tiokossi de Lomé. (Far from Mango. The Chokossi of Lomé.)
See item no. 389.

Anatomy of architecture: ontology and metaphor in Batammaliba architectural expression.
See item no. 491.

Moral architecture: beauty and ethics in Batammaliba building.
See item no. 494.

Artisanats traditionnels en Afrique noire, Togo. (Traditional artisans in Black Africa, Togo.)
See item no. 504.

Population and Demography

182 **Analyses des données du recensement général de la population et de la habitat 8-22 novembre 1981.** (Analyses of the data from the general census of the population and its habitat as of 8-22 November 1981.)

Lomé: Direction de la Statistique, 1989. 11 vols.

This is the most ambitious demographic analysis ever attempted by Togo, and is based on the census returns for 1981. The census listed the country's population at 2,719,567 people compared to the 1,950,646 of 1970. The densest prefecture, du Golfe, with 300 people per square kilometre was followed by the Lac, and Binah, both with densities of 100-200 people per square kilometre, while the centre of the country had the lowest figures, of around 25 people per square kilometre. The eleven volumes are all-encompassing in their analysis of the country's population, including areas such as economic activity and education. Each was prepared by an individual specialist. Several additional abbreviated summaries of the census results were also published.

183 **Analyse régionale du recensement de 1970.** (Regional analysis of the 1970 census.)

Mensah L. Assogba, Thérése Locoh, Koffi Adognon. Lomé: Direction de la Statistique, 1983. 245p. bibliog.

This volume is a comprehensive study of the results of the 1970 census, analysed by region.

184 **Enquête socio-démographique chez les Moba-gurma.** (Socio-demographic survey of the Moba-Gurma people.)

P. Levi, M. Pilon. Paris: ORSTOM, 1988. 187p. bibliog.

This book is an up-to-date detailed analysis of the demographics of the extreme north of Togo, where the Moba reside. As a group, they are often ignored due to the far greater population pressures in the Kabre areas further south.

185   **Perspectives de la population togolaise, 1971-2006.** (Prospects for
the Togolese population, 1971-2006.)
Messan L. N. Assogba.   Lomé: Université du Bénin, Unité de
Recherche Démographique, 1986. 36p.

Based on the results of the previous two censuses, the author of this brief study
projects the growth of Togo's population, by sex and age, up until the year 2006 when
it should reach a total of five million. The bulk of the study is composed of charts and
statistical tables.

186   **Population et progrès socio-économique au Togo.** (Population and
socio-economic progress in Togo.)
E. Y. Gu-Konu.   Lomé: Université du Bénin, 1980. 291p. bibliog.

This is a detailed analysis of Togo's census data, and their implications for the future.
The work, which is presented in six chapters, includes a multiplicity of statistical
tables, diagrams and maps.

187   **La population togolaise, 1967.** (Togolese population, 1967.)
Emmanuel Konu.   Lomé: Institut National de la Recherche
Scientifique, 1968. 44p. bibliog.

A review of the census of 1961, and an analysis of the population shifts and other
demographic changes that had transpired since the previous census.

188   **Surpression démographique et évolution foncière: le cas du sud-
est du Togo.** (Demographic pressures and the evolution of land
tenancy: the case of south-east Togo.)
Emile Le Bris.   *African Perspectives*, vol. 1 (1979), p. 107-25.
bibliog.

In this article the author carries out an investigation into what he regards as a cul-de-
sac. He discusses the pressure being exerted on existing arable land by a growing
large population which is no longer able to produce enough food surpluses to feed
itself. There is no real solution in sight but basic land reforms and these, the author
finds, are unpalatable to many.

189   **Togo: selected statistical data by sex.**
Agency for International Development.   Washington, DC: AID,
1981. various pagination.

A compendium of statistics on all aspects of Togo's population, based on a database
from 1970.

Enquête démographique et de santé au Togo: 1988. (Demographic and
health enquiry on Togo: 1988.)
See item no. 221.

Urban Studies

190 **Armature urbaine au Togo.** (Urban reinforcement in Togo.)
Yves Marguerat. Paris: ORSTOM, 1985. 166p. bibliog.

Since independence the capital of Lomé has seen phenomenal growth, transforming it from a charming, small sleepy town into a sprawling metropolitan centre. Major urban renewal was necessary in the 1970s, including the demolition and relocation of an entire indigenous trading quarter that had become a crowded slum on prime inner-city land. This study traces the demographic changes of urbanization in Togo since before independence. For an account of the origins of Lomé see Hermann Attignon, 'Lomé' *Le Mois en Afrique*, no. 81 (Sept. 1972), p. 49-57. A more detailed study of land-utilization in Lomé can be found in: Yves Marguerat, 'Logiques et pratiques des acteurs fonciers à Lomé' (Logic and practice of land actors in Lomé). In: *Strategies urbaines dans les pays en voie de développement: politiques sociales en matière d'urbanisme et d'habitat,* edited by Nicole Haumont, Marie Alain. Paris, Harmattan, 1987, p. 78-100.

191 **Dynamiques de villes secondaires et processus migratoires en Afrique de l'Ouest: le cas de trois centres en région de plantation au Togo: Atakpamé, Kpalimé, Badou.** (The dynamics of secondary towns and migration processes in West Africa: the case of three urban centres in plantation regions in Togo: Atakpamé, Kpalimé, Badou.)
Véronique Dupont. Paris: ORSTOM, 1986. 437p. bibliog.

While much of the uncontrolled rural-urban drift in West Africa in general, and in Togo specifically, has been towards the capital city, considerable migration has also taken place in the direction of regional centres, several of which have experienced significant growth. This massive work examines in detail the demographic patterns of internal migration that have led to the growth of three secondary towns in Togo that lie in prime agrarian country. The author analyses the reasons for these migrations, the attractions these centres have for new arrivals, and the resultant urban problems. See also: Philippe Antoine, Sidiki Coulibaly, *L'insertion urbaine des migrants en Afrique* (The urban influx of migrants in Africa). Paris: ORSTOM, 1989, 323p.

192 **Famille et residence dans les villes africaines: Dakar, Bamako, Saint Louis, Lomé.** (Family and residence in African cities: Dakar, Bamako, Saint Louis, Lomé.)
Emile Le Bris. Paris: Harmattan, 1987. 268p. bibliog.

This work, which includes Lomé as one of its case-studies, focuses on the rapid process of urbanization in francophone West Africa. It considers the social problems this has caused and some of its negative effects on family life and housing.

193 **Lomé, les étapes de la croissance: une breve histoire de la capitale du Togo.** (Lomé, the steps in its growth: a brief history of the capital of Togo.)
Yves Marguerat. Paris: Karthala, 1992. 64p. bibliog.

This slim volume constitutes an informative history of the evolution of Lomé, from a small village in the days when Aného was the capital of German Togo, to the metropolitan centre of today. The book contains several plates and maps, and a one-page bibliography.

194 **Les lotissements et leur destin: l'exemple de Sokodé au Togo.** (The building plots and their destiny: an example from Sokodé in Togo.)
Jean-Claude Barbier. In: *Strategies urbaines dans les pays en voie de développement: politiques sociales en matière d'urbanisme et d'habitat* (Urban strategies in the developing countries: social policies on matters of urbanization and housing.) Edited by Nicole Haumont, Marie Alain. Paris, Harmattan, 1987, p. 20-43. bibliog.

Barbier presents a detailed study of urban policy, city planning and housing policy in Sokodé which is located in the northern central area of the country. Over the years the city has grown in population, from 15,000 to 50,000 people in the early eighties (and more since) to become Togo's second-largest town. The author points out that it is relatively easy to obtain building plots in Sokodé, if only because its ten traditional chiefs are eager to expand their local authority over new arrivals, without ethnic discrimination. Reasonable building costs have resulted in better houses being built, and a spacious city centre has been maintained. This work includes plates, diagrams and urban plans. Another Togolese city studied in the same volume is Atakpamé, which is located further south of Sokodé, to which it ceded demographic primacy in the 1970s. See: G. Kwasi Nyassogbo, 'Juxtaposition de deux pratiques foncières et deux formes architecturales dans une ville secondaire au Togo' (Juxtaposition of two land policy practices and two architectural styles in a secondary town in Togo), p. 112-28. bibliog.

195 **Pour une analyse comparative de l'urbanisation en Afrique noire: le cas de Lomé et de Harare à travers leur quartiers.** (Towards a comparative analysis of urbanization in Black Africa: the case of Lomé and Harare through their quarters.)
Philippe Gervais-Lambony. In: *L'année africaine 1990-91.* Bordeaux, France: CEAN, 1991. p. 393-430.

This is a comparative analysis of the demographic growth of the capitals of Togo and Zimbabwe, the town structures and services, and how they are coping with the heavy influx of new arrivals. The work also surveys the history of the two towns, their urban layout and landscapes, the businesses established there, urban practices, and the scale of the neighbourhoods.

196 **Sokodé: un plan d'urbanisme contesté.** (Sokodé: a contested urbanization plan.)
Jean-Claude Barbier. *Cités Africains*, no. 2 (1985), p. 7-12.

Although this is a rather brief article, it is quite significant in that it illustrates, through the example of what transpired in Sokodé in north-central Togo, the kinds of unexpected, but nevertheless very obvious opposition that can be encountered, when urban renewal plans threaten established ethnic and religious 'zones'.

197 **L'urbanisation et son evolution au Togo.** (The evolution of urbanization in Togo.)
Kwasi Nyassogbo. *Cahiers d'Outre-Mer*, vol. 37, no. 146 (April-June 1984), p. 136-58.

Presents a survey of the origins and evolution of Togolese towns, covering the capital, Lomé, which began as an insignificant fishing village, with the onset of German colonial rule, and other secondary urban centres. Statistical data is provided on their demographic growth over the years.

198 **Usages d'espaces et dynamique du front d'urbanisation dans les quartiers periphériques de Lomé.** (Space utilization and the dynamics of urbanization in the peripheral quarters of Lomé.)
Emile Le Bris.   In: *Famille et residence dans les villes africaines: Dakar, Bamako, Saint Louis, Lomé.*   Edited by Emile Le Bris, et al. Paris: Harmattan, 1987, p. 13-69. bibliog.

This is a meticulously detailed study of space utilization (with many diagrams and photographs of actual individual houses) in the new outlying areas of Lomé. Their spatial demographics are assessed, and the author makes a number of suggestions regarding better zoning laws and policies of land allocation to avert any further spatial anarchy. For another study on Lomé in the same volume see Alain Narie 'Espace, structures et pratique sociales à Lomé' (Space, structures and social practices in Lome), p. 177-240.

Lomé: capitale du Togo. (Lomé: capital of Togo.)
See item no. 8.

Les pratiques foncières face à l'urbanisation. (Land tenure practices versus urbanization.)
See item no. 291.

Labour

199 **Crise économique et perspective de l'emploi dans une économie ouverte: le cas du Togo.** (Economic crisis and employment prospects in an open economy: the case of Togo.)
Bureau International du Travail. Addis Ababa: Bureau International du Travail, 1985. 457p.

This massive report by the International Labour Organization considers the economic crisis in Togo, its effects on the work force, and the increasing levels of poverty in the country. Replete with numerous diagrams and statistical tables, the work is much more than a labour survey, and offers a very thorough review of the economy's fluctuations, development planning and the successes and failures of the Eyadema regime. The study is extensive, commencing with an overview of the economic crisis and of the level of unemployment in the country (including graduates), and continuing with a sectoral analysis and critical assessment of salaries and state revenues. A large number of specific suggestions and recommendations are made throughout the text, some of which are summarized in the last few pages of the report.

200 **Eléments d'anthropologie des lieux de travail: le cas d'une brasserie au Togo.** (Anthropological aspects in workplaces: the case of a brewery in Togo.)
M. Agier, T. Lulle. *Anthropologie et Sociétés,* vol. 10, no. 1 (1986), p. 109-43.

Through a detailed analysis of a brewery employing several hundred workers, the authors emphasize the continued relevance, in modern Togolese workplace settings, of traditional patron-client authority relationships, and of inter-ethnic tensions and religious practices. For an account of working conditions in the agro-industries see: Jean-Maurice Derrien, *Conditions de travail et sous-développement: les industries agro-alimentaires au Sénégal et au Togo* (Conditions of work and underdevelopment: the food industries in Senegal and Togo). Paris: CNRS, 1981. 296p.

201 **Eléments pour une étude de l'emploi au Togo à l'horizon du quatrième plan quinquennal.** (Elements for a study of employment in Togo in the light of the fourth five-year plan.)
Alfred Schwartz. Paris: ORSTOM, 1982. 43p.

This study is a projection of the employment opportunities that should have been created in the light of the implementation of Togo's fourth Five-Year Plan, which commenced in 1981. However, that development Plan rested on the same faulty assumptions as the previous ones, that is to say, that there would be increases in global market prices of phosphates, and a commensurate pick-up in State revenues from phosphate exports. Most targetted projects were therefore not even commenced, and indeed, by the mid-1980s Togo was in a severe liquidity crisis, with higher levels of unemployment than before.

202 **Eléments pour une strategie d'emploi dans les zones rurales au Togo.** (Elements for an employment strategy for the rural zones of Togo.)
International Labor Office. Addis Ababa: International Labor Office, Jobs and Skills Programme for Africa, 1983. 80p. bibliog.

A report to the Togolese government on how to formulate a rural manpower strategy, both in terms of basic data collection and assessment, and with respect to rural job-creation. An appendix lists the documentation examined in Togo by the visiting ILO team. The work includes various statistical tables, and a large number of suggestions and recommendations are presented.

203 **Evolution de l'emploi dans les entreprises togolaises du secteur moderne de 1979 a 1982.** (The evolution of employment in enterprises in the modern Togolese sector between 1979 and 1982.)
Alfred Schwartz. Paris: ORSTOM, 1982. 12p.

Despite its brevity this contribution by an ORSTOM labour sociologist is valuable in that it provides a sectoral analysis, together with statistics, of the growth of the modern work force in Togo.

204 **Labor conditions in the Republic of Togo.**
Office of Foreign Labor and Trade. Washington, DC: United States Bureau of Labor Statistics, 1966. 23p.

This is a dated survey of the labour force and its conditions of work in Togo as of the early 1960s.

205 **L'organisation corporative des chauffeurs de taxis collectifs à Bamako et Lomé.** (Corporate organization of collective taxi drivers in Bamako and Lomé.)
Jean-Claude Pradeilles, et al. *Afrique Contemporaine*, no. 158 (April-June 1991), p. 4-13.

The communal taxi-drivers of Lomé and Bamako, Mali are studied in this work and comparisons made.

206 **Rapport d'enquête sur les travailleurs d'une industrie extractive du Togo.** (Survey on the workers in an extractive industry in Togo.)
A. Hauser. Paris: ORSTOM, 1974. 223p.

This work, research on which commenced at the end of 1968, is a massive study of the labour force of Togo's main industry, the phosphate mines near Lomé, that transformed Togo into the world's fifth exporter of that commodity. The book was simultaneously published in Togo by the local ORSTOM centre, with 326 pages. It includes a tremendous amount of detailed data on every aspect of the 1,000-man labour force, from their level of education, place of origin and working conditions, to their matrimonial and funerary practices. The work provides both comprehensive statistical data, and analysis and interpretation. Of some importance is the fact that by the time Hauser's work was published the mines had been nationalized, and a major increase in production taken place.

207 **Seminaire national sur 'liberté syndicale' — conditions préalables vers la justice sociale.** (National seminar on 'trade-union freedom' — necessary conditions for social justice.)
CNTT. Lomé: CNTT, 1989. 102p.

This book consists of the proceedings of a national conference held in Lomé, with the assistance of the Hans-Seidel Foundation of Germany, on the subject of social justice and trade-union independence from government controls.

208 **Seminaire national sur 'nouvelles strategies de l'éducation ouvrière' 1990.** (National seminar on 'new strategies of workers' education, 1990.)
CNTT-ATAO. Lomé: CNTT-ATAO, 1990. various pagination.

These are the proceedings of a national conference, arranged, with assistance from the Hans-Seidel Foundation in Germany, to assess the various methods of educating the workers in Togo. The work is composed of a number of presentations and an analysis on their applicability in Togo.

209 **The underdogs of the urban economy join forces: results of an ILO programme in Mali, Rwanda and Togo.**
C. Maldonado. *International Labour Review* (Geneva), vol. 128, no. 1 (1989), p. 65-84. bibliog.

With the acceleration of the rural-urban exodus, the decline in most African economies, and programmes of privatization rampant in public sectors, more and more Africans are moving into the informal sector and engaging in a variety of petty trades to survive. In some countries as many as seventy-five per cent of the urban labour force may be employed in this way. Since 1982 the ILO has been involved in programmes aimed at helping those in the informal sector to get organized. This article reports on the aims, results and effects of these programmes in the three countries concerned and based on evaluations carried out between 1986 and 1988.

Labour

210 **L'unité du syndicalisme togolais.** (The unity of Togolese
syndicalism.)
O. F. Natchaba. *Penant*, vol. 92, no. 777/778 (1982), p. 32-72.
A comprehensive overview of the role of organized labour in Togo from 1948 until
the 1980s. The article, representing the government point of view, argues that
organized labour has been behind the rise of every regime to come to power in Togo,
only to be later disillusioned. Efforts to unify organized labour were also thwarted in
the past until this goal was finally attained under General Eyadema who created the
single CNTT union confederation.

Le syndrome du diploma et le chômage des diplomés. (The syndrome of
the diploma and the unemployment of those with diplomas.)
See item no. 269.

Migration

**211   Aménagement de l'espace et mouvements de population au Togo:
l'exemple du pays Kabyé.** (Space management and migratory
movements in Togo: the example of Kabre country.)
Anne-Marie Pillet-Schwartz. *Cahiers d'Etudes Africaines*, vol. 26,
no. 3 (1986), p. 317-31. English summary.

Since the rise to power of the Kabre General Eyadema a great deal of effort has been
expended on establishing a region of economic development in north Togo, centred
around the Kabre in their home district. The objective was to create a counterbalance
to the south of the country which had previously attracted a disproportionate amount
of investment. This initiative revolves around the stabilization of population
movements and urbanization and has opened up the hitherto economically neglected
north. As a result it has enhanced the status of urban elements in the minds of the
rural population. Surprisingly, however, the new opportunities which have emerged in
their original ethnic heartland have not appealed to the hundreds of thousands of
Kabre who, over the years, have migrated to new lands in the south. It is this question
that forms the core of Pillet-Schwartz's analysis.

**212   L'ancienne colonisation kabré et ses possibilités d'expansion dans
l'Est-Mono.** (The former Kabre colonization and its possibilities of
expansion into eastern Mono.)
Jean Claude Pauvert.   Paris: ORSTOM, 1955. 96p. bibliog.

The Kabre's original habitat was in the north, where high population densities and soil
degradation created major pressures on the land. Therefore, in 1925, the French
administration initiated a Kabre resettlement programme that brought them into relatively
depopulated areas in the south, such as Sokodé and Atakpamé. This was followed by a
larger spontaneous migration in the 1950s. In this work Pauvert statistically assesses
precisely which groups were migrating, how many of them there were, and the reasons
why this was occurring. The objective was to avoid a repetition of the problems that
developed in one district where rapid soil degradation developed in the lifetime of one
generation and meant that yet another population relocation was necessary.

213 **La colonisation des terres neuves du Centre-Togo par les Kabre et les Losso.** (The colonization of new land in central Togo by the Kabre and the Losso.)
Bernard Lucien-Brun. Paris: ORSTOM, 1974. 293p. bibliog.

Originally a doctoral dissertation, this is a comprehensive study of the land and demographic pressures forcing the northern Kabre people out of their Kara redoubt into vacant land further south. With the aid of maps and thirty-two plates, the book examines in great detail the causes of the spontaneous migration, the manner in which it took place, the continued links that the displaced Kabre maintain with their heartland and original villages, and their agricultural practices on the new lands.

214 **External migration in Togo.**
Tom K. Kumekpor, Sylvere Issifou Looky. In: *Modern migrations in western Africa.* Edited by Samir Amin. London: Oxford University Press, 1974, p. 358-70.

This is a survey of the nature of, and reasons behind, labour migration from Togo to Ghana, which shows that different factors seem to have played a role at different times. During the colonial era the forced labour practised by the French in Togo, and the fact that they tended to employ French-speaking nationals from neighbouring Dahomey (Benin) rather than the German-speaking Togolese, played an important early role in labour migration, as did the generally poor employment prospects in Togo. After independence most of these labourers remained in Ghana since the currency exchange rates penalized those with Ghanaian capital. Their children were also unable to return to Togo since they now spoke no French. The close proximity between the new Kabre lands and their original home-villages meant that there was no problem in maintaining contact with their kin. Indeed, their success tended to provide a steady stream of Togolese hoping to emulate them. For another book that puts Togolese migration within a regional pattern see: K. C. Zacharia, Julien Condé, *Migration in West Africa: demographic aspects.* New York: Oxford University Press, 1981, 130p.

215 **L'impact de la migration sur la société villageoise: approche sociologique, exemple Togo-Ghana.** (The impact of migration in a village society: a sociological example from Togo-Ghana.)
Anani Ahianyo-Akakpo. In: *Modern migrations in western Africa.* Edited by Samir Amin. London: Oxford University Press, 1974, p. 156-69.

This article sets the sociological consequences of migration between Togolese and Ghanaian ruling areas in a historical perspective. Although migration affects demographic, economic, cultural and linguistic balances, it has not really changed the fundamental structure of traditional society in Ghana, since migrant groups have more often than not stayed with their ethnic kinsmen. This has had the effect of conserving 'the traditional and conservative features of their own society and personality' (p. 169). See also: Emile le Bris, 'Migrations and the decline of a densely populated rural area: the case of Vo Koutime in southeast Togo'. *African perspectives* (Leiden), vol. 1 (1978), p. 109-25.

216 **Les migrations des expulsées du Nigeria: aspects
demo-économiques.** (The migrations of those expelled from Nigeria:
demo-economic aspects.)
K. Ekouevi. Lomé: Université du Bénin, Unité de Recherches
Demographiques, 1985. 52p. bibliog.

Most of the states in West Africa have intermittently mounted drives to round up any
non-nationals illegally working in their countries and expel them. This study focuses
on one such incident, and the demographic and economic repercussions of the
resettlement of those Togolese expelled from Nigeria.

217 **Les migrations agricoles internes dans le sud-est du Togo.** (The
agrarian internal migrations in south-east Togo.)
Emile Le Bris. In: *Capitalisme négrier: la marche des paysans vers
le proletariat* (Black capitalism: the march of the peasants towards
proletarian status.) Edited by Pierre-Philippe Rey, Michel Samuel.
Paris: Maspero, 1976, p. 139-91. bibliog.

Although this book as a whole is anchored in a solid Marxist theoretical framework,
Le Bris' own case-study is, until the actual conclusion, a largely straightforward
extrapolation of migratory data from other studies (especially from Vogan) relating to
population movements towards Lomé and Ghana. Le Bris notes that very high
percentages of internal migration have been recorded in some districts and documents
the reasons that have been advanced for this. He concludes that 'simple explanations,
such as those by neo-malthusians or those of E. Boserup are unable to account for the
reality, because they confer on demographic pressure a direct causal value
camouflaging social relations of production' (p. 190). For another contribution on
migration in Togo in the same book see: Pierre-Philippe Rey, 'Les formes de la
décomposition des sociétés précapitalistes au Nord-Togo et les mécanismes des
migrations vers les zones de capitalisme agraire' (Forms of precapitalist societal
decompression in north Togo and mechanisms of migration towards the zones of
agrarian capitalism), p. 195-209.

218 **Les migrations rurales des Kabyé et des Losso.** (The rural
migrations of the Kabre and Losso.)
Bernard Lucien-Brun, Anne-Marie Pillet-Schwartz. Paris: ORSTOM,
1987. 391p. bibliog.

This is the definitive, and most up-to-date study (at the time of publication) of the
Kabre and Losso migrations to virgin territory, south of their original lands in the
Kara district. By the 1980s the diaspora in these areas outnumbered by nearly two to
one those remaining in their original habitat. Profusely illustrated, with a pocket
containing maps, and a large number of plates and diagrams, the study covers every
demographic aspect of the several waves of migration, and every detail of their
agriculture and building styles in the new locations. Also considered are Kabre and
Losso relations with the original inhabitants in their new lands, and their links with
their home-villages.

219 **Migrations togolaises: bilan et perspectives.** (Togolese migrations:
record and prospects.)
Emile Le Bris.   Lomé: Université du Bénin, Unité de Recherche
Démographique, 1986. 385p. bibliog.

This is a major study of the periodic waves of internal migrations within Togo, which
occur when primarily northern populations relocate from their overpopulated and
soil-degraded lands to relatively empty regions in the south. The work also surveys
official population policy and governmental encouragement of these demographic
dislocations, and attempts to assess the future prospects, and dimensions, of internal
migration in Togo.

**Dynamiques des villes secondaires et processus migratoires en Afrique
de l'Ouest.** (The dynamics of secondary towns and migration processes in
West Africa.)
See item no. 191.

Health and Medicine

220 **Alimentation en milieu rural au Togo: un modèle de prévention contre des maladies non-infectieuses?** (Nutrition in rural areas in Togo: a model for the prevention of non-infectious diseases?)
T. Teushcer, P. Baillod. In: *Les malnutritions dans les pays du Tiers Monde.* Edited by D. Lemonnier, Y. Ingenbleek. Paris: INSERM, 1986, p. 157-62. English summary.
Analyses the effect a high-fibre, carbohydrate and low animal protein dietary intake has on non-infectious diseases in a rural village in south-west Togo. It was discovered that a positive relationship existed, that cholesterol levels were low, and only one individual from the sample suffered from diabetes.

221 **Enquête démographique et de santé au Togo: 1988.** (Demographic and health inquiry on Togo: 1988.)
Akoua Agounké, Mensan Assogba, Kodjo Anipah. Lomé: Direction Générale de la Santé, Unité de Recherches Démographiques, 1989. 169p. bibliog.
Produced with the assistance of the Columbia (Maryland) Institute for Resource Development/Macrosystems, this work is a comprehensive statistical inventory and survey of human fertility and health demographics in Togo.

222 **Enquête sur la fécondité et la mortalité infantile à Lomé, novembre 1980 – fevrier 1981.** (Survey on fertility and child mortality in Lomé, November 1980 – February 1981.)
Dovi Kuevi. Lomé: Institut Nationale de la Recherche Scientifique, 1981. 109p.
Some 2,000 women who visited various clinics in Lomé were requested to complete a questionnaire being used in a scientific survey on birth control and related matters. This work is the report of that survey. Of that group of women, fifty-eight per cent

were illiterate and fifty per cent were traders or retailers. A very high percentage of the sample (seventy-two per cent) refused to answer the birth control question, and only 4.5 per cent acknowledged practising modern methods. Thirty-six per cent of the women aspired to have six or more children, and thirty-five per cent hoped to have between three and five. Although this is important because it is one of the few studies reporting on survey analysis, the work is somewhat disorganized, and may present some other problems.

223 **L'expérience des pharmacies d'état en République Togolaise.**
(The experience of state pharmacies in Togo.)
Françis Johnson-Romauld. *Coopération et Développement,* no. 38
(Nov.-Dec. 1971), p. 39-44.

An early discussion of the nationalized pharmacies in Togo, which were supposed to bring about reduced medical costs, and greater access to medications by the masses. Although some of these objectives were attained, the state pharmaceutical company finally went bankrupt. See also: 'Les pharmacies d'état du Togo ou l'expérience du Togopharma' (The state pharmacies in Togo, or the experience of Togopharma). *Nations Nouvelles,* no. 18 (Dec. 1968), p. 17-23.

224 **Facteurs étiologiques du goitre au Togo.** (The etiology of goitre in Togo.)
A. Doh, et al. In: *Les malnutritions dans les pays du Tiers Monde.*
Edited by D. Lemonnier, Y. Ingenbleek. Paris: INSERM, 1986.
p. 403-12. English summary.

A survey was carried out to discover the prevalence of goitre in Togo, and the reasons for it. The results indicated that there was a mean prevalence of 18.43 per cent, with women twice as affected, and those under nineteen years of age forming sixty-six per cent of those suffering from the illness. Several factors are identified as explaining the incidence of goitre in the country, the most important being the absence of iodine in the salt imported, whether from Europe or from Ghana.

225 **Niveaux et tendances de la mortalité dans l'enfance dans quelques régions rurales d'Afrique de l'Ouest.** (Trends and levels of child mortality in some rural areas of West Africa.)
Marc Pilon. *Cahiers ORSTOM,* vol. 20, no. 2 (1984), p. 257-64.
English summary.

This article reports on the declining child mortality rates between 1950 and 1974, as evident from data collected in four different population surveys conducted by ORSTOM, in Burkina Faso and Togo. For an examination of the relationship between household size, nutrition and child mortality levels in Togo, see: Dovi Placca, K. Sossah, 'L'espacement des naissances: les problèmes de nutrition au Togo' (The spacing of births: problems of nutrition in Togo). *Etudes Togolaises* (Lomé), no. 27/30 (1984-85), p. 17-51.

226 **La répartition par sexe des enfants hospitalisés à Lomé.** (A division by sex of children hospitalized in Lomé.)
Thérèse Locoh. *Population* (Paris), vol. 42, no. 3 (1987), p. 549-57. bibliog.

Locoh suggests some possible reasons for the large disparity in the sex of those children hospitalized for various medical problems at the pediatric ward of Lomé's general hospital. An earlier study had revealed that of 1,700 children in hospital between the ages of one and four, sixty-one per cent were boys and only thrity-nine per cent were girls, at a time when demographic data indicated near numerical parity in Lomé's child population. The author suggests that anthropological research is necessary in order to discover the reason for the disparity, which could be a function of the greater value attached to the health of boys.

227 **Single-dose chloroquine therapy for *plasmodium falciparum* in children of Togo, West Africa.**
J. G. Breman, et al. *Journal of Tropical Medicine and Hygiene* (Baltimore), vol. 36, no. 3 (1987), p. 469-73. bibliog.

This is a report on a sequential analysis of 174 children treated with chloroquine medication, with near-universal success. For an account of the emergence of a chloroquine-resistant malaria strain see: A. R. Gbary, et al., 'Emergence du paludisme chloroquinorésistant en Afrique de l'Ouest: le cas de Sokodé, Togo' (The emergence of chloroquine resistant malaria in West Africa: the case of Sokodé, Togo). *Tropical Medicine and Parasitology* (New York), vol. 39, no. 2 (1988), p. 142-44.

228 **Situation épidemiologique 1967.** (Epidemiological survey 1967.)
G. F. Glokpor. Lomé: Ministère de la Santé Publique, 1969. 69p.

This is a comprehensive health study of Togo, which reports on the prevalence of communicable diseases and levels of mortality in the country. Much of the book consists of tables of medical data. For another article on medical problems in Togo see: M. A. Mijiyawa, et al. 'Rheumatic diseases seen in hospital outpatient clinics in Lomé, Togo'. *Revue de Rhumatisme et des Maladies Osteo-Articulaires* (Paris), vol. 58, no. 5 (1991), p. 349-54.

229 **Tendances et facteurs de la mortalité dans l'enfance sur le plateau de Dayes, sud-ouest Togo.** (Trends and determinants of child mortality on the Dayes plateau of south-west Togo.)
Patrice Vimard. *Cahiers ORSTOM*, vol. 20, no. 2 (1984), p. 185-206. bibliog. English summary.

This is a retrospective (1930-1976) analysis of child mortality patterns on the Dayes plateau which fell from rather high levels to very low ones. A detailed investigation of the data reveals that much of the decline happened prior to 1965, emphasizing the difficulty of attaining subsequent improvements. The data also demonstrates that there are differences between the mortality levels of separate ethnic groups, with those of the Ewe substantially lower than those of the Kabre. These differences are seen as stemming from cultural, social and economic reasons, that allow the Ewe to seek health care and medical facilities to a much greater degree than the Kabre who are constrained from doing so.

230   **Togopharma et le problème du médicament au Togo.** (Togopharma
       and the problem of medicines in Togo.)
       Françis Johnson-Romauld.   *Afrique Contemporaine*, vol. 20, no. 116
       (1981), p. 13-16.

This article briefly looks at the state pharmaceutical monopoly in Togo, and suggests
some reasons why medications are not as universally available in the country as they
should be.

Médecine et 'remèdes miracles' des plantes chez nous. (Medicines and
'miracle cures' of plants among us.)
See item no. 51.

Medicinal plants in tropical West Africa.
See item no. 52.

L'anthropologie de la maladie. (The anthropology of disease.)
See item no. 136.

Gender Issues

231 **Die rolle der Frau bei den Kabre in Nord-Togo.** (The role of the
   woman among the Kabre in north Togo.)
   Ruth Vermot-Mangold.   Basel, Switzerland: Museum für
   Volkerkunde, 1977. 253p. bibliog. plates.
Originally the author's 1972 PhD dissertation, this book has a large number of tables,
diagrams and plates, and an extensive bibliography. It is a comprehensive and very
detailed study of the multiple activities – household, commercial, artisanal – of Kabre
women in northern Togo.

232 **Le divorce chez les Evé du Togo: note ethno-sociologique.** (Divorce
   among the Ewe of Togo: an ethno-sociological note.)
   Claude Rivière.   *Le Mois en Afrique,* no. 203/4 (Dec. 1982-Jan. 1983),
   p. 118-28.
This is an analysis of the phenomenon, and incidence, of divorce among the Ewe, in
terms of traditional law and social custom. On the one hand marriage is viewed as an
absolutely permanent union, but on the other discrete separation or divorce can be
accomodated.

233 **L'emploi des femmes.** (The employment of women.)
   Bureau International du Travail.   Addis Ababa: Bureau International
   du Travail, 1985. 7 vols.
This seven volume study on francophone Africa focuses on the role of women in the
national economy, the specific activities (in both the traditional and modern sectors)
they engage in, and the problems and advantages they have. Volume six of the series
is devoted to the employment of women in Togo.

234 **Etude socio-démographique du mariage chez les Coniagui et Bassari.** (Socio-demographic study of marriage among the Coniagui and Bassari.)
Monique Gessain. *Cahiers du Centre de Recherches Anthropologiques*, vol. 2 (1963), p. 123-222.

Gessain provides a comprehensive comparative analysis of marriage practices, marriage rites, divorce and separation among the Bassari. For another study of gender issues focusing on this group see: Gessain's 'A propos de l'évolution actuelle des femmes coniagui et bassari' (In connection with the evolution of women anong the Coniagui and Bassari). *Journal de la Société des Africanistes,* vol. 34, no. 2 (1964), p. 255-76.

235 **Fecondité et famille en Afrique de l'Ouest: le Togo méridional contemporain.** (Fertility and family in West Africa: contemporary southern Togo.)
Thérèse Locoh. Paris: Presses Universitaires de France, 1984. 182p. bibliog.

This is a seminal study on marriage and female fertility in Togo, a country that has the third-highest female fertility rates in Africa (an average of seven children per woman), surpassed only by Rwanda and Burkina Faso. Locoh, a well-known sociologist, focuses on this phenomenon, studying it not in isolation, but as part of several deep-rooted and shared social and cultural imperatives. As she points out, despite their lower status, women nevertheless possess part of the land in Togo, and petty trade is overwhelmingly dominated by women, something that in fact gives them great independence. The modest title of Locoh's work belies its contents, since this is a very comprehensive study of many aspects of Togolese life, such as: marriage customs and expectations; different kinds of conjugal unions; the role of polygamy; common child-spacing practices (between thirty-five and thirty-nine months); and birth and death rates. See also: Edoh Adjakly, *Pratique de la tradition religieuse et réproduction sociale chez les Guen/Mina du sud-est du Togo* (Traditional religious practices and social reproduction among the Guin/Mina of south-east Togo). Geneva: IUED, 1985, 156p.

236 **Femmes africaines et commerce: les revendeuses de tissu de la ville de Lomé.** (African women and commerce: textile retailers in the city of Lomé.)
Rita Cordonnier. Paris: Harmattan, 1987. 2nd ed. (First edition published in 1982 by ORSTOM.) 190p. bibliog.

This is a seminal study, originally a doctoral dissertation, of one of the most important retail forces in Lomé, the *Nana Bentzes* (or female textile retailers) and their trading monopoly in the city. Cordonnier commences with a thorough introduction to the historical, economic and anthropological reasons for female participation in business and trade, noting the evolving role of Ewe and Mina women as traders, especially after their migration to Lomé. She then sympathetically explores their simultaneous, and demanding, roles as traders, mothers and wives, and their commercial links, activities, outlets, mutual-aid structures, and the economic underpinnings of their activities.

237 **La femme en droit coutumier togolais, son rôle en tant qu'épouse et mére.** (The woman in customary Togolese law, her role as both wife and mother.)
Véronique Dadadzi. *Revue Juridique et Politique*, vol. 12, no. 4 (Oct.-Dec. 1974) p. 801-07.

This article is a study of the legal status of women in Togo, according to traditional law.

238 **Femmes de Lomé.** (Women of Lomé.)
Suzanne Comhaire-Sylvain. Bandundu, Zaire: Ceeba [distributed by Steyler Verlag], 1982. 287. bibliog.

The conditions, social life and customs of women in Lomé's urban area are considered in detail in this work which deals chronologically with the various stages in a woman's life. The author commences with the birth of the baby and an examination of the mortality rates of female babies and family attitudes on their birth. She continues with a discussion of the kinds of values girls are expected to acquire as they grow up, and their household and sex education at home. A consideration of the role of women in higher education follows, and Comhaire-Sylvain provides details on the number of scholarships they obtain and the fields in which they specialize. There is also an analysis of their role in the workforce – in trade, the civil service, and education for example. For another excellent study on urban women in both Cameroon and Togo see: Raymond Deniel, *Femmes des villes africaines*. Abidjan: Inades, 1985. 220p.

239 **Frauen und landliche Entwicklung in Afrika: Fallbeispiele aus Ghana und Togo.** (Women and rural development in Africa: examples from Ghana and Togo.)
Agnes Klingshirn. Cologne, Germany: Welforum, 1982. 334p. bibliog.

This work, which is supplemented by maps and plates, studies the productive role of women in rural areas in Ghana and Togo. For a shorter, English-language discussion of this topic see: Kate Young, 'Women's participation in development'. In: *Women and economic development*, edited by Kate Young. Paris: UNESCO, 1986, p. 171-208.

240 **Le mariage traditionnel au Togo: traditions togolaises.** (Traditional marriage in Togo: Togolese customs.)
Claude Durand. *Annales de l'Université du Bénin* (Lomé), 1979. special issue.

This entire issue is devoted to an enumeration and examination of customary marriage practices among several of the main peoples in Togo. In addition, an early article in English on the role of women in Togo is available. See: Ferdinand N'Sougan Agblemagnon, 'Research on attitudes towards the Togolese women'. *International Social Science Journal*, vol. 14, no. 1 (1962), p. 148-56.

241 **Mariage traditionnel dans les pays ewe.** (Traditional marriage in Ewe country.)
Nyaletasi Akakpo. Kpomé, Togo: [n.p.], 1976. 42p.

Since it bears no imprint this work may prove difficult to locate, although a copy can be found in the Library of Congress, Washington, DC. It is a most remarkable detailed enumeration of Ewe courtship rites, marriage procedures, nuptial practices and conjugal expectations and is written by an individual who describes himself as 'an Ewe writer', and who is a member of a small traditional Ewe village in the Tsévié district.

242 **Mobilité conjugale et divorce en milieu rural au sud-est du Togo.**
(Conjugal mobility and divorce in a south-eastern Togo rural setting.)
Alain Mignot. *Penant,* vol. 91, no. 771 (1981), p. 23-64.

A provocative consideration of divorce and separation in southern Togo in the light of the fact that, at the time of writing, in the age group forty-five to forty-nine, forty-eight per cent of females were no longer living with their first husband. The author examines traditional Mina customs in the area, that regard conjugal separation solely in terms of the two immediate partners, and the role of the modern court in Aného in pronouncing such couples as formally divorced. Several tables illustrate the dimensions of the problem.

243 *Nanas* **et pêcheurs du port de Lomé: une exploitation de l'homme par la femme?** (The *Nanas* and the fishermen of the port of Lomé: an exploitation of men by women?)
Jean-Yves Weigel. *Politique Africaine*, no. 27 (Sept.-Oct. 1987), p. 37-46.

This is a study of the powerful *nanas* (women-traders and commercial entrepreneurs of Togo) who control much of the commerce of Togo, focusing specifically on the field of fishing. While it is well known that 'commercial activity in Togo is the work of women in practically all sectors' (p. 37), especially in the case of textiles, their role as entrepreneurs has not been studied as extensively. Weigel focuses on the *nanas* who invest in the fishing industry by purchasing boats and sponsoring the fishing activities of their crews, many of whom are Ghanaian, under extremely stringent conditions and at exhorbitantly high interest rates. For an examination of the role of the *nanas* in the textile trade see: Egboni Ayina, 'Pagnes et politique' (Loin-clothes and politics). *Politique Africaine*, no. 27 (Sept.-Oct. 1987), p. 47-54. See also: L. Bellow, 'Je cours plus vite que ma rivale: paroles chez les Gen-mina du Sud-Togo' (I run faster than my competitor: sayings among the Gen-Mina of southern Togo). *Cahiers de Littérature Orale*, no. 19, 1986, p. 29-67.

244 **La nuptialité au Togo. Evolution entre 1961 et 1970.** (Marriage in Togo. Development between 1961 and 1970.)
Thérèse Locoh. *Population*, vol. 31, no. 2 (March-April 1976), p. 379-98. English summary.

In this article Locoh makes a study of marriage patterns in Togo during the 1960s. The results revealed that there was a high level of conjugal mobility, linked to the prevalence of polygamous practices, which were, however, beginning to decline, with the age of females marrying for the first or subsequent times increasing.

245 **La participation des femmes à la vie économique en milieu rural: le cas du sud-est Togo.** (The participation of women in economic life in rural areas: the case of south-east Togo.)
Thérèse Locoh. Lomé: Université du Bénin, Unité de Recherche Démographique, 1979. 29p.

This is a discussion of the role women play in the trade, commerce and agriculture of south-eastern Togo.

246 **Quelques aspects de la socialisation traditionnelle des enfants chez les Ewe dans la vie moderne.** (Some aspects of traditional child socialization among the modern Ewe.)
Svetlana Koudolo. Lomé: DIFOP, 1987. 49p. bibliog.

A very interesting study of child socialization among the Ewe, based on fieldwork conducted in the region of Zio. It includes an overview of the social life, customs and gender and family relationships among modern Ewe parents, their child-rearing practices, and the values which are transmitted to the next generation. In 'La participation des institutions d'afa et du vodu dans les processus de la socialisation de enfants en milieu Ewe' (q.v.) the author looks at the perpetuation of vodun practices as a function of the early socialization of children in its rites.

247 **Rites du mariage chez les Evé du Togo.** (Marriage rites among the Ewe of Togo.)
Claude Rivière. *Anthropos,* vol. 79, no. 4/6 (1984), p. 377-95. bibliog.

In this article Rivière analyses in detail the various stages in traditional marriages, from asking for the hand of the bride and negotiating the marriage, to the legitimation of the marriage contract and the presentation of the bride price to her father. Once this is agreed the ceremonies commence. They include: revealing the bride price to everyone; accompanying the bride to her new domicile; and the communal celebrations. Notwithstanding the strong power of custom, Rivière notes how the growing modern influences in Ewe society make marriage increasingly fragile, multiplying the instances of divorce, desertion, concubinage and polygamy.

248 **Rural women and attitudes to family planning, a contraceptive practice, and abortion in southern Togo.**
Tom. K. Kumekpor. Legon, Ghana: University of Ghana, Department of Sociology, 1970. 30p.

This monograph is the first of a socio-demographic survey series on Togo, and is based on an attitudinal survey of Ewe women in the country's Maritime region around Lomé. The survey looked at 293 females over the age of fifteen, of whom eighty-one per cent had no schooling, fifty-two per cent were already married between the ages of fifteen and nineteen, and another twenty-two per cent between the ages twenty and twenty-four years. The author briefly notes the methodological problems involved in asking questions about family planning and abortions, which in the past have resulted in many misleading conclusions. Of his sample group, the results indicated the overwhelming desire of the respondents for birth-spacing, with twenty-three per cent preferring two-year intervals and fifty per cent three-year intervals between births. However, in order to attain this preference contraception was practised by only eight per cent, and abortion by only one per cent of the women. The majority (sixty-two per cent) resorted to abstinence, either in agreement with their husbands (that may involve the husband seeking other partners, or polygamy), or through actual physical separation for the duration of the desired intervals.

249 **Structures des ménages dans les populations rurales du sud Togo.**
(Household structures among the rural populations of southern Togo.)
Daniel Benoit, et al. *Cahiers ORSTOM*, vol. 19, no. 3 (1983),
p. 321-33. bibliog,

The authors examine variations in family sizes and family structures in southern Togo. Using factor analysis this data is correlated with the social mores of the population groups and the characteristics of the head of the household, establishing several household types.

250 **Union et procréation en Afrique: rites de la vie chez les Evé du
Togo.** (Union and procreation in Africa: rites of passage among the
Ewe of Togo.)
Claude Rivière. Paris: Harmattan, 1990. 233p. bibliog.

Written by one of the foremost scholars of the Ewe people, who was formerly department head at the University in Togo, and is currently teaching at the Sorbonne, this is a masterful and detailed analysis of all aspects of marriage, childbirth and childrearing customs and rites among the Ewe in Togo. Supplemented by eight pages of plates and other illustrations, the work discusses issues such as: bride-prices; marriage ceremonies; conjugal stability and instability; adultery of both men and women; the significance of twins; social and religious rites that are undertaken to protect newborns; and early child socialization practices. The highly stylized manner in which children are given names (depending upon the day of the week, sex, and priority of birth) is particularly well outlined.

251 **Les unions au Togo: changement et permanences.** (Marriages in
Togo: changes and permanence.)
Thérèse Locoh, Marc Pilon, L. N. Messan Assogba. Lomé:
Université du Bénin, Unité de Recherche Démographique, 1990. 150p.
bibliog.

This monograph includes three important separate articles on matrimonial unions in various parts of Togo. Locoh (p. 5-33) reports on her research in Lomé, where new forms of unions are taking place and attitudes towards childbirth have changed. She bases her conclusions on research with a large sample of 3,600 mothers; Pilon (p. 34-53) describes the matrimonial system and attitudes towards marriage among the Moba in north Togo; and Assogba (p. 53-75) presents the results of his research on the changing status of women and changes in family structures in southern Togo. The book concludes with a particularly comprehensive bibliography (p. 76-105).

La répartition par sexe des enfants hospitalisés à Lomé. (A division by
sex of children hospitalized in Lomé.)
See item no. 226.

La fille et l'école. (The girl and school.)
See item no. 259.

The impact of western schools on girls' expectations.
See item no. 260.

L'instruction des filles à Lomé. (The education of girls in Lomé.)
See item no. 261.

Unequal knowledge distribution.
See item no. 271.

La vocation héréditaire de la femme dans le droit positif. (The hereditary role of women in Togolese positive law.)
See item no. 299.

Education

252 **Bildung und Kolonialismus in Togo (1850-1914).** (Education and
colonialism in Togo [1850-1914].)
Christel Adick.   Basel, Switzerland: Beltz Verlag, 1981. 364p.
bibliog.

This book, an abridged version of Adick's 1979 doctoral dissertation, discusses the
early decades of European contact with Togo, the German colonial era, and especially
the educational policies pursued in the territory during that time. A very
comprehensive bibliography (p. 315-29) completes the study. Adick has written a
number of additional articles on this theme. See: 'Padagogische Idylle und
Wirtschaftswunder im deutschen Schutsgebeit Togo' (Pedagogic ideal and economic
wonders in the German protectorate of Togo). *Die Dritte Welt*, vol. 5, no. 1 (1977),
p. 27-46; and 'Theorie und Analyse kolonialer Lehrplane: Beispiele aus Deutsche-
Togo' (Theory and analysis of colonial education: example from German Togo).
Bildung und Erziehung (Cologne), vol. 34, no. 4 (1985), p. 513-29.

253 **Cent cinquante ans de scolarisation au Togo: bilan et perspectives.**
(One hundred and fifty years of schooling in Togo: record and
prospects.)
Marie-France Lange.   Lomé: Université du Bénin, Unité de
Recherche Démographique, 1991. 174p. bibliog.

Lange presents a comprehensive history of education in Togo, from the earliest
mission-schools at the time of the German colonial era, to the 1990s. The work
contains illustrations and statistical data showing the progressive expansion of
schooling in the country. Attention is also devoted to the social aspects of education,
its implications for the economy, projections of future educational enrolments and
needs, and the stresses that will be placed on tertiary education, which has already
reached record-high levels.

254   **Conceptions et attitudes des élèves togolais au lendemain de l'independence (1961), à l'égard de leur avenir.** (Conceptions and attitudes of Togolese students in the aftermath of independence, 1961, on their future.)
Roland Devauges.   Paris: ORSTOM, 1973. 154p.

This study, based on empirical research in Togo, agrees with considerable similar research that was conducted in the 1970s in a number of other African states. It attempts to assess the views of the young about themselves and their future following independence. For a more recent attitudinal survey of Lomé youth, which reveals its materialism, see Comi M. Toulabor, 'L'énonciation du pouvoir et de la richesse chez les jeunes de Lomé' (Expression of power and wealth among Lomé youth). *Revue Français de Science Politique* (June 1985), p. 446-58.

255   **Dualisme de l'éducation dans les pays de la côte du Benin (Togo).**
(Dualism in education in the Bight of Benin states, Togo.)
Louise Kayissan Houenassou.   Lomé: Institut National de la Recherche Scientifique, 1973. 144p. bibliog.

A survey of rural education in Togo during the first decade of independence. See also: Adjo M. Quashie, Ahloko M. Komlan, *Précis d'histoire de l'enseignement au Togo des origines à 1975* (Historical summary of education in Togo from its origins to 1975). Lomé: Université du Bénin, 1986. 104p; and A. Akakpo, 'The interaction of education, culture and communications in Africa: the Togolese experience'. *Educafrica*, no. 11 (1984), p. 138-46.

256   **Educational guidance and students' personal satisfactions.**
Gnansa C. Djassoa.   *Journal of Negro Education* (Washington, DC), vol. 53, no. 4 (1984), p. 481-90.

The author looks at the University of Benin (Lomé) and its formal educational and vocational guidance system, in order to explore the reasons for high failure rates, especially among first-year students, their frustrations and opposition to the courses they are studying, and their claims that they are forced to take courses which are not of their choice. The author, who teaches in the university's department of psychology, reaches the conclusion that at least fifty per cent of all first-year students at the university are completely unmotivated, and disillusioned, because they are forced into academic programmes not of their choice, with the result that they tend to fail them.

257   **L'énonciation du pouvoir et de la richesse chez les jeunes 'conjoncturés' de Lomé.** (Expressions of power and wealth among the young in Lomé.)
J. F. Bayart, M. Mbembe, C. M. Toulabor.   In: *La politique par le bas: contribution à une problematique de la démocratie en Afrique noire* (Politics from below: contribution to a problem of democracy in Black Africa.)   Paris: Karthala, 1986. p. 131-45.

This is a study of the mix of acute apathy and materialistic attitudes that have spread throughout the youth population in Lomé. Apathy is a dynamic in and of itself, while wealth is seen as stemming primarily from political interaction. The article is written by a Togolese scholar in self-imposed exile in France who has provided some of the most penetrating insights into the Togolese context.

258 **Evolution des dépenses publiques d'éducation au Togo et influence des deperditions scolaires sur les coûts unitaires dans l'enseignement général du troisième degré.** (The evolution of educational public expenditures in Togo and the influence of the scholarly allowances on unit costs of general education for the tertiary degree.)
Yawovi Tchamegnon. Quebec: Université Laval, Centre d'Etudes et de Documentation sur le Développement de l'Education en Afrique, 1991. 41p. bibliog.
This is a financial analysis of the cost of secondary education in Togo, with projections in terms of fiscal needs to satisfy all those interested in, and qualified for higher education.

259 **La fille et l'école: étude comparative de la situation scolaire des filles de l'enseignement du premier degré en Côte d'Ivoire, au Tchad et au Togo, 1965-1970.** (The girl and school: comparative study of the situation of girls in primary education in Côte d'Ivoire, Chad and Togo, 1965-1970.)
Ministère de l'Education Nationale. Lomé: Ministère de l'Education Nationale, 1973. 133p.
A comparative study of the integration of girls in primary education in three countries, including Togo, and the problems they face in remaining in the educational system. Apart from providing a wealth of statistics and diagrams on enrolment levels, the study focuses on the reasons why girls do not enrol, and when they do, why they drop out from primary school. In general, girls have needed to make much more of an effort in their studies than boys, partly due to lack of motivation and partly because they are needed at home for a variety of household duties, all leading to premature drop-out levels. A comparison is made in particular of Côte d'Ivoire and Togo, which shared more similarities than Chad. It was found that although female enrolment levels were similar in both countries (twenty-four and twenty-five per cent) in Côte d'Ivoire the problem has been improved, whereas in Togo it remains a persistent phenomenon. See also: K. Houenassou-Houangbé, 'Intégration de la jeune fille aux institutions éducatives au Togo' (The integration of the young girl in the educational institutions in Togo). In: *AAWord in Nairobi*. Dakar: AAWord, 1986, p. 47-53.

260 **The impact of western schools on girls' expectations: a Togolese case.**
Karen C. Biraimah. *Comparative Education Exchange* (Chicago), vol. 24, no. 2, pt. 2 (June 1980), p. 196-208.
Biraimah assesses the degree to which peer-group relations, formal curricula and female role-models affect the impact of western schools on Third World women's expectations, relating it specifically to Togo. The data collected in Togo indicates that more research is necessary. Although factors such as personal determination and outside role-models do indeed internationalize the attitudes and expectations of girls

in Togo's schools, the schools, and their teachers have, for a variety of reasons, difficulties in bringing about the true internationalization of values among their female students.

261 **L'instruction des filles à Lomé.** (The education of girls in Lomé.)
Suzanne Comhaire-Sylvain. *Problèmes Sociaux Congolais* (Lubumbashi, Zaire), no. 8 (Sept. 1968), p. 93-122.

This article constitutes a comprehensive study of the role of gender in education during Togo's first decade of independence. The title is somewhat misleading since, although the author considers gender (and ethnicity) in the distribution of children in (Catholic and Protestant) primary, secondary and higher education she also examines the gender/ethnic distribution among teachers. Gender attitudes, values and preferences are also analysed. One conclusion of the study is that conditions favour a powerful increase in the scholarization of girls and their continuing education at university. In general, since the publication of this article, there have been massive increases in the numbers attending schools and university in the 1970s and 1980s.

262 **Des jardins d'enfants au Togo et au Tchad.** (Kindergartens in Togo and Chad.)
Bernadette Moussy. *Les Carnets de l'Enfant*, no. 21 (Jan.-March 1973), p. 63-75.

A comparative study of facilities for pre-school children in the urban areas of Togo and Chad. See also: *L'enfance et la jeunesse dans le développement national du Togo* (Childhood and youth in the national development of Togo). Paris: SEDES, 1966.

263 **The planning of an adult literacy project.**
Eric Packham. *Community Development Journal* (Manchester), vol. 3, no.1 (Jan. 1968), p. 22-28.

Details about a UNESCO-sponsored mission to Togo for the purpose of mounting an adult literacy progamme are presented here.

264 **Le programme des études de lettres modernes à l'Université du Bénin.** (The programme in modern literature at the University of Benin.)
G. O. Midiohouan. *Peuples Noirs – Peuples Africaines*, vol. 9, no. 52 (1986), p. 41-55.

Midiohouan takes a detailed look at the modern literature programme of studies at the University of Benin in Togo, which is one of the most popular on campus.

265 **Qui a peur de la philosophie?** (Who is afraid of philosophy?)
Estelle Floriani. *Politique Africaine*, no. 27 (Sept.-Oct. 1987), p. 67-72.

Philosophy is taught in Togo from the first year onwards, unlike in France where it is only taught during the last year of school. In this article the author assesses the problems of teaching the subject in Togolese schools. These include the fact that the subject is completely divorced from the cultural background of most students, causing major problems, which are compounded by their poor command of French. In addition, the atmosphere in schools is not conducive to the discussion of basic philosophical themes because of the constraint on freedom of expression in Togo and Eyadema's all-pervasive personality cult.

266   **The reform of the educational system of Togo.**
Koffi Atignon.   In: *Educational reforms and innovations in Africa.*
Paris: UNESCO, 1978, p. 38-47.

This is a report on the planned educational reform in Togo. Prior changes in primary education in 1959 and 1967, in secondary education in 1967, and in higher education in 1971, were all slight modifications of the content of the original system inherited from France. The plan Atignon is concerned with was for a major structural overhaul of education that, *inter alia*, would have assured universal education until the age of fifteen. This would have had major implications for society itself. See also: Togo, Ministère de l'Education Nationale, *La reforme de l'enseignement au Togo* (The educational reform in Togo). Lomé, 1975.

267   **Le refus de l'école: pouvoir d'une société civile bloquée.** (The refusal of schooling: the power of a blocked civil society.)
Marie-France Lange.   *Politique Africaine,* vol. 27 (1987) p. 74-86.

Although in 1980 Togo had one of West Africa's highest school enrolment ratios (seventy-two per cent of school-age children), in 1981 a sudden decline started, with the percentage dipping to fifty-two per cent in 1984. The author analyses the reasons behind these drops, and reaches the conclusion that they are a direct result of the economic crisis in the country, which ushered in a freeze on hiring in both public and private sectors. In turn, this led parents to judge that there was 'no purpose' in their children obtaining schooling, and they shifted them into more productive agricultural work. See also: Marie-France Lange, 'Diderot au certificat d'étude togolais'. *Politique Africaine,* no. 33 (1989), p. 33-47.

268   **Statistiques scolaires.**
Direction Générale de la Planification de l'Education.   Lomé: [n.p.], 1965. annual.

This is the annually-published government compendium of statistics on all educational issues and details.

269   **Le sydrome du diploma et le chômage des diplomés: rapport.** (The syndrome of diplomas and the unemployment of those with diplomas: report.)
Bureau International du Travail.   Addis Ababa: Bureau International du Travail, 1982. 5 vols.

Volume five of this multi-country study focuses on Togo. It examines one of the more poignant aspects of modern urban life in Africa: the frenzied rush of young people for a modern secondary or higher education, followed by unemployment, under-employment, or manual work. The work surveys the educational degrees granted in the countries concerned and the employment possibilities there, emphasizing that the economies of some countries, such as Togo, are simply incapable of absorbing into the modern sector the large surplus of qualified individuals the educational system continues to churn out year after year.

270 **Togo.**
Martena Tenney Sasnett, Inez Sepmeyer. In: *Educational systems of Africa: interpretations for use in the evaluation of academic credentials.* Berkeley, California: University of California Press, 1967, p. 729-37. bibliog.

Part of a directory of education in Africa, this offers a somewhat dated description of the Togolese educational system and an assessment of its curricula. Since 1967, when this was published, primary, secondary and tertiary education in Togo has dramatically improved, and new structures have emerged; an updated assessment is therefore now needed. For a snapshot of education during the 1960s, however, the material is useful, as is 'Togo'. In: *The educated African*, edited by Helen A. Kitchen. New York: Praeger, 1962, p. 513-18. For an updated outline of the levels of education in the country see: Thérèse Locoh, F. B. Dovi-Sodemekou, *Evolution de la scolarisation au Togo vue à travers les statistiques scolaires 1971-1984* (The evolution of school attendance in Togo as perceived through the school statistics of 1971-1984). Lomé: Université du Bénin, Unité de Recherche Démographique, 1986. See also: Akrima A. Kogoe, 'Perceived administrative needs of school executives in Togo'. *Comparative Education,* vol. 22, no, 2 (1986), p. 149-58.

271 **Unequal knowledge distribution: the schooling experience in a Togolese secondary school.**
Karen C. Biraimah. Buffalo, New York: SUNY/Buffalo Faculty of Educational Studies, 1984. 55p. bibliog.

This is an occasional paper based on the author's PhD dissertation and it represents a wide-ranging and important survey of sex discrimination in Togolese secondary education. The author analyses the textbooks used in schools, quantifying the gender of the characters that appear in the texts, to validate her contention that there is much role-stereotyping and even a hidden-agenda in Togolese schooling.

272 **La violence à l'école: le cas d'un village au Togo.** (Violence in school: the case of a Togolese village.)
Comi Toulabor. *Politique Africaine,* vol. 2, no. 7 (Sept. 1982), p. 43-49.

Toulabor provides an account of corporal punishment in primary schools in Togo, from his own experience in a rural village school, to modern-day practices.

La participation des institutions d'afa et de vodu dans les processus de la socialisation des enfants en milieu Ewe. (The participation of afa and vodu institutions in the socialization process of children in an Ewe context.) *See* item no. 126.

Law and
The Constitution

273 **Changing views about the restitution of marriage payments among the Tyokossi of northern Togo.**
E. A. B. van Rouveroy van Nieuwaal. Leiden, Netherlands: Afrika Studiecentrum, 1974. 44p. bibliog.

This is a study of traditional law and the changing customs about marriage payments among the Chokossi in north Togo. Modernization has slowly eroded past views and posed basic questions about the permanence of bride-prices in society.

274 **Chef coutumier: un métier difficile.** (Traditional chiefs: a difficult job.)
E. A. B. van Rouveroy van Nieuwaal. *Politique Africaine,* no. 27 (Sept.-Oct. 1987), p. 19-29.

In this study the author examines the conflicting pressures on customary chiefs in Togo, whose judicial role has not been recognized by the government since 1961. Notwithstanding this, they have continued to play a major role in the arbitration of small claims, disputes, land issues, and in maintaining law and order. With the creation by General Eyadema of the National Union of Traditional Chiefs they have received token consideration of their status but at the expense of a demand for their unflinching loyalty to the regime. See also: the author's earlier 'Chefferie au Nord-Togo: la position ambigué d'un chef supérieur des Anufom à N'Zara (Sansanné-Mango)' (Chiefdom in north Togo: the ambiguous position of a superior chief of the Chokossi in N'Zara [Sansanné-Mango]). *Revue Française d'Histoire d'Outre-Mer,* vol. 68, no. 250/253 (1981), p. 204-12. bibliog.

275 **Un code de la famille au Togo.** (Family statutes in Togo.)
Bernard Connen. *Penant,* vol. 9, no. 774 (1981), p. 5-22.

Connen is a magistrate, and in this article he discusses the significance of the personal and family judicial code in Togo that was promulgated on 31 January 1980, and that includes 727 articles. The new code aimed at modernizing family law and emancipating women, a difficult task in view of the fact that the country has numerous ethnic groups with quite diverse customary laws. The author dissects the various statutes, highlighting their significance and starting with the first requirement – that every person have a surname. See also: Focanem Mayemba, 'Quelques aspects du code togolais de la famille' (Several aspects of the Togolese family statutes). *Penant*, vol. 96, no. 791 (July-Oct. 1986), p. 228-56. An earlier article discussing the former legal status in Togo is by Théodore Acoutey, 'Unité ou dualité des statuts dans le droit de la famille au Togo' (Unity or duality of the statutes on the law of the family in Togo). *Revue Juridique et Politique*, no. 1 (Jan.-March 1967), p. 34-47. For a specific analysis of the issue of divorce see: Kouévi Agbekponou, 'La détermination de la loi applicable au divorce international et le nouveau code togolais de la famille' (A resolution of international law on divorce and the new Togolese family statutes). *Penant*, vol. 93, no. 781/2 (Aug.-Dec. 1983), p. 283-305.

276 **Code des investissements: investment code.** (Investment code.)
Lomé: Chambre de Commerce d'Agriculture et d'Industrie, 1989. 44p.
This booklet, that includes a section in English, summarizes the grand outlines of Togo's economic policy, and existing law and legislation with regard to foreign investments.

277 **Code des personnes et de la famille.** (Personal and family law.)
République Togolaise.   Lomé: Editogo, 1990. 170p.
This publication is the most recent official codification of personal and family law in Togo, and includes changes in the legal codes which were passed in the 1980s. Togo's new family code, in particular, has also been the subject of a lengthy analysis: Alain Mignot, *Le droit de la famille au Togo: textes et documents* (Family law in Togo: texts and documents). Lomé: Presses de l'Université du Bénin, 1990. 451p.

278 **La condition juridique de l'enfant en Togo et son évolution.** (The juridical status of the child in Togo and its evolution.)
Lucien Olympio.   *Revue Juridique et Politique*, vol. 20, no. 1 (Jan.-March 1966) p. 85-95. bibliog.
A brief overview of the changing statutes on the rights of children in Togo as of the mid-1960s. They are intended to be seen in conjunction with the revisions in the legal code of the family in the 1980s.

279 **La constitution de la IIIe République togolaise.** (The constitution of the 3rd Togolese Republic.)
Lomé: Secretariat Administratif, 1982. 15p.
This is the official text of the Togolese constitution adopted by referendum on 30 December 1979, and implemented as from 13 January 1980. For an analysis of the constitution see: Claude Leclercq, 'La constitution togolaise du 13 Janvier 1980' (The Togolese constitution of 13 January 1980). *Revue Juridique et Politique*, vol. 34, no. 4 (Oct.-Dec. 1980), p. 817-24. For Togo's earlier constitution see: *inter alia* 'Togo'. In: *Constitutions of nations*, edited by Amos Peaslee. The Hague: Martinus Nijhoff, 1965. vol. 3.

280 **Constitution de la République togolaise (mai 1963).** (The constitution of the Togolese republic [May 1963].)
Notes et Etudes Documentaires, no. 3175 (1965), p. 34-42.

The 1963 constitution was adopted after the the *coup d'état* that saw the murder of President Olympio. It set up a presidential system that pitched within it two incompatible leaders, Grunitzky and Meatchi. The constitution was abolished after Eyadema's second military intervention, in 1967.

281 **La Cour Supreme du Togo.** (The Supreme Court of Togo.)
M. Kekeh. In: *Les cours supremes en Afrique.* Edited by Gérard Conac, Jean du Bois de Gaudusson. Paris: Economica, 1988, vol. 2, p. 366-79.

Written by the president of the Judicial Chamber of the Supreme Court of Togo, this is a definitive outline of the evolution of the court, and its areas of competence. The chapter describes the manner in which the court selects its cases, its personnel (both magistrates and paralegal), the role of lawyers and interpreters in its proceedings, and procedural issues that determine hearings and decisions.

282 **Detournement des deniers au Togo.** (Embezzlement of funds in Togo.)
Messanvi Foli. Lomé: Institut National de la Recherche Scientifique, 1975. 127p. bibliog.

A legal study of criminal law, and the specific provisions and legislation that exist relating to embezzlement of public funds in Togo.

283 **Droit moderne et droit coutumier au Togo.** (Modern and traditional law in Togo.)
E. A. B. van Rouveroy van Nieuwaal. *Penant,* vol. 85, no. 747 (Jan.-March 1975), p. 5-18.

Outlines the judicial organization in Togo in civil matters, and how the conflict between traditional and modern law is resolved. Although theoretically the two systems of personal statutes are legally equal, both the legislature and the judicial bodies, in fact, give precedence to modern statutory law. For an account of the perceptible changes in attitudes that the spread of the modern system of law has caused among the Chokossi in north Togo see: E. A. B. Rouveroy van Nieuwaal, E. van Rouveroy van Nieuwaal-Baerends, 'The plot of the sophisticated son-in-law: old and new ways of establishing rights over land in N'Zara, north Togo'. In: *Anthropology of law in the Netherlands,* edited by K. von Benada-Beckmann, F. Trijbosch. Dordrecht, Netherlands: Foris, 1986, p. 175-194.

284 **Le droit successoral chez les ewe.** (The law of succession among the Ewe.)
J. Binet. In: *Etudes de droit africain et de droit malgache* (Studies in African and malagasy law.) Edited by Jean Poirier. Paris: Cujas, 1965. p. 307-15.

The traditional law of succession varies from society to society, and in this chapter Binet surveys the law of succession among the Ewe. See also: Binet's 'Le droit successoral chez les Ewe de Tsiévé' (The law of succession among the Ewe of Tsieve). *Penant*, vol. 76, no. 710 (Jan.-March 1966), p. 127-31; 'Le droit foncier des Ewe de Tsivié' (Land law among the Ewe of Tsivie). *Cahiers de l'Institut de Science Economique Appliquée*, vol. 9, no. 166 (Oct. 1966), p. 101-18.

285 Ewe law of property.
A. K. P. Kludze.   London: Sweet & Maxwell, 1973. 324p. bibliog.

This pioneering work, which is based on the author's dissertation for the University of London, codifies the law of property among the Ewe which has not received much attention apart from early missionary reports. There are some limitations to the book, that should be kept in mind. As the author himself notes, the work is really only valid with respect to what is referred to as the 'northern Ewe' of Ghana although, as Kludze also notes, with minor variations of detail 'the rules stated are applicable throughout Eweland' (p. xi). The book is organized around thirteen tersely-written chapters dealing with the role of the family and the head of the family; the nature of land titles; family property and its alienation; the sale of land; the role of the stool (the chief); and issues relating to gifts, pledges and tenancies of land.

286 La justice traditionnelle, une justice parallèle. (Traditional justice, a parallel justice.)
Alain Mignot.   *Penant*, vol 92, no. 775 (1982), p. 5-30.

Mignot's study relates only to southern Togo, and outlines the nature of the country's parallel traditional and modern legal codes. Notwithstanding their divergences which have narrowed anyway, these two systems do not necessarily conflict, since different sets of populations often seek redress from one or the other, and in any case modern law is supreme.

287 Les mécanismes juridiques de la protection des droits de la personne au Togo. (The judicial mechanism for the protection of human rights in Togo.)
Atsu Koffi Amega.   *Revue Juridique et politique*, vol. 36, no. 1 (Feb. 1982), p. 250-56.

Written by the long-standing President of the Togolese Supreme Court, this brief article provides an outline of the legal statutes protecting human rights in Togo. The analysis is only of legalistic and/or structural interest since massive abuses of human rights have been frequent under the regime of General Eyadema.

288 L'organisation judiciaire au Togo en matière civile. (Judicial organization in civil issues.)
Messanvi Foli.   Lomé: Institut Nationale de la Recherche Scientifique, 1978. 43p.

This is an outline of the court system in Togo, and the procedures for civil litigation.

289 **La parcelle de gendre comploteur: manières coutoumières et modernes d'acquirir des droits sur la terre.** (The plot of the scheming son-in-law: customary and modern ways to acquire land-rights.)
E. A. B. Rouveroy van Nieuwaal, E. A. van Rouveroy van Nieuwaal-Baerends. Leiden, Netherlands: Afrika-Studiecentrum, 1982. 31p.

This brief monograph illustrates, through a case-study of a legal conflict resolved in Mango, in the far north, the complexity of the relationship between modern and traditional land-tenure law in Togo. In this specific case the insistence of the claimant, who had received a plot of land, that it be properly demarcated and registered in Lomé, led to the revocation by the traditional authorities of his right to the land.

290 **Une pratique foncière dans le sud-ouest du Togo: le dibi-ma-dibi.** (Land use in south-west Togo: the dibi-ma-dibi.)
E. Y. Gu-Konu. In: *Espaces disputés en Afrique noire: pratiques foncières locales* (Disputed spaces in Black Africa: local land practices.) Edited by Bernard Crousse, Emile Le Bris, Etienne Le Roy. Paris: Karthala, 1986. p. 243-52.

This is a discussion of customary land law usage, which accommodates two seemingly incompatible elements in south-west Togo. On one hand, there is a large amount of land which is unused because of the lack of manpower in the area, whereas on the other hand, the land is agriculturally productive (coffee and cacao) but its ownership cannot be transferred. The practice which has been adopted to overcome this gives those cultivators who migrate from the land-hungry north the right to cultivate the land and retain half the harvest for the lifetime of the trees. This right was transferable but ownership of the land could never be transferred. The practice is not to be confused with share-cropping or tenant-farming.

291 **Les pratiques foncières face à l'urbanisation dans la région maritime du Togo.** (Land practices in the face of urbanization in the Maritime region of Togo.)
Do Felli. In: *Espaces disputés en Afrique noire: pratiques foncières locales* (Disputed spaces in Black Africa: local land practices.) Edited by Bernard Crousse, Emile Le Bris, Etienne Le Roy. Paris: Karthala, 1986. p. 41-49.

Felli considers how customary law has been widely subverted by claims on modern law, leaving scores of festering legal conflicts in the Maritime region of Togo, where sale (or expropriation) of land for urban purposes has taken place contrary to traditional custom.

292   A la recherche de la justice: quelques aspects du droit
      matrimonial et de la justice du juge de la paix et du chef
      superieur des Anufom à Mango dans le nord du Togo. (In search of
      justice: several aspects of marriage law and the justice of magistrates
      and of the superior chief of the Anufom in Mango in northern Togo.)
      E. A. B. van Rouveroy van Nieuwaal.   Leiden, Netherlands: Afrika-
      Studiecentrum, 1976. 268p. bibliog.

This is a comprehensive study of the structures and methods involved, and the general
rules pertaining to, the application of customary and modern law to matters relating to
family disputes among the Chokossi of northern Togo. In order to better understand
the conflict between modern and customary law the author provides a broad survey of
the Chokossi which covers their: lineage system; traditional chiefly system;
customary law, and norms pertaining to the different kinds of marriage among them;
and methods of resolving family disputes. For two other studies by this prolific author
see: *Essai sur quelques aspects du droit matrimonial des Tyokossi: réglement d'un
litige à la cour du chef supérieur de Sansanné-Mango'* (Essay on several aspects of
Chokossi marriage law: the resolution of one litigation at the court of the superior
chief of Sansanné-Mango). Leiden, Netherlands: Afrika-Studiecentrum, 1973. 51p.
bibliog.; and *Conciliation et la qualité des rélations sociales chez les Anufom du
Nord Togo en Afrique de l'Ouest* (Conciliation and the quality of social relations
among the Anufom of north Togo in West Africa). Leiden, Netherlands: Afrika-
Studiecentrum, 1981. 38p. bibliog.

293   **La reforme foncière togolaise.** (Land-tenure reform in Togo.)
      Marc Ducat.   *Penant,* vol. 85, no. 749 (July-Sept. 1975), p. 291-307.

Ducat reviews the system of land tenure inherited by Togo following independence,
and outlines how, after considerable hesitation and assessment, it was finally changed
by ordinance 12-74 of February 1974. The ordinance is reprinted at the end of the
article.

294   **La réforme agrofoncière au Togo.** (The agrarian land tenure reform
      in Togo.)
      Kokou Koffigoh.   In: *Enjeux fonciers en Afrique noire* (Stakes in land
      tenure in Black Africa.)   Edited by Emile Le Bris, et al.   Paris:
      Karthala, 1982. p. 240-52.

This is a description of the important February 1974 land tenure reforms in Togo.
Half the article consists of the actual decree. Another article in this book surveys the
effect of the reforms on traditional land law.

295   **La réforme agrofoncière et droit coutumier en Togo.** (The agrarian
      land law reform and customary law in Togo.)
      Messanvi Foli.   In: *Enjeux fonciers en Afrique noire* (Stakes in land
      tenure in Black Africa.)   Edited by Emile Le Bris, et al.   Paris:
      Karthala, 1982, p. 253-62.

Foli surveys the conflict between customary land law and the agrarian land reforms of
February 1974 decreed in Lomé, and the manner in which it was greeted in the
countryside. The author notes that while in general the reforms were beneficial, they

confused farmers, and should have been applied gradually and from region to region, allowing the population to became used to them.

296 **Les relations entre la France et le Togo en matière de securité sociale.** (The relations between France and Togo on the matter of social security.)
A. Mignot. *Penant,* no. 758 (Oct. 1977), p. 450-85.

Constitutes a review of the history of social security in Togo and the relevant statutes and agreements made between France, who bears most of the costs, and Togo on these matters.

297 **Sherea: justice du chef supérieure à N'zara.** (Sherea: justice of the superior chief at N'zara.)
E. A. B. van Rouveroy van Nieuwaal. Leiden, Netherlands: Afrika-Studiecentrum, 1975. 70p. bibliog.

Written in conjunction with a film made about the Chokossi chiefdom in Mango (N'Zara), this book outlines the nature of traditional law and the powers of the superior chief. It is illustrated with photographs, includes genealogies of the dynasty that arrived from Côte d'Ivoire in the 18th century, and outlines the procedures adopted during judicial sessions, and the punishments meted out. The author also assesses the role of sorcery in: 'Sorcellerie et justice dans une société togolaise: une quantité négligeable' (Sorcery and justice in a Togolese society: a negligible quantity). *Penant,* vol. 99, no. 778 (Aug.-Dec. 1989), p. 433-53. bibliog.

298 **Togo: la constitution de la IVe République.** (Togo: the constitution of the Fourth Republic.)
Afrique Contemporaine, no. 170 (1994), p. 54-74.

This is the full text of the current constitution of Togo, which was adopted by referendum in September 1992 and promulgated the next month, following the part-liberalization of the political system under General Eyadema between 1991 and 1992. The constitution contains 159 articles, including forty-one entrenching civic and human rights. It provides for a head of state (currently General Eyadema, who intimidated the country's other major political contenders so that they did not run against him), and a prime minister (currently Edem Kodjo, head of a minority party in alliance with Eyadema's RPT party), who is responsible to a national assembly. The text of the constitution has been reprinted elsewhere as well, but this source is the most widely available in libraries.

299 **La vocation héréditaire de la femme dans le droit positif togolais des successions.** (The hereditary role of women in the Togolese positive law of succession.)
Kouévi Agbekponou. *Penant,* vol. 98, no. 798 (Oct.-Dec. 1988), p. 424-52.

In this article the author enters into a detailed discussion of the conflict arising from the status of Togolese women as potential inheritors of estates under modern and customary law. The author pinpoints several areas requiring additional legislation to protect or entrench prior rights gained under constitutional provisions.

La femme en droit coutumier togolais. (The woman in Togolese customary law.)
See item no. 237.

Administration and Local Government

300 **La commune togolaise.** (The Togolese administrative district.)
Léonidas Quashié. *Revue Juridique et Politique*, vol. 22, no. 2
(April-June 1968), p. 397-406.
Written by the Attorney General of Togo, this article discusses two approaches to
local public administration, the pre-independence heritage, and, using the Lomé
'commune' as an example, outlines the rules and regulations governing its
organization and administration.

301 **Enquête sur les agents (salariés) de l'etat et les collectivités locales
et para-publiques.** (Inquiry into [salaried] state agents and local and
para-statal organs.)
Togo. Direction de la Statistique. Lomé: Division Documentation et
Publications, 1973. 53p.
Although dated, this work allows easy comparison with subsequent data on the
dramatic evolution of Togo's civil service and public finances. It is essentially a
detailed census of the country's civil service and employees in para-statal organs as
of 1972. Supplemented by tables and diagrams the data is broken down by such
factors as: nationality; occupation; salary; years of employment ; age; and sex.

302 **L'etat et l'organisation territoriale du Togo.** (The state and
territorial organization in Togo.)
Yves Marguerat. *Afrique Contemporaine*, vol. 27, no. 1 (1988),
p. 47-56.
Marguerat makes a critical examination of the territorial organization and structures
of power in Togo. He argues that the country's poorly-defined basic units (such as
villages and cantons), the inadequate resources allocated to the prefectural and
cantonal administrative levels, and the absence of any real power in the hands of
regional hierarchies, including in the main towns, reveals that the State is more

94

concerned with control than administration, and the perpetuation of territorial divisions.

303 **Die Evolution der politisch-administrativen Structuren in Togo.**
(The evolution of the politico-administrative structures in Togo.)
Jurgen Theres. Munich: V. Florenz, 1989. 199p. bibliog.

A revised version of the author's 1988 PhD dissertation for the University of Munich, this work is supplemented by illustrations and an extensive bibliography (p. 186-99). In part the book is a study of political anthropology in that it looks at both the traditional context and the political culture that affects Togolese developments, as well as the modern adaptations of the country's political and administrative structures.

304 **Institutions politiques et organisation administrative du Togo.**
(Political institutions and administrative organization in Togo.)
Agbodjan Combévi. Lomé: A. Combévi, 1987. 247p.

A detailed presentation of the Togolese constitution of 1980 and an analysis of the executive, legislative and judicial branches of government, with their compositions, powers and procedures. The study also examines the country's central administration, territorial and local authorities, and the role played by chiefs and other traditional leaders. A special chapter is devoted to the country's sole party, the RPT, and its ancillary structures (for example, women and youth organizations). Much, although not all, of the material is now only of historical or academic interest, in view of the political changes that occurred in the country between 1992 and 1993. The 1980 constitution can be found in its entirety at the end of the work, together with other important acts, laws and decrees.

305 **Plaidoyer pour le fonctionnement de la juridiction administrative au Togo.** (A plea for enabling administrative jurisdiction in Togo.)
Palouki Massina. *Penant*, vol. 100, no. 804 (Oct.-Dec. 1990), p. 403-21.

An analysis of the reasons why regional and local administrative jurisdictions find it very difficult to operate in Togo, causing both administrative problems and blockages higher up in the system. The author maintains that this is because General Eyadema, resisting any change of empowerment, has avoided establishing any new structures.

306 **République du Togo.** (Republic of Togo.)
Walter Z. Duic. In: *Africa administration: directory of public life, administration and justice for the African states.* New York: K. G. Saur, 1978, vol. 1, p. 845-904.

This is a unique directory in six different languages: English; Dutch; German; Italian; Serbo-Croat; and Spanish. It contains compactly organized but very detailed data on Togo's administrative regions and provides a wealth of information on: their capitals, towns, villages, and city quarters; names of cabinet ministers; radio and television stations; embassies; local government authorities; international representation; mayoral offices; the gendarmerie and rural constabulary; regional army commands; hospitals; and banks. The work also includes a list of all professional offices such as lawyers, engineers, doctors, and architects, as well as lists of all schools, sports clubs, hotels, waterworks and electricity plants. Some of the information is obviously dated, but most cannot be easily found elsewhere.

307 **La région des savanes au Togo: l'état, les paysans et l'intégration régionale, 1885-1985.** (The Savanes region of Togo: the state, peasants and regional integration, 1885-1985.)
Léo De Haan. Paris: Karthala, 1993. 353p. bibliog.

This book provides a comprehensive historical account of a century of colonial and post-colonial administration in Togo's northern Savanes region. The study outlines the socio-economic nature of the region, its unique problems, and the kinds of administrative and economic policies pursued by the various governments to bring about its development and national integration. For purposes of in-depth analysis the author focuses on the canton of Kantindi in the Savanes region.

308 **Rôle de préfets et chefs de régions au Togo.** (The role of prefects and regional chiefs in Togo.)
A. Apati-Bassah. *Revue Juridique et Politique*, vol. 36, no. 2 (June 1982), p. 797-810.

In this article the author analyses the evolving role of prefects and regional heads as administrative agents in Togo since independence. He notes that prefects carry out more or less the same duties as their predecessors did during the colonial era, especially in financial matters. On the other hand, regional heads, who were placed above the prefects following the 1981 administrative reforms, have been allocated economic and developmental duties.

309 **Sokodé, capitale administrative, ou, Le destin d'une hégémonie au Nord-Togo.** (Sokodé, an administrative capital, or, the destiny of a north Togolese hegemony.)
Jean-Claude Barbier. *Revue Française d'Administration Publique*, vol. 42 (June 1987), p. 353-64. bibliog.

In assessing the administration of the town of Sokodé in north Togo, the author argues that history shows that the current administrative divisions were not the product of either rationality or artificiality, even though they were created by an outside power. Rather, they reflect inter-group cleavages and strategies of privileged social actors to maximize or conserve power and authority.

Chef coutumier: un métier difficile. (Customary chief: a difficult job.)
See item no. 274.

La justice traditionnelle, une justice parallèle. (Traditional justice, a parallel justice.)
See item no. 286.

L'organisation judiciaire au Togo en matière civile. (The judicial organization in Togo in civil issues.)
See item no. 288.

A la recherche de la justice. (In search of justice.)
See item no. 292.

Sherea: justice du chef supérieure à N'Zara. (Sherea, justice of the superior chief of N'Zara.)
See item no. 297.

Politics

310 **Les actes de la Conference Nationale Souveraine (1991).** (The acts
of the Sovereign National Conference [1991].)
Lomé: Editogo, 1992. 80p.

This volume includes the text of the twenty-two acts passed by the National
Conference, which was convened in 1991 and then promptly declared itself sovereign
and decreed the end of General Eyadema's reign. These acts include the dissolution
of Eyadema's RPT party, restructuring of the public sector, and reversing the early
edict on the adoption of indigenous names. There is also a full list of the members of
the Haut Conseil de la République, the new interim government. Some of this
material is also found in: Togo, *Résolutions, declarations et appel* (Resolutions,
declarations and an appeal). Lomé: Conference Nationale Souveraine, 1991. 64p. See
also: Kokou Koffigoh, *Le nouveau contrat social pour une transition pacifique:
programme minimum du gouvernement pour sauver la democratie au Togo* (The new
social contract for a peaceful transition: minimal governmental programme for saving
democracy in Togo). Lomé: République Togolaise, 1991. 25p. The latter, written by
the interim Prime Minister chosen by the National Conference, outlines a programme
of action to assure a democratic transition in Togo, and includes photographs of all
members of Koffigoh's interim government.

311 **Allocutions et discours du Général d'Armée Gnassingbé Eyadema,
1969-1979.** (Speeches and addresses of Army General Gnassingbe
Eyadema, 1969-1979.)
Lomé: RPT Secretariat Administratif, 1979. 3 vols.

This bulky three-volume set is a collection of the speeches made by General Eyadema
during 1969-1979, chronologically arranged. Part of the personality cult that
Eyadema fostered throughout the country, and also, allegedly, in preparation for an
expected nomination for a Nobel Peace prize, many of the speeches are banal and/or
trivial. Subsequently, additional, though much smaller, volumes have been published,
with the same title, such as the one for 1982.

312 **Bilan de la 1ère législature de la 3ème République Togolaise.**
(Record of the 1st legislature of the 3rd Togolese Republic.)
O. F. Natchaba. *Revue Juridique et Politique,* no. 3-4 (1985),
p. 860-70.
Natchaba presents an overview of the activities of the Togolese national assembly during the five years ending December 1984. The author maintains that the assembly showed a great deal of caution ('prudence') amounting to virtual 'self-limitation' in its activities, the reasons for which he outlines in the article.

313 **Conference Nationale Souveraine (1991).** (Sovereign National
Conference [1991].)
Lomé: Secretariat Général, Conference Nationale Souveraine du Togo,
1991. various pagination.
This 300-page volume is a remarkable collection of the minutes of the sessions of the National Conference that was convened in Lomé between 2 July and 21 July 1991, and that, declaring itself independent, paved the way for the partial relaxation of the grip of the dictatorship of General Eyadema. The documents in the book include numerous critiques of the failings of the Eyadema regime, including (on the last page) of the latter's economic policies. Numerous other publications resulted from the National Conference. See in particular: *Conference Nationale Souveraine: 8 juillet-28 aout 1991: comptes rendus* (Sovereign National Conference: July 8 – August 28, 1991: proceedings). Lomé: Secretariat Général, Conference Nationale Souveraine du Togo, 1991. various pagination; *Les actes de la Conference Nationale Souveraine du Togo* (The acts of Togo's Sovereign National Conference). Lomé: Secretariat Général, Conference Nationale Souveraine du Togo, 1991, 80p.; *Résolutions, declarations et appel.* Lomé: Secretariat Général, Conference Nationale Souveraine du Togo, 1992. 64p. An episcopal conference also took place in 1991 in which the Catholic Church issued a strong appeal to its faithful to work for a new society of law, peace and brotherhood. See: Conference Episcopale du Togo, *Démocratie: orientations pastorales pour une société de droit, d'amour, de solidarité et de paix* . Lomé: La Conference, 1991. 42p.

314 **Conference Nationale Souveraine (1991). Commission III –
affaires économiques et financières.** (Sovereign National Conference
[1991]. Committee III – economic and financial matters.)
Lomé: Secretariat Général, Conference Nationale Souveraine du Togo,
1991. 206p.
This document is the analysis of Togo's economic and fiscal situation, as assessed by a committee created by the National Conference in 1991.

315 **Un despotisme à visage humain: le Togo.** (A despotism with a
human face: Togo.)
Kwam Azé Kwam. Lomé: K. A. Kwam, 1991. 139p.
With the gradual disintegration of the Eyadema dictatorship in Togo and the political liberalizations of 1990, a variety of sharply critical works on his reign began to openly appear for the first time in Togo. This book, self-published by the author but available at the time in Lomé bookshops and in major academic centres overseas, is a

biting criticism of Eyadema's twenty-five-year reign and an enumeration of many of the crimes that Kwam accuses him off.

316 **Development in francophone Africa.**
Lapido Adamolekun, M. Laleye. In: *Local government in West Africa.* Edited by Lapido Adamolekun, D. Oluwu, M. Laleye. Lagos: Lagos University Press, 1988, p. 310-41.

This chapter begins with a concise overview of French Africa's political context at independence, and continues with a brief description of the major trends in the evolution of local government in each country since then.

317 **Deuxième congrès statutaire du Rassemblement du Peuple Togolais.** (Second statutory congress of the Assembly of the Togolese People.)
Rassemblement du Peuple Togolais. Lomé: Nouvelles Editions Africaines, 1979. 163p.

This is the record of the important RPT congress held in the northern town of Lama Kara between 26 and 29 November 1976. For the first statutory congress, in the southern town of Kpalimé in 1971 see: *Premiere congrès statutaire du Rassemblement du Peuple Togolais* (First statutory congress of the RPT). Lomé: Secretariat Administratif du RPT, 1972. 93p. For the third (held in Lomé) see: *Troisieme congrès statutaire du Rassemblement du Peuple Togolais* (Third statutory congress of the RPT). Lomé: Secretariat Administratif du RPT, 1979. 233p. For the final congress, before the party's dominance in Togo ended, see: *Quatrieme congrès statutaire du Rassemblement du Peuple Togolais: tenu à Lomé les 4, 5, 6, et 7 decembre 1986* (Fourth statutory congress of the RPT: held in Lomé on 4, 5, 6, and 7 December 1986). Lomé: Secretariat Administratif du RPT, 1987. 183p. Various similar publications have been issued since the RPT was set up, summarizing either the debates of statutory congresses or of their national councils. One example of the latter literature is: Rassemblement du Peuple Togolais, *Cinquieme conseil national du Rassemblement du Peuple Togolaise: Lomé 17-18 fevrier 1981* (Fifth national council of the Rassemblement du Peuple Togolaise). Lomé: Secretariat Administratif du RPT, 1981. 141p.

318 **Le deuxieme congrès statutaire du RPT.** (The second statutory congress of the RPT.)
Raymond Verdier. In: *L'évolution récente du pouvoir en Afrique noire* (The recent evolution of power in Black Africa.) Bordeaux, France: Centre d'Etude d'Afrique Noire, 1977, p. 153-61.

An early laudatory assessment of General Eyadema's leadership in Togo, and his role in guiding the country's single party. The account was written before revelations of some of Eyadema's more brutal atrocities came to light. With respect to the RPT the author maintains that 'the personality of its founding-President . . . and its progressive institutionalization permitted it in 7 years to revive a profound renewal in the country' (p. 153).

319 **The dictator's duet.**
Peter Da Costa. *Africa Report* (Nov.-Dec. 1993), p. 61-65.
Da Costa provides a concise description of the background to Togo's first-ever multi-party presidential elections, and the reasons for the victory of the incumbent dictator, General Gnassingbe Eyadema, *albeit* with a low (39.5 per cent) voter turnout, and after a policy of intimidation and exclusion that led to the withdrawal from the race of all but two independent candidates.

320 **Dix ans de 'démocratisation' au Togo: les faussaires de la démocratie.** (Ten years of 'democratization' in Togo: the falsifications of democracy.)
Comi M. Toulabor. In: *Année africain 1989*. Paris: Pedone, 1990, p. 287-310.
This is a highly critical review of General Eyadema's previous decade in power, and especially of Togo's political evolution during 1989, which was to lead to the National Convention ushering in multipartyism. Toulabor, a Togolese scholar living in France, traces in detail the gyrations of Eyadema and how he tried at the outset to avoid, and later to accomodate, external pressures for democratization.

321 **Forces armées togolaises.** (Togolese armed forces.)
René Bail, Jean Warren. Paris: Afrique Biblio Club, 1977. 143p.
This glossy publication gushes with admiration for the 'glorious' leadership of the armed forces by their 'founder', General Eyadema, who was actually a Sergeant when he first seized power in 1963. Aimed at reinforcing the personality cult established by Eyadema in Togo, the book opens with a double-page photograph of Eyadema and concludes with a similar one of his Kim-il-Sung-style statue (carved in North Korea), which was erected in Lomé but has since been removed. The book includes various colour photographs, organograms of the armed forces, and is interspersed with various 'sayings' of Eyadema.

322 **Eyadema's nightmare.**
Richard Everett. *Africa Report*, Nov.-Dec. 1986, p. 14-17.
The author presents a brief discussion of the insecurity of the Eyadema regime in view of the September coup attempt that was assisted by neighbouring countries. For a similar discussion, see: Richard Gerster, 'How to ruin a country: the case of Togo'. *IFDA Dossier*, no. 71 (May-June 1989), p. 25-36.

323 **Les hésitations au Togo: les obstacles à la transition.** (Hesitations in Togo: obstacles to the transition.)
Christian Komi Soglo. In: *Les nouvelles constitutions africaines: la transition démocratique* (The new African constitutions: the democratic transition.) Edited by Henry Roussillon. Toulouse: Presses de l'Institut d'Etudes Politiques de Toulouse, 1993. p. 163-72.
Set within the context of a continental survey of the changing array of political power, democratization and constitutional change, this is an analysis of the reasons for the resistance to change in Togo. The author emphasizes the degree to which events in neighbouring Benin inspired the Togolese movement for holding a National

Conference in Lomé. He points out that General Eyadema's unwillingness to ste[
down from power assured that the Beninois outcome (the ouster of General Kerekou
would not be replicated in his own country.

324 **Histoire du Togo. Il était une fois . . . Eyadema.** (History of Togo.
Once upon a time . . . Eyadema.)
Serge Saint-Michel. Paris: ABC, 1976. 48p.

This remarkable book is an example of General Eyadema's cult of personality at it
height. It is a colour, comic-strip epic rendition of the life of the former sergeant
portraying events in his life from birth, through military service in the French colonia
armies, his two takeovers of power, and several miraculous escapes from designs o.
his life, to the widespread admiration with which he was regarded in Togoles
society. Commissioned by Eyadema, the work was aimed at spreading the myth o
Eyadema's invincibility, and garnering the regime support.

325 **The iron hand rusts.**
Mark Huband. *Africa Report* (Nov.-Dec. 1991), p. 18-20.

Huband briefly reviews the events leading up to the convening of the Nationa
Conference in Lomé, which stripped General Eyadema of all powers in 1991. Se
also: A. Lee, A. Astrow, 'In search of friends'. *Africa Report*, vol. 32, no. 2 (Feb
1987), p. 51-53.

326 **Jalons pour une sociologie électorale du Togo: 1958, 1985.**
(Towards an electoral sociology of Togo: 1958, 1985.)
Jean-Claude Barbier. *Politique Africaine*, no. 27 (Sept.-Oct. 1987),
p. 6-18. English summary.

This article is part of a special issue of this important journal on Togo. The autho
analyses the 1958 and 1985 legislative elections in Sokodé, paying particula
attention to the levels of voter participation and degree of ethnic (and cross-ethnic
voting. He reaches several conclusions about electoral motivations.

327 **Jeu de mots, jeu de vilains: lexiques de la derision politique au**
Togo. (Games of words, games of villains: the language of political
derision in Togo.)
Comi Toulabor. In: *La politique par le bas: contribution à une*
problematique de la démocratie en Afrique noire (Politics from below.
contribution to a problem of democracy in Black Africa.) Edited by
J. F. Bayart, M. Mbembe, Comi Toulabor. Paris: Karthala, 1986,
p. 109-30.

Originally published as a shorter version in 1981 (see *Politique Africaine*, no. 3
1981. p. 55-71) and by a Togolese scholar in self-imposed exile in France, thi
important article helped to open a new analytical trail in African studies. The autho
deals with the language of 'low politics', explaining and decoding the hidde
meaning of the derogatory language used in political discourse in Togo, an
indicating how in many societies, such as Togo, rumour, barbed puns and jokes ar
the popular lexicon of political conflict over legitimacy.

328 **La JRPT hier, aujourd'hui, demain.** (The JRPT yesterday, today, tomorrow.)
Lomé: Bureau Executif de la Jeunesse du RPT, 1975. 52p.

Including an organogram and photographs, this publication outlines the structures of the RPT party's ancillary youth organization, its role in political life and programme manifesto.

329 **Les militaires au Dahomey et au Togo.** (The military in Dahomey and Togo.)
Robert Cornevin. *Revue Française d'Etudes Politiques Africaines* (Dec. 1968), p. 65-84.

This is a very perceptive comparative study of the armed forces of these two neighbouring countries, how they differ, the reasons for their several coups, and the role the armed forces may be expected to play in the future.

330 **The politics of military rule in Togo.**
Samuel Decalo. *Genève-Afrique* (Geneva), vol. 12, no. 2 (1973), p. 1-35.

The early political history of Togo is outlined in this article, which considers Eyadema's two military coups (in 1963 and 1967) and their specific motivations, as well as the nature of the political system he established.

331 **Le president Olympio vous parle: recueil des allocutions importantes de 1961.** (President Olympio speaks: collection of important speeches of 1961.)
Sylvanus Olympio. Lomé: Service de l'Information et de la Presse du Gouvernement du Togo, 1962. 74p.

Information and knowledge of the brief Olympio presidency (1960-63) in Togo is relatively sparse. This volume is a collection of the speeches delivered by Olympio in 1961 on a variety of themes.

332 **Le renouveau démocratique au Togo.** (The democratic renewal in Togo.)
Yves-Emmanuel Dogbé. Lomé: Editions Akpagnon, 1991. 83p.

Written by one of Togo's best-known authors, this is a brief review of Togo's history leading up to the 1991 National Conference, and an account of Dogbé's own six-month detention without trial under the Eyadema regime between 1976 and 1977.

333 **Rumour and power in Togo.**
Stephen Ellis. *Africa*, vol. 63, no. 4 (1993), p. 462-76.

This article focuses on the mass challenge that developed in 1991 to General Eyadema's continued rule in Togo. The author discusses how popular perceptions about what was transpiring were formed, in a country with tight news censorship, via 'radio trottoir' ('bush telegraph', or urban gossip), and how by manipulating various myths Eyadema managed to cling to a measure of power. By extension, Ellis indicates that by eroding the myths that sustain Eyadema's claim to legitimacy –

spread throughout the latter's lengthy reign – the dictator's continuing position at the pinnacle of power in Togo can be challenged successfully. The author has written another article on this theme: 'Tuning to pavement radio'. *African Affairs*, vol. 88, no. 352 (1989), p. 321-30.

334 Sieges and scapegoats: the politics of pluralism in Ghana and Togo.
David Brown. *Civilisations* (Brussels), vol. 33, no. 2 (1983), p. 71-112.

Brown's article is a comparison of the role of politicized ethnicity as an explanatory variable for a better understanding of the different political evolutions of Ghana and Togo.

335 Stability and stagnation under a military brokerage system.
Samuel Decalo. In: *Coups and army rule in Africa: motivations and constraints.* New Haven, Connecticut: Yale University Press, 1990. 2nd ed. p. 205-40. bibliog.

This chapter is one of five case-studies (four from francophone Africa) in a book focusing on military systems, the motivations of army leaders for seizing power, the constraints on effective military regimes, and the modalities of military rule illustrated by each regime within a three-fold typology. Togo is placed within the 'brokerage' modality, where, while maintaining supreme authority, military leaders stabilize themselves by satisfying basic societal demands to a certain degree. The chapter outlines the basic socio-economic and historical background of Togo, pinpoints the motives for General Eyadema's twin coups (1963 and 1967) and describes the kind of political system he set up, and with what results up to 1988. The author periodizes Eyadema's lengthy reign, illustrating how progressively the latter dissipated whatever social support he might have garnered in the early 1970s, and how by overextending the economy through bouts of massive spending, patronage, and unchecked rampant corruption, he set in motion the forces that were to challenge him later on. An earlier version of this material, for the period up to 1975, is found in the first edition (1976) of this work, with a slightly different title.

336 Sylvanus Olympio: un destin tragique. (Sylvanus Olympio: a tragic destiny.)
A. K. Agbobli. Dakar: Nouvelles Editions Africaines, 1992. 198p.

For decades after Sergeant Eyadema's first assault on legitimate power in Lomé in 1963, little was written about Togo's first president, Olympio, who was murdered at the time by Eyadema. This work by Agbobli, who played a role in liberalizing Togo's political system during 1991 and 1992, is one of several much-belated re-assessments of Olympio the man, his regime and his tragic fate. Of some interest is the fact that for the first time the question is raised as to whether there was any indirect French involvement in Eyadema's attack.

337 **Togo.**
   In: *Academic freedom and human rights abuses in Africa*.   London:
   Human Rights Watch, 1991, p. 115-18.

A succinct review of censorship in Togo under General Eyadema, and the travails of
the academic community. The author notes 'On campus free discussion was allowed
only in non-political disciplines . . . anyone writing a book, an article, a play, or
producing a film was required to submit his or her work to a censor [and any author of
critical material] was subjected to arrest and detention, beatings and other forms of
mistreatment.' (p. 115).

338 **Le Togo du Sergeant en Général.** (Togo, from Sergeant to General.)
   Andoch Nutépé Bonin.   Paris: Lescaret, 1983. 231p.

This book was one of the first of the highly critical mass of literature about General
Eyadema that began to appear in the 1980s and is written by a Togolese who knew
Eyadema intimately. Bonin was his interpreter, attached to the Presidential Office,
between 1979 and 1982 after which he fled to exile. The book was banned in Togo,
and representations were made to have it banned in France as well, because it
revealed and/or reminded readers of a variety of unflattering personal details about
the Togolese military leader. This included information such as: that his real name is
Gnassingbe, 'Eyadema' being adopted for its connotation of bravery; that the 1963
coup did not take place as Eyadema had planned; that former President Olympio was
murdered in his own palace by a nervous Eyadema, and his corpse moved to reflect
better on the coup leaders; and details about people Eyadema subsequently had
liquidated.

339 **Le Togo 'en général': la longue marche de Gnassingbé Eyadema.**
   (Togo in general: the long road of Gnassingbe Eyadema.)
   Claude Feuillet.   Paris: ABC, 1976. 190p.

A flattering biography of General Eyadema, this work follows the official line about
his role in the 1963 and 1967 coups, and his subsequent leadership of Togo.

340 **Togo: Eyadema – 20 ans de pouvoir.** (Togo: Eyadema – 20 years in
   power.)
   Europe-Outremer (Paris), no. 675-76 (April-May 1986), Special issue.

This special issue of the Parisian glossy monthly is composed of a collection of brief,
largely laudatory articles on all aspects of Togo's political and economic evolution
under General Eyadema.

341 **Togo: game, set and match.**
   Africa Confidential, vol. 32, no. 24 (Dec. 6 1991), p. 4-6.

Articles in this bi-weekly newsletter are always perceptive and this is no exception. It
is a detailed and succinct overview of the process by which the beleaguered General
Eyadema utilized his solid control of the armed forces to engineer his political
comeback in Togo, after being stripped of all powers by the National Conference of
1991. Among the several other brief reviews of ongoing events in Togo in this
publication, one stands out: 'Togo: leaders at daggers drawn'. *Africa Confidential*,
vol. 33, no. 22 (Nov. 20 1992), p. 4-5.

342 **Togo: impunity for killings by the military.**
Amnesty International. New York: Amnesty International, 1993.
23p. plates.

Despite formal 'democratization' in 1991, power and especially command of the
northern-packed armed forces has remained in the hands of General Eyadema. This
report, which is accompanied by photographs, enumerates various atrocities
committed by the security forces both during the 'transitional' phase of liberalization
and after it. The report concludes with recommendations for the respect of basic
human rights in Togo. Amnesty International has published two earlier highly critical
reports on abuses of human rights in Togo, the largest number on any African
country. For the earlier ones see: *Togo: report of a government commission of inquiry
into torture.* New York: Amnesty International, 1986. 14p.; and *Togo: impunity for
human rights violators at a time of reform.* New York: Amnesty International, 1992.
20p. The latter details the widespread use of human torture in Togolese detention
centres, and the death by starvation in 1984 of former Vice-President Meatchi.

343 **Le Togo sous Eyadema.** (Togo under Eyadema.)
Comi M. Toulabor. Paris: Karthala, 1986. 332p. bibliog.

No author has done more to de-mystify the lengthy dictatorial rule of General
Eyadema and the aura of stable and effective (if firm) government he succeeded in
projecting abroad, than Comi Toulabor, a Togolese scholar teaching in France. The
book, when published, also sent shock-waves through academic circles, paving the
way for greater realism in African Studies. Toulabor's work was the harshest
indictment of Eyadema's dictatorship until the National Conference in Lomé in 1991
publicly revealed gruesome details about the regime's misdeeds. Toulabor's
devastating critique does not focus on policies pursued in Lomé, but rather on
Eyadema as an individual. He underscores how Eyadema, seen by the Togolese as a
mediocre, crude and vain personality, deftly exploited, by brute force and by twisting
the truth to his advantage, a series of events to build a grotesque personality cult (with
an element of cultural-religious symbolism, meaningful in Togo) 'proving' his
invincibility. These included Olympio's murder in 1963 (an act of panic on the part of
Eyadema) and the 1974 Sarakawa air-crash, where a mausoleum was erected to which
youth were compelled to make pilgrimages.

Dream of unity: pan-Africanism and political unification in West Africa.
See item no. 66.

The Ewe unification movement.
See item no. 74.

Naissance d'un état africain. (Birth of an African state.)
See item no. 89.

Le referendum du Togo (28 Octobre 1956). (The Togolese referendum [28
October 1956].)
See item no. 94.

Qui a peur de la philosophie? (Who is afraid of philosophy?)
See item no. 265.

Institutions politiques et organisation administrative du Togo. (Political institutions and administrative organization in Togo.)
See item no. 304.

Historical dictionary of Togo.
See item no. 541.

Togo.
See item no. 557.

Togo.
See item no. 562.

Foreign Relations

344 **African problems and the Cold War.**
Sylvanus Olympio. *Foreign Affairs,* vol. 40 (1961), p. 50-57.
This article constitutes a rare discussion of the problems of Togo and Africa, in general, and their suggested international role, by the country's first president.

345 **Le Bénin dans les rapports ouest-africaines: stratégie d'insertion, bilateralisme sous-régional et engagements régionaux.** (Benin in West African relations: entry strategy, sub-regional bilateralism and regional relations.)
Leon C. Codo. Talence, France: University of Bordeaux, Centre of African Studies, 1987. 267p. bibliog.
Written from a Beninois perspective, this is a comprehensive study of that country's foreign relations with neighbouring African states, including Togo. Chapter seven (p. 169-88) specifically deals with the history of Benin-Togo relations, although there are references to Togo throughout the volume. Relations between the two neighbouring countries have been difficult (especially between 1975 and 1977), with their common border frequently closed to the detriment of mutual trade and human contact, because of mutual accusations that each regime was supportive of opposition groups in exile.

346 **Borderline politics in Ghana: the National Liberation Movement of western Togoland.**
David Brown. *Journal of Modern African Studies,* vol. 18, no. 4 (1980), p. 575-609.
This is an erudite and sympathetic study of the problem of the Ewe people who were separated by the Ghana/Togo boundary following the pre-independence plebiscite that merged the former British Togoland with the Gold Coast to form Ghana. Brown surveys: Ewe unification efforts from as early as 1919; the emergence of the All-Ewe Conference; and finally the rise of the CUT political party in French Togoland that

led that country to independence. He then focuses on the emergence in Ghana of TOLIMO, the latest unification movement to come to global attention. In 1972 they presented a petition to the Organization of African Unity to sanction the unification of all Ewe within the republic of Togo, and this put great strains on Ghana-Togo international relations.

347 **La coopération germano-togolaise de 1960 à nos jours.** (German-Togo co-operation from 1960 to this day.)
Mavor Tetey Agbodan. *Le Mois en Afrique,* no. 235/36 (Aug.-Sept. 1985), p. 52-63.

Although the German colonial era in Togo was very short, ending with the onset of the First World War, when Togo became the first of the Allied military successes, Germans have always retained a surprising nostalgia for their former possession. This became visible after Togo's independence when Germany extended various programmes of technical co-operation to the government. This article surveys German-Togolese social, economic, cultural, religous and diplomatic relations between 1960 and 1982, with particular attention paid to trade and commerce. See also: Jean Hegba, 'La place de l'Afrique dans la politique des investissements privés allemands à l'étranger' (The place of Africa in the politics of private German investments abroad). *Revue Française d'Etudes Politiques Africaines* (April 1971), p. 36-65.

348 **Deutchland und Togo 1847-1987.** (Germany and Togo 1847-1987.)
Raphael Quarshie Avornyo. Frankfurt: Peter Land, 1989. 541p. bibliog.

Originally the author's 1987 doctoral dissertation, this is a history of German-Togolese relations, from the first German explorers, through pacification and German colonial rule, to the era of mutual co-operation after Togo's independence. A solid bibliography that notes most of the literature in German and French is appended.

349 **Entre Israel et le Togo: une experience de coopération entre deux états petits et jeunes.** (Between Israel and Togo: co-operation between two small and young states.)
B. A. Awesso. *Espoir de la Nation Togolaise* (Lomé), no. 5/6 (April-May 1970), p. 2-34.

Until Togo was forced to join the near continent-wide diplomatic rupture of relations with Israel in the early 1970s, relations between the two countries were particularly close, and were even commemorated in Togo by a series of postage stamps. This article discusses Israel's multifaceted programmes of international co-operation in Togo, and the lessons Togo expected to learn from the Israeli developmental experience.

350 **The Ghana-Togo boundary 1914-1982.**
R. Bagulo Bening. *Afrika-Spectrum* (Hamburg), vol. 18, no. 2 (1983), p. 191-209.

This article recounts the history of the evolution of the boundary between Togo and Ghana that artificially divides a number of ethnic groups. This caused periodic problems during the colonial era, and inter-state tensions after independence. Ewe unificationist sentiments have periodically been kindled on both sides of the border to the detriment of stable international relations, and friction between the leaders of the two countries, notably between Nkrumah and Olympio, and between Rawlings and Eyadema, have likewise caused tensions. In north Togo, Konkomba crossed into Ghana to assist their kinsmen during the bloody Nanumba-Konkomba ethnic violence of 1981, and more recently they have sought refuge in Ghana from the tumult in Togo in the 1990s. For more on this complex issue see: Saadia Touval, 'Ghana and Togo'. In: *The boundary politics of independent Africa*. Cambridge, Massachusetts: Harvard University Press, 1972, p. 203-11; and Amouzouvi Maurice Akakpo, 'La delimitation des frontières togolaises'. In: *Symposium Leo Frobenius*. Cologne: UNESCO, 1980, p. 92-109.

351 **La politique extèrieure du Togo.** (The foreign policy of Togo.)
Robert Cornevin. *Revue Française d'Etudes Politiques Africaines*, no. 82 (Oct. 1972), p. 59-71.

Written by one of France's top Africanists, this article surveys the variables that have determined Togo's foreign policy, and especially with regard to neighbouring Ghana and the Council of the Entente, dominated by the Ivory Coast. Cornevin traces many frictions that developed with Ghana, considering the different world-views of the two countries' first presidents, Olympio and Nkrumah. Problems were exacerbated by irredentist claims arising from the division of the Ewe between the two states at the end of the colonial period.

352 **Si la maison de votre voisin brûle . . . : Eyadema et la politique extèrieure du Togo.** (If your neighbour's house is burning . . . : Eyadema and Togo's foreign policy.)
Georges Ayache. Paris: ABC, 1983. bibliog.

This is a highly laudatory assessment of General Eyadema's first fifteen years in office. Although the author's main thrust is allegedly to analyse Togo's foreign policy and diplomatic history, the over-riding theme that emerges is his admiration of Eyadema who gave Togo decades of internal peace after the political strife of the preceding civilian era. The negative aspects of the Eyadema reign are not touched. The book includes a political chronology and many photographs.

353 **Le Togo dans le monde: recueil des actes diplomatiques interesant le Togo.** (Togo in the world: collection of diplomatic treaties of interest to Togo.)
E. Kwam Kouassi, Alain Mignot. Lomé: Université du Bénin, Institut de Recherche et de Documentation, 1978. 3 vols.

A collection of the texts of all the international treaties and accords to which Togo is a signatory actor.

354 **Togo, the Entente's fifth member.**
Virginia Thompson. In: *West Africa's Council of the Entente*. Ithaca: Cornell University Press, 1972, p. 75-90.

This is a study of Togo's political evolution, foreign policy, and uneasy international relations within the regional West African Council of the Entente.

355 **The uncertain frontier: Ghana-Togo.**
Denis Austin. *Journal of Modern African Studies*, vol. 1, no. 2
(1963), p. 139-45.

Since independence the boundary between Ghana and Togo has been closed on
several occasions for varying periods of time. This has been at the instigation of one
or the other side and is a symptom of the intermittently poor relations between the
two countries. This article discusses the early years of Ghana-Togo diplomatic
relations, when the border between the two countries was closed due to multi-faceted
friction between presidents Olympio and Nkrumah.

Les migrations des expulsés du Nigeria. (The migrations of those expelled
from Nigeria.)
See item no. 216.

Les relations entre la France et le Togo en matière de securité sociale.
(Relations between France and Togo on social security issues.)
See item no. 296.

Economy and Economic Development

356 **Activités d'exportation de produits primaires et développement économiques: l'exemple du Togo.** (Export of primary products and economic development: the example of Togo.)
Monique Anson-Meyer. *Mondes et Devéloppement* (Paris), no. 29/30 (1980), p. 163-200.

This article examines the role of export-revenues in driving the economic expansion of Togo, and the excessively-high expectations of a continued boom of phosphate-generated revenues in the mid-1970s that misled the government into massive expenditures that could not be sustained once revenues plummeted.

357 **Aspects du développement récent de l'économie togolaise.** (Aspects of the recent economic development of Togo.)
Philippe Roudie. *Les Cahiers d'Outre-Mer*, vol. 31 (Oct.-Dec. 1978), p. 359-74.

Roudie reviews the Togolese government's efforts, as of the late-1970s, to develop the economy based on its royalties from the sale of phosphates. The specific policies embarked upon are discussed, including industrialization, agricultural development and the establishment of regional development structures. The former glossy Parisian monthly *Europe-Outremer* has also published a number of special issues devoted specifically to Togolese developments. For two such issues see: 'Togo: priorité au développement intégral' (Togo: priority on integral development), no. 594 (July 1979); and 'Togo: vers une croissance durable' (Togo: towards a sustained growth), no. 667/668 (Feb. 1986).

358 **The economy of Togo.**
U. Tun Wai, et al. *IMF Staff Papers* (Washington, DC), vol. 12,
no. 3 (Nov. 1965), p. 406-69.
This early and dated paper is still a very useful overview of the Togolese economy in
the early 1960s, before phosphates came onto the export market.

359 **Effet de la recession sur l'économie togolaise: évolution recente et**
perspective de croissance économique. (The effect of the recession
on the Togolese economy: recent events and prospects of economic
growth.)
K. M. Gozo. Addis Ababa: Bureau International du Travail, 1985.
74p. bibliog.
This ILO publication focuses on the deteriorating economic conditions in Togo since
1979 that led to a decline in exports and state revenues, postponement of payments of
international debts, and a very strong contraction of public and private investments
and consumption. The report assesses the possibilities of a moderate economic pick-
up in the short term. There are numerous tables, and comprehensive economic figures
for the years 1966 to 1983.

360 **Une étude de micro-centrales hydroélectriques au Togo et au**
Bénin. (A study of a small hydro-electric centre in Togo and Benin.)
R. Sokal. *Académie Royale des Sciences d'Outre-mer* (Brussels),
vol. 32, no. 3 (1986), p. 479-97.
Sokal has made a study of the water and energy resources of Togo, and in particular
the hydro-electric plant that produces power for both Benin and Togo, and its role in
the Togolese economy.

361 **L'etat et le secteur non structuré au Togo.** (The state and the non-
structured sector in Togo.)
K. M. Gozo, A. Dravié. Addis Ababa: Organisation Internationale de
Travail, Programme des Emplois et des Competences Techniques pour
l'Afrique, 1990. various pagination. bibliog.
This represents a concerted attempt to quantify the dimensions and characteristics of
Togo's sizeable informal sector, and to analyse its significance. In 1984 there were
209,000 people, three-quarters of them in the country's rural areas, involved in the
informal sector, amounting to twenty-three per cent of the economically active
population. This book, which has different internal paginations, comprises of a
twenty-eight-page study that summarizes most of the findings of the research,
providing details such as: the age of those involved; their capital resources; field of
endeavour; and whether they have available electricity or running water in their
enterprise. Nineteen pages of annexes containing mostly statistical tables, and a nine-
page reproduction of the questionnaire used for the research are also included. The
study includes several specific proposals aimed at encouraging and enhancing the role
of the informal sector in Togo.

362 **Institutional development and technical assistance in macro-economic policy formulation: a case study of Togo.**
Sven B. Kjellstrom, Ayité-Fily d'Almeida.   Washington, DC: The World Bank, 1987. 69p.

This World Bank discussion paper assesses the contributions made by IDA-financed technical assistance programmes to the institutional development in macro-economic policy formulation in Togo during the period of 1983-1985. It discusses the first structural adjustment programme that was necessitated because of the 1974 collapse of phosphate prices, and the excessive State expenditures that were made in anticipation of continued high prices.

363 **International development and technical assistance in macro-economic policy formulation: a case study of Togo.**
Sven B. Kjellstrom, Ayité-Fily d'Almeida.   Washington, DC: The World Bank, 1985. 85p.

In a remarkably succinct manner, this World Bank staff working paper (no. 786) pinpoints Togo's economic problems, blaming them on the excessive spending on the State sector after the phosphate price boom of 1974, and the unwillingness of the government to accept the fact that those sharply higher producer prices were temporary, thus aggravating deficit-spending. The paper outlines the requirements for a successful programme of technical assistance to the Togolese government. See also: a briefer account by the same authors, 'Aid coordination: a recipient's perspective'. *Finance and Development*, vol. 23 (Sept. 1986), p. 37-40.

364 **A la limitation des risques dans la pratique des crédits traditionnels en Afrique noire: quelques réflexions sur la base de l'expérience togolaise.** (Towards risk limitation in the practice of traditional credits in Black Africa: some reflections on the basis of the Togolese experience.)
K. I. Egbeto, A. Bender.   *Genève-Afrique* (Geneva), vol. 26, no. 2 (1988), p. 29-46.

The authors of this article focus on the banking sector in Africa, that is afflicted by a variety of risks and problems, including bad repayment ratios by borrowers, especially by those in the rural sector. The authors suggest that the alternative is to use traditional forms of credit, analogous to the exchange of labour in times of need. Resting on moral and social pressure the latter is always honoured: it benefits all participants, and if renegued upon would lead to complete isolation and ostracism of the offending party. The authors suggest that although there may be limits to the expansion of traditional credit systems, since they greatly limit risk, they should be studied for possible implementation.

365 **Les limites sectorielles de l'expérience togolaise de vingt ans de 'planification': l'agriculture, 1966-1985.** (The limits of twenty years of Togolese sectoral planning: agriculture, 1966-1985.)
Ewihn-Liba Pana. *World Development,* vol. 14, no. 3 (1989), p. 63-77. English summary.

The head of the department of economics at the University of Benin in Lomé has written this important article, which outlines in a rather stark manner the record of twenty years of planning in Togo's key sector of agriculture, which has always been defined by the regime as the 'priority of priorities'. Planning came to an end in 1985 when, faced by a major liquidity crisis, the country had to accept a World Bank structural adjustment programme. The author emphasizes how there has always been a huge gap between official pronouncements and development plans, and reality. Thus, notwithstanding large investments in agriculture, progress has been modest, and a drastic regression in production took place in the 1980s as farmers were marginalized. Contrary to the proclaimed policy of attaining food self-sufficiency by 1980, the food subsector actually recorded a decline, which was the result of misconceived policies that placed much greater value on export crops that would bring in foreign exchange, than on basic staple crops and foodstuffs. Moreover, as the author concludes, the 'production of provisional statistics in the cosy atmosphere of ministerial offices neglects the human factor in rural development. Without the knowhow and consent of the peasantry, nothing can be achieved in the rural areas.' (p. 63.)

366 **Le marché togolais.** (The Togolese market.)
Marchés Tropicaux et Mediterranéens, no. 1,308 (Dec. 5 1970), p. 3,455-528.

Published in one of the most important economic periodicals for francophone Africa, this article comprehensively surveys Togo's different economic sectors: trade; commerce; industry; and manufacturing. Periodic updates and news items appear frequently in this journal, which since the 1990s has also been published as a monthly in English.

367 **Le mouvement cooperatif d'espargne-crédit au Togo.** (The savings credit co-operative movement in Togo.)
Nukunu Kodjovi. *Communautés,* no. 77 (1986), p. 68-85.

This is a history of the savings and credit co-operative movement in Togo. Its inception was in 1969, when in a village near Badou, at the initiative of an American missionary, the first credit union was founded. Their rapid proliferation brought about formal recognition by the government, and the creation of a federation of credit unions, which in 1983 numbered 111, and encompassed 10,169 members and 240 million CFAF in savings. Some of the problems faced by credit unions are also discussed. Credit unions are also surveyed in another article, in English: G. Almeda de Stemper, 'The role of credit in development projects: the credit union movement in Togo'. *African Review of Money, Finance and Banking,* no. 1 (1987), p. 27-44.

368 **Les moyens financiers du devéloppement au Togo: breviaire des services techniques.** (The financial means of development in Togo: a handbook of technical services.)
Edo Kodjo Agbobli.   Lomé: Editions du Togo, 1978. 144p. bibliog.

This is a handbook of sources of international technical economic assistance in Togo. See also A. J. Barry, *Coordination et efficacité de l'aide* (Co-ordination and aid efficiency). Paris: OCDE, 1988.

369 **La pêche traditionnelle sur le littoral Evhe et Mina.** (Traditional fishing on the Ewe and Mina littoral.)
Albert de Surgy.   Paris: Groupe de Chercheurs Africanistes, 1966. 157p. bibliog.

De Surgy reports on a 1965 Conseil National de Recherches Scientifiques-sponsored research mission, starting with a survey of the historical Ewe dispersal from Notsé (then Nuatja), and the ethnic mix that arose along the Togo-Benin coast. He then focuses on the structures involved in lagoonal and deep sea fishing, the role of women and of fishermen chiefs, and the manner in which earnings from the catch are divided.

370 **The privatization drive.**
P. M. Hirschoff.   *Africa Report,* vol. 31, no. 4 (1986), p. 89-92.

In the 1980s the fiscally-strained Togolese state began an effort to privatize its largely deficitory state sector. This article is a brief review of the after-effects of the successful privatization of one of Togo's white elephants, the State steel mills, which encouraged Togo to seek other partners for its privatization drive. The author argues, however, that there are potential drawbacks in investing in the country's manufacturing and industrial sectors that might limit further western interest in the country. For an early report on Togo's state sector see: the World Bank, *Report on State-owned companies in Togo.* Washington, DC: The World Bank, 1981. A more general article which focuses on Togo and sets the entire recent privatization issue in proper perspective can be found in Jacques Alibert, 'La privatisation des entreprises publiques en Afrique noire francophone' (The privatization of public enterprises in French Black Africa). *Afrique Contemporaine,* July-Sept. 1987, p. 35-50.

371 **Privatization through leasing: the Togo steel case.**
Ivan Bergeron.   In: *Privatization and control of state-owned enterprises.*   Edited by Ravi Ramamurti, R. Vernon.   Washington, DC: The World Bank, 1991, p. 153-75.

Togo's State steel-processing plant (the SNS) was built at great cost and had a capacity for producing 20,000 tons of steel a year. However, after inauguration it was hardly operational. This is a detailed examination of how in 1984 Togo leased the closed-down deficient SNS to an American entrepreneur for ten years. The leasing arrangement was the first instance of its kind in Africa, and in itself of great interest. In addition to this, the new company promptly turned a profit in its very first year of operation, suggesting that with the proper kind of managerial talent, Africa's State enterprises need not be perennial money-losers. This study is thus of great importance for all African states, that are reeling with deficitory state sectors and are under IMF/World Bank pressures to withdraw from economic activities. It illustrates an alternative, more palliative approach, to total privatization, which is repugnant to

African leaders since it alienates economic sectors to foreign capital. The study is quite specific since it addresses such issues as: under what conditions leasing is a viable option; and what specific clauses need to be built into leasing arrangements to assure equity to both sides. See also: R. Everett, 'Privatization: a case study'. *Africa Report*, vol. 32, no. 6 (1987), p. 59-61.

372 **Quatre plan quinquennaux de développement au Togo (1966-1985): les politiques sectorelles, mythes et réalités.**
(Four five-year development plans in Togo (1966-1985): sectoral policies, myths and realities.)
Alfred Schwartz. Lomé: ORSTOM, 1984. 231p. bibliog.

This book, written by a sociologist with ORSTOM in Lomé, is an incisive analysis of Togo's twenty-year record of development planning. The author dissects each plan and its sectoral allocations, noting how in each case, and especially in the last development plan, by which time Togo was fiscally ailing, actual expenditures fell far short of those originally projected, with the result that only modest results were accomplished.

373 **Quel Togo dans 25 ans? Seminaire national à Atakpamé du 9 au 14 juin 1986: document final.** (What Togo in 25 years? National seminar held in Atakpamé from June 9-14, 1986: final document.)
Ministère du Plan et d'Industrie. Lomé: Ministère du Plan et d'Industrie, 1987. 483p.

Records the proceedings of a national conference that took place in Atakpame, with the assistance of the United Nations Development Project and certain regional African bodies. The conference concentrated on the kinds of social policies, regional planning initiatives and general economic stimuli that would be necessary to attain maximal development in Togo.

374 **Le rôle des sociétés transnationales dans l'économie togolaise.**
(The role of transnational societies in the economy of Togo.)
Economic Commission for Africa. Addis Ababa: Economic Commission for Africa, 1984. 39p.

This is an overview of the multinational companies that are established in Togo, and their role in the national economy. Most of the companies are French.

375 **Social security in Togo and the national economy.**
Bassabi Kagbara. *International Social Security Review*, vol. 30 (1977), p. 21-51.

This is a comprehensive description of Togo's social security system as it existed in the late 1970s. Kagbara discusses the system in the context of both the economic conditions which prevailed at the time and the country's demographic characteristics. He also makes several pertinent suggestions for the future restructuring of the social security system.

376 **A structural adjustment that destabilises economic growth.**
Jan Toporowsky. *IDS Bulletin* (Brighton), vol. 9, no. 1 (Jan. 1988), p. 17-22.

The author presents a somewhat over-sympathetic lament of the stiff structural adjustment conditionalities imposed by the World Bank on Togo in the 1980s. Toporowsky surveys the regime's poor economic record of the 1970s that 'produced little in the way of GDP or exports, but much in the way of deficits and debt service problems' (p. 17), but still argues that the stiff price it has had to pay has led to 'unstable stagnation' (p. 21). This, he argues, is 'indefensible, from a humanitarian as well as from a more strictly economic point of view' because it is based on the '*institutionalisation* of irrational decision-making in international banking and development aid organisations' (p. 21, emphasis in original.)

377 **Techniques of privatization.**
Helen Nankani. In: *Techniques of privatization of state-owned enterprises. vol. 2: selected country studies.* Edited by Helen Nankani. Washington, DC: The World Bank, 1988, p. 137-46.

From the mid-1980s the fiscally hard-pressed Eyadema regime was forced to commence a forced liquidation sale of a variety of bankrupt or deficitory (and some closed-down) state enterprises. This chapter briefly reports on the various kinds of arrangements possible, and actually implemented (outright sale, lease, mixed-economy, etc.) with respect to those enterprises already privatized (ITT, Togotex, SODETO, IOTO, SNS, STH), and the new private investments expected, or being solicited, for some other companies such as the ITP and SOTOMA.

378 **Togo.**
International Monetary Fund. Washington, DC: International Monetary Fund, 1970. vol. 3. p. 613-88.

Part of a major economic survey of the entire continent, this chapter, although very dated, is still a useful overview of the Togolese economy of the late 1960s.

379 **Togo.**
Carlos E. Cuevas. In: *Rural finance profiles in African countries.* Edited by Mario Masini. Milan: Finafrica, 1990. vol. 2. p. 209-306. bibliog.

This is part of an FAO survey of African rural economies aimed at understanding why normal financial institutions have universally failed to make any impact in assisting in rural development, while *ad hoc* institutions have usually gone bankrupt. Although the chapter is geared specifically to the study of financial policy and financial structures in the rural economy, it nevertheless provides excellent general overviews of the Togolese economy. Topics exhaustively covered include monetary policy, financial development, the performance of banks, rural credit organizations, and agricultural policy in general. The study emphasizes that, notwithstanding government rhetoric, less than three per cent of total institutional credit goes to the primary sector where the majority of society is found, and that sum accounts for ninety-five per cent of the credit available to that sector. The other five per cent originates in rural credit unions. Togo's banks, including 'development' ones, are therefore not funding development but private urban housing.

380 **Togo 1987.**
Robert Cornevin. *Marchés Tropicaux et Méditerranéens*, no. 2,148
(Jan. 9, 1987), p. 53-73.

Appearing in one of the best weekly journals devoted to African economies, this
article provides a broad overview of Togo's social, political and economic
development since the 1970s.

381 **Togo 2000. Planification togolaise et voie africaine de**
développement. (Togo 2000. Togolese planning and the African way
of development.)
Koudjolou M. Dogo.   Lomé: Nouvelles Editions Africaines, 1983.
376p.

This is a comprehensive and well-written history of economic planning in Togo since
1966, with an introductory section that discusses planning initiatives in the German
and French colonial eras. The bulk of the work discusses both basic planning
guidelines and objectives, and specific projects completed, and recently commenced,
as well as projects planned for the future. These projects are in the fields of
infrastructure-building and communications which include roads, railroads and the
expanding port of Lomé, as well as in agriculture.

382 **Togo: suffit-il d'être Kabyé pour acceder au devéloppement?**
(Togo: does it suffice to be Kabre to attain development?)
Anne-Marie Pillet-Schwartz. *Politique Africaine*, no. 32 (Dec. 1988),
p. 85-90.

Pillet-Schwartz comments briefly on allegations that the developmental policies of
General Eyadema (who is a Kabre himself) grossly favour his northern ethnic region.

383 **Troisième plan de devéloppement économique et social, 1976-1980.**
(Third plan of economic and social development, 1976-1980.)
Togo, Direction Générale du Plan et du Développement.   Lomé:
Ministère du Plan, 1976. 491p.

This massive volume is a comprehensive guide to the projected expenditures, and the
socio-economic sectors targeted to benefit, under Togo's third development plan for
the years 1976 to 1980. It is produced in much glossier format than previously, as if
to attest to Togo's coming of age as a result of the 1974 phosphate boom. In fact
many of the projects scheduled for the period 1976-1980 had to be scaled down or
cancelled, since the ambitious plan was based on the faulty premise that the
quadrupling of revenues from phospates, Togo's main export, would continue. Togo's
1974 financial bonanza, however, was a temporary aberration, the result of Morocco's
(a major producer) unsuccessful attempt to manipulate global prices by reducing
output. When the ploy failed, phospate prices normalized and Togolese revenues
returned to their old levels. Nevertheless, the Eyadema regime estimated that prices,
and revenues, would rise again, and continued some of the projected Plan's
expenditures, only to end up with a massive, and unmanageable, national debt by the
mid-1980s. For Togo's previous development plan, much more modest and itself not
fully attained, see: 'Togo, 2ème plan quinquennal, 1971-1975' (Togo's second five-
year plan, 1971-1975). In: *Les plans de développement des pays d'Afrique noire.*
Paris: Ediafric, 1975.

384 **Vingt ans d'efforts de planification pour le développement du Togo.** (Twenty years of planning efforts for the development of Togo.) Direction Générale du Plan et du Développement. Lomé: Ministère du Plan et d'Industrie, 1988. 202p.

This official publication is a comprehensive summary of guidelines adopted for development planning in Togo since inception to 1967. The material includes an overview of the Togolese economy and resources, infrastructure, social attributes, and limitations, and details on specific legislation adopted to develop the human and economic resources of the country.

The People's Republic of Benin and the Republic of Togo.
See item no. 9.

Togo.
See item no. 10.

Crise économique et perspective de l'emploi dans une économie ouverte. (Economic crisis and employment prospects in an open economy.)
See item no. 199.

The underdogs of the urban economy join forces.
See item no. 209.

L'expérience des pharmacies d'état en République Togolaise. (The experience of state pharmacies in the Republic of Togo.)
See item no. 223.

Les désillusions de phosphate. (The disillusionment with phosphates.)
See item no. 391.

Les entreprises industrielles togolaises. (The Togolese industrial enterprises.)
See item no. 393.

Le guide bancaire du Togo. (Banking guide to Togo.)
See item no. 540.

Togo.
See item no. 555.

Togo.
See item no. 557.

Togo.
See item no. 562.

Trade and Commerce

385 **Approvisionnement, commercialisation et demande des engrais en République du Togo.** (Supplying, marketing and demand for fertilizers in the Republic of Togo.)
Marc André.   Muscle Shoals, Alabama: International Fertilizer Development Center, 1990. English summary.
Unpaginated, this brief work surveys the fertilizer industry in Togo from the point of view of existing supply and demand, prospects for a growing need for fertilizers by Togolese agriculture, and the actual marketing channels for the sale of fertilizers in the country.

386 **Centres urbaines sécondaires et commercialisation des produits vivriers au Togo.** (Secondary urban centres and the marketing of foodstuffs in Togo.)
F. Lançon.   *Economie Rurale*, no. 190 (1989), p. 33-39.
In this brief article Lançon outlines the channels through which small urban centres are supplied with food supplies by rural producers.

387 **Les commerçants ouest-africaines entre marchés formels et informels.** (West African merchants between the formal and the informal markets.)
Rita Cordonnier.   *Cahiers de Sociologie Economique et Culturelle*, no. 5 (1986), p. 115-36.
Cordonnier provides in this article perceptive insights into the plight of traders within the context of a large competitive informal sector. Many customers interact with this sector and she discusses the strategies they employ to stay competitive. The article deals specifically with the situation in Lomé.

388 **Commerce et sociabilité: les negociants soudanais du quartier zongo de Lomé (Togo).** (Commerce and sociability: Sudanese traders of the zongo quarter of Lomé, Togo.)
Michel Agier. Paris: ORSTOM, 1983. 317p. bibliog.

The *zongo* are quarters for strangers, found in all but the smaller villages in Togo (and indeed throughout much of West Africa), where non-indigenous people can settle, ruled by their own quarter's chief. Historically the *zongo* have been centres for trade and commerce. The *zongo* quarter in Lomé, until it was relocated in 1977, due to its position on prime land, was by far the largest of its kind, with over 7,500 people living there in 1975. Agier's work, originally his PhD dissertation, is a fascinating study of Togo's *zongo*, with particular attention to Lomé. His work outlines: its structure and organization; the trade networks that radiate from the Lomé *zongo*, to the north as well as along the coast; the social and religious life in these quarters; their hierarchy of power; and how conflicts (and theft) are resolved. The work includes maps, diagrams, tables and plates, and Agier also provides profiles of the individuals who actually served as chiefs of Lomé's *zongo*, as well a breakdown of the social composition of the trading community. His figures reveal that traders in the Lomé *zongo* are a multi-ethnic group (although half are Hausa) with a number of Ewe or Mina women. Over seventy-five per cent of the traders are non-Togolese in origin, with many of the rest Muslim Kotokoli from the north of the country.

389 **Loin de Mango. Les Tiokossi de Lomé.** (Far from Mango. The Chokossi of Lome.)
J. M. Gibbal. *Cahiers d'Etudes Africaines*, no. 81/83 (1981), p. 25-51.

This article concentrates on the small Chokossi community resident in Lomé, many of whom are merchants. The author examines how they are socially organized, how they retain links with their distant homeland, and their economic preoccupations.

390 **Les marchés ruraux dans la circonscription de Vo, République du Togo.** (Rural markets in the district of Vo, Republic of Togo.)
Emile Le Bris. Paris: ORSTOM, 1984. 93p. bibliog.

In this volume Le Bris makes a historical and contemporary study of trade and markets in south-east Togo. He looks at both the geographical and economic factors behind the markets in Vo, that have evolved in conformity with the agrarian conditions in the region, which is characterized by an extreme dispersal of producers and consumers. The study includes many maps and diagrams.

Colonial distortion of the Volta river salt trade.
See item no. 64.

The Hausa kola trade through Togo, 1899-1912.
See item no. 83.

Rélations commerciales entre l'Allemagne et le Togo, 1680-1914. (Commercial relations between Germany and Togo, 1680-1914.)
See item no. 95.

Femmes africaines et commerce: les revendeuses de tissu de la ville de Lomé. (African women and commerce: textile retailers in the city of Lomé.)
See item no. 236.

Nanas **et pêcheurs du port du Lomé.** (Nanas and the fishermen of the port of Lomé.)
See item no. 243.

Le marché togolais. (The Togolese market.)
See item no. 366.

Togo.
See item no. 557.

Togo.
See item no. 562.

Togo.
See item no. 564.

Industry

391 **Les désillusions du phosphate.** (The disillusions with phosphate.)
Claude Mijoux. *Revue Française d'Etudes Politiques Africaines*,
no. 264 (Oct. 1977), p. 13-16.

This article discusses Togo's sole major exploitable mineral resource. Phosphate
deposits, used in the production of fertilizers, and conveniently located in large
amounts in Togo near the coast, have long been the country's sole hope for economic
upliftment. After a quadrupling of global market prices in 1974 ambitious
development plans were formulated on the assumption that these prices would remain
high, but they fell back to their old levels. Unwilling to accept the permanence of this
drop, and continuing an economic expansion based on loans, the Togolese
government eventually entered a period of acute fiscal imbalance from which it has
not yet extracated itself.

392 **Directoire des industries et activités du Togo.** (Directory of
industries and industrial activity in Togo.)
Service d'Etudes Economiques de Côte d'Ivoire. Abidjan, Côte
d'Ivoire: Service d'Etudes Economiques de Côte d'Ivoire, 1982. 54p.

An inventory of Togo's various industrial enterprises, their business figures, and an
overview of the Togolese economy in general.

393 **L'entreprise industrielle togolaise.** (Togolese industrial enterprises.)
In: *Entreprises et entrepreneurs d'Afrique noire.* Paris: Ediafric,
1984. p. 493-506.

Provides an overview of Togo's industrial and manufacturing sector, which is
dwarfed by the coastal phosphate mines.

394 **Livre blanc sur les phosphates de Kpemé et la C.T.M.B.** (White
paper on the Kpeme phosphates and the C.T.M.B.)
Togo, Ministère du Plan. Paris: Editions Africaines du Flamboyant,
1975. 115p.

The Togolese government commissioned this glossy publication after General
Eyadema's aeroplane crash of 24 January 1974 at Sarakawa. The crash, seen as part
of a conspiracy by French phosphate interests, led to the nationalization of the mines,
Togo's sole natural resource. Eyadema's survival was seen as a miracle and Sarakawa
became glorified as a place of pilgrimage for youth. This book includes photographs
of the phosphate mines, as well as an array from the scene of the crash. A brief article
on the nationalization of the mines is by Phillipe Decraene, 'Togo: eviction des privés
du secteur minier' (Togo: evicting private companies from the mining sector). *Revue
Française d'Etudes Politiques Africaines*, no. 98 (Feb. 1974), p. 15-16.

395 **Lome's informal industrial sector.**
E. Demol, et al. In: *Industry and accumulation in Africa.* Edited by
Martin Fransman. London: Heinemann, 1982, p. 372-84. bibliog.

This is one of the few articles on the highly archaic informal petty industry sector in
Lomé. The author outlines both the kinds of products produced and the specific
problems faced by the informal sector in Togo.

396 **Mineral industry of Togo.**
Bureau of Mines. Washington, DC: Department of Interior, 1965.
18p.

An early survey of the mineral resources of Togo, this brief study also considers the
possibilities of their exploitation from the early 1960s.

397 **La mise en valeur des phosphates du Togo.** (The exploitation of
phosphates in Togo.)
Max Robert. *Annales des Mines* (March 1965), p. 11-34.

This article was written in 1964 on the occasion of phosphates entering the export
markets in Togo. Robert surveys the history of the discovery of phosphate deposits,
and the investment group that was brought together to build the plant, as well as
providing technical details about the plant itself.

**Rapport d'enquête sur les travailleurs d'une industrie extractive du
Togo.** (Report of an inquiry on the workers in an extractive industry.)
See item no. 206.

Agriculture

398 **Une action de développement à Dzobegan (Togo).** (Development action in Dzobegan [Togo].)
Marc Bouffel.   Abidjan, Côte d'Ivoire: Institut Africain pour le Développement Economique et Social, 1967. 70p.

This is a description of an unusual case-study of community development, radiating outwards from a Benedictine monastery at Dzobegan on the Dayés plateau near the border with Ghana.

399 **Agbetiko: terroir de la basse vallée du Mono (Sud-Togo).**
(Agbetiko: land at the base of the Mono valley [south Togo].)
Benoit Anthéaume.   Paris: ORSTOM, 1978. 126p. bibliog.

The fourteenth in a series of in-depth studies of specific agrarian regions under ORSTOM's 'Atlas des structures agraires au sud du Sahara', this work is a comprehensive, multi-faceted study of the population and economy of an area near Tabligbo in Togo. Photographs, maps and numerous statistical tables present data on a wide array of facts, including: soil conditions and precipitation; the composition of the population; its density and patterns of polygamy; the nature of employment broken down by age and sex; land ownership and crops produced; and levels of trade.

400 **Agricultural pricing in Togo.**
David Bovet, Laurian Unnevehr.   Washington, DC: The World Bank, 1981. 76p. bibliog.

This is an analysis of Togo's pricing policies with respect to cotton, coffee and cocoa. The authors suggest certain alternative models and policies to enhance productivity, based on the fact that, in Togo in particular, producer prices have a major effect on whether crops are cultivated by farmers or not.

401 **L'agriculture urbaine à Lomé.** (The urban agriculture of Lomé.)
C. Schiller. Paris: Karthala, 1991. 320p. bibliog.

Schiller provides an in-depth analysis of agriculture and the dairy industry in Lomé and in its immediate proximity, which supplies the capital with its daily necessities.

402 **Atlas agro-économique de la region sud-ouest Togo: essai de traitement infographique de données statistiques.** (Agro-economic atlas of Togo's south-west region: a graphical treatment of statistical data.)
A. Leplaideur, P. Charmasson, et al. Montpellier, France: Institut de Recherches Agronomiques Tropicales et des Cultures Vivrières, 1988. 144p. bibliog.

This is an unusual book, aimed at presenting researchers, for the first time, with comprehensive 'cartographical statistics' on a specific region in Togo. The bulk of the work comprises of tables and maps on every imaginable topic or dimension relating to a region that includes Wawa, Amou and Kloto in south-west Togo. The manner in which the data is presented allows both for the inclusion of a large amount of information and for easy readability.

403 **Boua, village de Koudé: un terroir kabye.** (Boua, village of Koude: a Kabre territory.)
Claude Sauvaget. Paris: ORSTOM, 1981. 78p. bibliog.

ORSTOM publish a series of comprehensive socio-agrarian studies under the title of 'Atlas des structures agraires au sud de Sahara'. This multi-faceted study forms part of the series and considers the Kabre people, their land settlement patterns and their agrarian practices. It also looks at the basic social aspects of their agriculture, as manifest from an in-depth analysis of one village. The work is supplemented by a pocket of thirteen large-scale maps and four pages of plates. For an account of Kabre patterns of agriculture, see also: A. K. Akibodé, *Colonisation agraire et essor socio-économique dans le bassin de la Kara* (Agrarian colonization and socio-economic development in the Kara basin). Lomé: Université du Bénin, 1987. 88p. bibliog.

404 **Centre bloqué, périphérie liberée: le terroir et ses marges. L'exemple de Béna.** (Blocked centre, liberated periphery: the territory and its edges. The example of Bena.)
Benoit Anthéaume. In: *Le devéloppement rural en question. Paysages, espaces ruraux, systèmes agraires.* Edited by Chantal Blanc-Pamard, et al. Paris: ORSTOM, 1984, p. 313-22. bibliog.

This is an examination of agrarian behaviour and land tenure patterns, as exemplified by one village, Bena, on the Akposso plateau in west-central Togo. As Anthéaume points out, such patterns vary according to location; in the middle of the village's 'terroir' (zone of exploitation), attitudes are frozen along accepted social norms, but towards the outer periphery they are free from social pressures.

405 **La cooperative agricole d'Agu-Nyogbo, ou, Quelques problèmes du développment rural au Togo.** (The agricultural co-operative of Agu-Nyogbo, or, Several problems of rural development in Togo.)
Emmanuel Konu. Lomé: Institut d'Enseignement Superieur du Bénin, 1969. 57p.

This work consitutes a study of the problems of rural agrarian development in Togo, and the role of producers co-operatives, as manifest from an analysis of the activities of one of them. The agricultural and artisanal co-operative chosen for detailed analysis was created during the German colonial era. After focusing on its activities over the years, and its successes and failures, the author comes up with some concrete proposals to enhance its role.

406 **Cotton development programs in Burkina Faso, Côte d'Ivoire and Togo.**
The World Bank. Washington, DC: The World Bank, 1988. 126p.

Since the 1970s cotton cultivation has slowly increased in the Kabre areas in north Togo. This report is an evaluation of the increased production of cotton in all three countries due to 'a development strategy integrating technical, financial and marketing services to farmers' (p. vii). Togo is assessed on pages 99-126. It is noted that notwithstanding rising revenues from cotton production since 1980, surpluses were not set aside as stipulated for stabilization purposes, but instead were absorbed in the government's budget. Thus when global prices dropped in 1986 deficits began to be recorded for which the government was liable.

407 **Cultures vivrières, cultures de rente: cas des zones cotonniers au Togo.** (Foodstuff crops, cash crops: the case of the cotton zones in Togo.)
Mawuena Kokouvi Oni. Montpellier, France: Institut Agronomique, 1986. various pagination.

This work is an analysis of whether cash crops, and specifically cotton, should continue to be planted in Togo, or be replaced by subsistence crops that would be of direct benefit to farmers as well as being exportable. The author argues that cotton production can only be sustained if Togo's foodstuff production is augmented.

408 **Des hommes à la rencontre des arbres: le cacaoyer et les Akposso dans le centre-ouest du Togo.** (Men's encounter with trees: the Akposso and cacao-trees in west-central Togo.)
Benoit Anthéaume. *Cahiers ORSTOM*, vol. 18, no. 1 (1981-82), p. 47-62. bibliog.

Including photographs, diagrams and maps, this is a study of cacao cultivation in west-central Togo. Cacao-trees, that had indigenously spread from Ghana to neighbouring regions in Togo, were utilized by the Akposso people, who began to descend from their inaccessible plateau after their migration from Ghana to escape perennial enemy attacks.

409 **Evaluation de l'effet de l'arachide comme précédent cultural au Togo.** (Evaluation of the effect of a preceding groundnut crop in Togo.)
J. Marquette. *Agronomie Tropicale*, vol. 41, no. 3/4 (1986), p. 231-41.
This is an agronomic assessment of the effect on production levels of alternating peanuts and maize planting in south and central Togo. The study indicated that planting peanuts prior to maize often increased maize yields by thirty-four per cent, compared to no crop rotation whatsoever.

410 **Un objectif atteint: l'autosuffisance alimentaire.** (An attained objective: self-sufficiency in foodstuffs.)
Europe-Outremer (Paris), no. 632 (Sept. 1982), 48p. Special issue.
A special issue of this glossy journal, it includes a number of short articles focusing on Togolese agricultural advances, aimed at attaining food self-sufficiency.

411 **Le paysan et la culture du coton au Togo.** (The farmer and cotton cultivation in Togo.)
Alfred Schwartz. Paris: ORSTOM, 1985. 106p. bibliog.
In many African countries farmers have a basic dilemma in choosing between planting staple foodstuff crops, for which they usually receive no particular State benefits, but which assure their subsistence, and cash crops, which while they cannot be consumed, produce revenues and are often promoted by governmental organizations. This volume discusses the tension between staple and cash crop farming in Togo, with specific reference to cotton. For another similar analysis see: C. Raymont, J. M. Funel, J. P. Schulman, A. Schwartz, *Evaluation économique de l'activité coton au Togo* (Economic evaluation of cotton in Togo). Paris: Ministère des Rélations Extérieures, Cooperation et Développement, 1983. 312p. bibliog.

412 **Une politique de développement dans le sud-est du Togo: l'operation 'régénération des terres de barre'.** (A developmental policy in south-east Togo: operation 'regeneration of the *barre* lands'.)
Emile Le Bris. *Cahiers ORSTOM*, vol. 14, no. 2 (1977), p. 127-39. bibliog.
Le Bris outlines in detail the government's policy of regenerating the soils of the coastal strip of *barre* land in South Togo, for purposes of enhancing crop productivity, especially of maize. The same topic is covered in J. Marquette, 'Maintien et amélioration des rendements du mais sur les terres de barre dans le sud du Togo' (Maintenance and amelioration of maize yields on the *barre* lands in south Togo). *Agronomie Tropicale*, vol. 41, no. 2 (1986), p. 132-48. bibliog. See also: M. Kirk, 'Technological innovations and changes in agrarian structures: the diffusion of animal traction in Cameroon and Togo'. *Quarterly Journal of International Agriculture*, vol. 27, no. 1 (1988), p. 52-63; and P. Baudin, 'Pathologie de la canne à sucre en Côte d'Ivoire, Dahomey et Togo' (Pathology of sugar cane in Côte d'Ivoire, Dahomey and Togo). *Agronomie Tropicale*, vol. 19, no. 8/9 (Aug.-Sept. 1964), p. 747-55.

413 **Pour une anthropologie de la pluralité technique: le cas de la culture d'igname au Sud-Togo.** (Towards an anthropology of technical diversity: the case of yams in south Togo.)
Bruno Martinelli. *Cultures et Développement* (Louvain), vol. 13, no. 4 (1981), p. 633-59.

In this article Martinelli argues that there are different ways to cultivate and harvest agrarian crops, and that these are intimately tied to the cosmologies of various ethnic groups. They need to be given attention, especially by foreign development planners. He illustrates his argument by focusing on the way yams are grown by the Ewe in southern Togo.

414 **Révolution verte et autosuffisance alimentaire au Togo.** (Green revolution and food self-sufficiency in Togo.)
Alfred Schwartz. *Politique Africaine,* no. 36 (1989), p. 97-107.

This article assesses the implementation and results of General Eyadema's declared policy that Togo should become self-sufficient in foodstuffs by the end of the decade.

Paysans africains. (African peasants.)
See item no. 3.

Les plantations allemandes du Mont Agou, 1884-1914. (The German plantations of Mont Agou, 1884-1914.)
See item no. 92.

Les limites sectorielles de l'expérience togolaise de vingt ans de planification: l'agriculture, 1966-1985. (The limits of twenty years of Togolese sectoral planning: agriculture, 1966-1985.)
See item no. 365.

Language

415 **Anecho-Ewe/Ge-Mina: Mina basic course.**
Gabriel Kwaoui Johnson.   Bloomington, Indiana: University of
Indiana, African Studies Program, 1967. 2 vols.
Written by a former editor and minister of information, this is a basic series of
grammar and phonology lessons in the dialects of the Aného region.

416 **Basic mood in Ife.**
Hélène Boethius.   *Journal of West African Languages* (Dallas), vol.
17, no. 2 (Nov. 1987), p. 43-70.
A linguistic study of a Yoruba dialect spoken by some 100,000 people in the
Atakpamé region in Togo. The article includes a basic description of Ife verb
phraseology, its structure, and five forms of basic moods.

417 **Bibliography of Gbe (ewe, gen, aja, xwla, fon, gun, etc.):**
publications *on* and *in* the language.
A. S. Duthie, R. K. Vlaardingerbroek.   Basel, Switzerland: Basler
Afrika Bibliographien, 1981. 229p. bibliog.
This book, invaluable not only for students of the linguistics of Togo, but also for
those interested in the indigenous languages of neighbouring Ghana and Benin, is part
of a series (no. 23) of communications from the Basel Africa Bibliography. The work
is a monumental effort, compiling 516 publications translated into this important
coastal language cluster (spoken in Togo by the Ewe, Mina, Adja, Nuatja and other
related groups), 379 original publications in these dialects, and 550 items on the
language. Listed works are indexed in a variety of ways in an eighty-one-page
appendix.

418 Bimoba syntax: a syntagmatic analysis.

Gillian Jacobs. Legon, Ghana: University of Ghana, Institute of African Studies, 1970. 285p.

Although this comprehensive study is dated, it is still valuable since it is written in English. It treats the Bimoba language spoken by the Moba people in north Ghana and in Togo, where they are concentrated around Dapaong. The study analyses sentence construction, clauses, phrases and word-usage, with a discourse narrative at the end of the book.

419 The central Togo languages.

M. E. Kropp Dakubu, Kevin C. Ford. In: *The Languages of Ghana.* London: Kegan Paul International, 1988, p. 118-54.

This chapter is a linguistic survey of several languages that are spoken by ethnic groups that live on both sides of the Ghana-Togo border. Another, briefer chapter (p. 91-101), by Alan S. Duthie, covers the Ewe.

420 La classification nominale en proto-guang. (Nominal classification in proto-guang.)

G. Manessy. *Afrikanistische Arbeitspapiere* (Cologne), no. 9 (1987), p. 5-49.

In this linguistic study Manessy considers the Gonja dialects spoken both in northern Togo and in neighbouring countries. The classic work on the language, which includes a German-Gonja-German dictionary, was published by the German linguist Diedrich Westermann (1875-1956) in 1922, and has since been reprinted. See: Diedrich Westermann, *Die Sprache der Guang in Togo und auf der Goldkuste und fünf andere Togosprachen* (The language of the Guang in Togo and in the Gold Coast, and five other Togolese languages). Nendeln, Liechtenstein: Kraus Reprint, 1974. 268p. For a shorter linguistic study in English see: Colin Painter, *Linguistic field notes from Banda. Language maps of the guang speaking areas of Ghana, Togo and Dahomey.* Accra: Institute of African Studies, University of Ghana, 1966. 43p.

421 Collected field reports on the phonology of Basari.

Mary Abbott, Monica Cox. Legon, Ghana: University of Ghana, Institute of African Studies, 1966. 59p.

This is a basic phonology of the Bassari language that is spoken by the small Gur ethnic group residing on both sides of the Ghana-Togo border. For another work see: Monica Cox, *La phonologie du bassari* (Bassari phonology). Lomé: Institut National de Recherche Scientifique, 1974. 41p.

422 Collected field reports on the phonology of Konkomba.

Mary Steele, Gretchen Weed. Legon, Ghana: University of Ghana, Institute of African Studies, 1966. 77p.

Steele and Weed provide a basic phonology of the Konkomba language that is spoken by the small but important ethnic group residing on both sides of the Ghana-Togo border. It includes a word-list of 200 Konkomba words.

423   **A comparative phonology of Gbe.**
Hounkpati B. C. Capo.   Berlin; New York: Foris Publications, 1991.
238p. bibliog. maps.
Gbe is a dialect cluster that includes the Ewe, Adja, Gen and Fon and it is spoken by
fifty-one coastal ethnic groups found in eastern Ghana, through Togo and Benin and
into western Nigeria. This is a methodologically-rigorous and intricately-complex
linguistic study on the comparative phonology of Gbe, and one of the few written in
English. The study, which includes a lengthy bibliography (p. 197-220) and index,
meticulously provides general typological features of Gbe phonology as a whole. The
author merges two linguistic approaches: that of classical comparative linguists
pioneered by Diedrich Westermann, and that of classical generative phonology
pioneered by Noam Chomsky, arguing for the linguistic unity of the various Gbe
dialects.

424   **Une comparaison entre les systèmes phonologiques du Kabiyé, de
l'Ewe et du Bassar.** (A comparison between the phonological systems
of Kabre, Ewe and Bassari.)
Sheila Crunden.   *Etudes Togolaises* (Lomé), Dec. 1981, p. 102-16.
This article is a basic comparison of tonality in three important Togolese languages.

425   **Les constructions possessives prédictatives et nominales en kabiye.**
(Nominal and predicative possessive compositions in Kabre.)
Kézié K. Lebikaza.   *Journal of West African Languages* (Dallas),
vol. 21, no. 1 (May 1991), p. 91-104.
This article is a study of Kabre linguistics, a language spoken in north and central
Togo.

426   **Critères de distribution des affixes en Lama.** (Distributive criteria
of affixes in Lama.)
Méterwa A. Ourso.   *Journal of West African Languages* (Dallas),
vol. 19, no. 1 (May 1989), p. 35-56.
The Lama language is spoken by an ethnic group closely related to the Kabre in
northern and central Togo. This study is a synoptic description of their language, and
a survey of the major morphological and semantic traits of its affixes.

427   **Les dialectes du Moyen-Togo.** (The dialects of central Togo.)
Jacques Bertho.   *Bulletin d'IFAN,* vol. 14, no. 3 (1952), p. 1,046-107.
Written by the prolific scholar, Bertho, this is one of the seminal examinations of a
number of languages found in central Togo.

428   **A dictionary of the Chokossi language.**
A. C. Krass.   Legon, Ghana: University of Ghana, Institute of African
Studies, 1970. 99p.
This is a basic English-Chokossi dictionary.

429 Dictionary of Ewe homonyms.
J. K. Adzomada.   Accra: Waterville Publishing House, 1969. 52p.

Pastor Adzomada has compiled this slim volume, which is presented in the form of a brief introduction to the richness of the Ewe language and homonyms, followed by the dictionary with parallel translations of the homonyms into English, French and German.

430 Dictionnaire des particularités du français au Togo et au Dahomey. (Dictionary of peculiarities of French as spoken in Togo and Dahomey.)
Suzanne Lafage.   Abidjan, Côte d'Ivoire: Université d'Abidjan, Institut de Linguistique Appliquée, 1975. 222p. bibliog.

Languages transposed into completely different cultural settings universally tend to metamorphose, to a certain degree, into virtual dialects of the original. This has happened with the French language in Africa. Lafage's study constitutes a detailed alphabetical dictionary of Africanized French words and terms currently used in Togo and Benin (then known as Dahomey), with their local meaning, origins, and usage. Her material was culled from francophone African literature and from oral discourse. She has also published a shorter version of her work as 'Le dictionnaire des particularités du français au Togo et au Dahomey' (A dictionary of peculiarities of French in Togo and Dahomey). *Annales de l'Université d'Abidjan*. Abidjan, Côte d'Ivoire, vol. 9, no. 1 [1976], p. 131-41.

431 Dictionnaire français-evé. (French-Ewe dictionary.)
J. Kofi Adzomada.   Lomé: Imprimerie de l'Alphabétisation, 1983. 3rd ed. 245p. bibliog.

This is the third edition of the much-expanded classic French-Ewe-French dictionary, first published in 1975.

432 Dictionnaire moba-français. (Moba-French dictionary.)
Pierre Reinhard.   Bombwaka, Togo: Mission Catholique, 1978. 121p.

Reinhard has compiled a basic Moba-French dictionary. The Moba reside in the extreme north of Togo, and are regarded by some anthropologists as among the few autochtonous peoples of the country.

433 Die Ewe-Sprache in Togo. (The Ewe language in Togo.)
Diedrich Westermann.   Berlin: De Gruyter, 1961. 95p.

This is a basic study of the grammar of the Ewe language in Togo, by the most influential linguist of West African languages, and the major writer on the Ewe cluster of languages. The work, a reprint of a 1939 edition, concludes with a thirty-five-page Ewe-German-Ewe vocabulary. The material is partly drawn from the author's earlier study *Grammatik der Ewe-Sprache* (Grammar of the Ewe language.) Berlin: D. Reimer, 1907. 158p. See also: his *Der Wortbau des Ewe* (Word formation in Ewe.) Berlin: De Gruyter, 1943. 23p.

434 **Die verhinderte Mitsprache: Aspekte zur Sprachpolitik in Ghana,
Togo und Obervolta.** (Prevention with language: aspects of language
policy in Ghana, Togo and Upper Volta.)
Gunther Rusch. Hamburg, Germany: Institut für Afrika-Kunde, 1984.
214p. maps. bibliog. English and French summaries.

Rusch makes a comparative study of the history of government language policy in
Ghana, Togo and Burkina Faso. He includes an extensive bibliography (p. 195-213).
By adopting the former colonial language as the official language of the country, and
limiting (in varying degrees, depending upon the country concerned) the degree to
which indigenous languages can be taught (usually at primary level) governments
impose a measure of uniformity on a vibrant cultural mosaic of peoples with different
languages. The author sharply contrasts the policies pursued in the three countries,
which stem in part from the different nature of their societies. For a briefer look at
language policy in Togo see: Haig Der-Houssikian, 'Togo's choice'. In: *The linguistic
connection.* Edited by Jean Casagrande. Lanham, Maryland: University Press of
America, 1983, p. 73-82.

435 **Displaying the semantic structure of an Ewe text.**
Alan S. Duthie. *Journal of West African Languages* (Dallas), vol. 14,
no. 1 (April 1984), p. 57-80.

Using text in the Ewe language, Duthie analyses its semantic structure and rules.
There are several additional linguistic articles on the Ewe and Gbe languages in the
same issue of this important periodical. For adverb usage in Ewe see: Kokou Sénamé
Agbadja, 'Pour une approche nouvelle des prétendus "adverbes" évé' (Towards a new
approach to the so-called Ewe adverbs). *Afrique et langage*, vol. 19, no. 1 (1983),
p. 32-51. See also: Felix Ameka, 'How discourse particles mean: the case of the Ewe
"terminal" particles'. *Journal of African Languages and Linguistics* (Leiden), vol. 12,
no. 2 (1990/91), p. 143-70; and Hounkpati Capo, 'The bilabial fricatives in Ewe,
innovation or retention?' *Journal of African Languages and Linguistics* (Leiden),
no. 134 (1992), p. 41-58.

436 **Essai pour une phonologie du gurma parlé à Kpana (Nord-Togo):
lexique gurma-français.** (Tentative phonology of Gurma spoken in
Kpana [north Togo]: Gurma-French lexicon.)
Nicole Tersis-Surugue. Paris: Société pour l'Etude des Langues
Africaines, 1967. 73p. map. bibliog.

This work is a basic phonological study of a Gur dialect spoken in a certain area in
north Togo, accompanied by 950 Gur words translated into French. See also Marcel
Gasser, 'The use of completive and incompletive aspect in Nawdm narrative discourse'. *Journal of West African languages* (Dallas), vol. 18, no. 1 (1988), p. 73-88.

437 **Etudes linguistiques préliminaires en quelques langues du Togo.**
(Preliminary linguistic studies in several Togolese languages.)
Edited by Jacques Nicole. Lomé: Société Internationale
Linguistique, 1984. 259p. bibliog.

Consists of twelve papers presented at a 1981 linguistics workshop organized in
Lomé by SIL. There are four papers on phonology, five on tonology, one on

morphology, and two on text-analysis. The languages analysed include Moba, Kabre and Chokossi. For another article on Kabre sentence construction see: Kézié K. Lébikaza, 'L'alternance consonantique et le problème de l'interaction entre traits segmentaux et suprasegmentaux en Kabye' (Alternating consonants and the problem of interaction between segmented and supersegmented hyphens in Kabre). *Afrikanische Arbeits-papiere* (Cologne), vol. 19 (1989), p. 147-63.

438 Evegbe nuti nunya: an eve grammar book with glossary.
Accra: Sedco, 1990. 80p.

This is a popular recent grammar, and basic Ewe-English glossary, of the Ewe dialect spoken across the Togo border in east Ghana by the large Anlo clan.

439 Ewe basic course.
Irene Warbuton, Prosper Kpotufe, Roland Glover.   Bloomington, Indiana: Indiana University, African Studies Program, 1968. 271p.

Prepared under the auspices of the US Department of Health, Education and Welfare, this book is a basic grammar textbook for non-Ewe speakers. It includes several appendices and a small Ewe-English dictionary.

440 Le français écrit des élèves bassari. (Written French of Bassari students.)
I. Takassi.   Abidjan, Côte d'Ivoire: Université d'Abidjan, Institut de Linguistique Appliquée, 1971. 99p. bibliog.

This linguistic study commences with a basic phonal and grammatical analysis of the Bassari language in northern Togo, and evolves into an exploration of how the language affects Bassari pupils learning French as a foreign language. The work is interspersed with numerous examples of grammatical errors commonly made by Bassari children as a result of their bilingualism.

441 Français écrit et parlé en pays ewe (Sud-Togo). (French as written and spoken by the Ewe [south Togo].)
Suzanne Lafage.   Paris: Société d'Etudes Linguistiques et Anthropologiques de France, 1985. 605p. bibliog. English summary.

This massive work is a comprehensive and seminal socio-linguistic study of the Ewe-speaking areas of southern Togo and includes maps, diagrams, and a brief summary in English. The author assesses the Ewe people and their language, which is linguistically compared and contrasted (especially in terms of phonemic and prosodic systems) to French. This is followed by a socio-linguistic analysis of the precise kinds of French-Ewe bilingualism that have emerged. Lafage considers the difficulties encountered (and why) by Ewe-speakers in grasping, let alone mastering, certain structural and functional features of the French language, which are totally absent in their own native language, and with what consequent mutations (loanwords, non-French neologisms, derivatives and compounds). The author then sharply distinguishes between the use of French in Togo's Ewe areas with the language as spoken/written in both France and in other francophone African states, where different metamorphoses have taken place. She emphasizes the fact that while clearly the degree of the Ewe-French inter-lingual 'interferences' depends upon the level of linguistic competence in French of the individual concerned, it nevertheless arises in all instances and in all countries, the specific manner being dictated by the phonetic and lexical structure of the indigenous language. Moreover, among the lesser educated masses in Togo's Ewe regions, major pidginization is rapidly proceeding as a deeply acculturated French language spreads as a major lingua franca.

442   **Ga-English Dictionary.**
      M. E. Kropp Dakubu.   Legon, Ghana: Institute of African Studies, 1973. 248p. bibliog.
Constitutes a comprehensive dictionary of the Ga language. For a 3,327-word glossary of Ga and Ewe by the same author see his *Ga, Adangme, and Ewe (Lomé) with English gloss.* Legon: Institute of African Studies, 1966, 79p.

443   **Le Gbe est une langue unique.** (Gbe is a distinct language.)
      Hounkpati B. C. Capo.   *Africa* (London), vol. 53, no. 2 (1983), p. 47-57. bibliog.
Takes a methodological position that linguists need be more rigorous in differentiating between 'languages' and dialects (mutually understandable linguistic mutations) lest African languages fail to be properly identified. Capo highlights the criteria he uses to reach the conclusion that a wide array of 'languages' previously identified along the Ghana-Nigeria coast of Africa (including Ewe, Adja, Fon and Gen) should really be considered as cluster dialects of one language, Gbe.

444   **Grammaire de la langue ikposso, Togo.** (Grammar of the Ikposso language in Togo.)
      Franz Wolf.   Lomé: Cercle d'Etudes Akposso, 1981. 72p. bibliog.
This work, translated from the German original, *Grammatik der Kposo-Sprache,* is one of the few works on the language of the Akposso that reside in central Togo and in neighbouring Ghana.

445   **Grammaire évé: aide-memoire des règles d'orthographe de l'évé.** (Ewe grammar: a study-guide to Ewe spelling rules.)
      J. Kofi Adzomada.   Lomé: Imprimerie Evangélique, 1980. 50p. bibliog.
Adzomada has produced an easy grammatical guide to the syntax and grammar construction rules of Ewe, with numerous examples throughout.

446   **Initiation à la langue ewe-mina; methode-nature pour étrangers.** (Introduction to Ewe-Mina: a natural approach for foreigners.)
      Gabriel Segbe, Roberto Pazzi.   Lomé: ABC, 1967. 126p.
Organized in the form of twenty-nine lessons and including a vocabulary of 365 words, this is a language textbook for foreign speakers wishing to learn the Mina dialect of Ewe.

447 **Le Kabiye.** (Kabre.)

J. Delord. Lomé: Institut de la Recherche Scientifique, 1976. 465p.
bibliog.

The seminal study of the phonology, tonality, syntax and morphology of the Kabre language of north Togo, this work is written by a pastor who worked among the Kabre people. See also the author's other works: *Morphologie abregée du Kabré* (Abridged Kabre morphology). Dakar: IFAN, 1964; 'Le Kaure de la Polyglotta africana et le Kabré d'aujourd'hui' (The Kaure of the African polyglot and today's Kabre). *African Language Review*, vol. 7 (1968), p. 114-39; 'Les mots-voyageurs en Kabré' (Transferable words in Kabre). In: *Wort und Religion* (Word and Religion). Edited by H. J. Greschat. Stuttgart: Evangelische Missionsverlag, 1969, p. 133-38; and 'Sur le kabré du Togo, jeu de tons' (On the Kabre of Togo, play of tones). *Bulletin d'IFAN*, vol. 30 (Jan. 1968), p. 256-68. See also: Méterwa A. Ourso, 'Root control underspecification and ATR harmony'. *Studies in Linguistic Sciences*, vol. 18, no. 2 (1988), p. 111-27, and the same author's 'Critères de distribution des affixes en Lama' (Criteria for the distribution of affixes in Lama). *Journal of West African Languages*, vol. 19, no. 1 (1989), p. 35-56.

448 **Le kabiye standard.** (Standard Kabre.)

M. Tetveehaki Paaluki. Lomé: Imprimerie de l'Alphabétisation, 1982. 47p.

Written by a local teacher and former ideologue of General Eyadema'a political party, this is a brief introductory linguistic and phonetic guide to the Kabre language of northern Togo. See also: Kézié K. Lebikaza, 'Les constructions possessives prédicatives et nominales en Kabiye' (Possessive and nominal predicative constructions in Kabre). *West African Languages* (Dallas), vol. 21, no. 1 (1991), p. 91-103.

449 **Konkomba-English dictionary.**

Ghana Institute of Linguistics. Tamale, Ghana: Ghana Institute of Linguistics, 1981. 209p.

This work is a Konkomba-English-Konkomba dictionary, with appendices containing vocabulary specifically relating to animals, insects and vegetation. The dictionary is of the Satoba dialect of the Konkomba peoples residing in Ghana: their brethren across the border in Togo have a dialect differing in some respects but which is mutually understandable.

450 **The languages of West Africa.**

Diedrich Westermann, Margaret A. Bryan, supplementary bibliography compiled by D. W. Arnott. Folkestone, England: Dawsons, 1970. 277p. bibliog.

Superbly organized, with a map and a supplementary bibliography of more recent linguistic research, this is a reprint of the most important classificatory text on the languages of West Africa. It provides data on the various Ewe dialects spoken by over one million people along the coast of West Africa.

451 **Lexique français-kabiye-ewe.** (French-Kabre-Ewe lexicon.)
Bassari Ebia. Lomé: Institut National de la Recherche, 1974. 130p.
This book is an extremely valuable double dictionary of French and Togo's two main languages, Ewe and Kabre.

452 **Li-timari, langue des Tamberma du Togo.** (Li-Timari, language of the Tamberma of Togo.)
André Prost. Dakar: IFAN, 1964. 245p.
This linguistic study and dictionary is written by one of the foremost scholars of the Somba, or Battamariba people of the Atakora mountains. See also: Prost's *Li-Timari, documents linguistiques* (Li-Timari, linguistic documents). Dakar: University of Dakar, 1983.

453 **Proverbes Moba.** (Moba proverbs.)
Pierre-Marie Carros, Pierre Reinhard. Dapaong, Togo: P. M. Carros, 1974. 3 vols.
These three volumes are available in several research libraries, including the US Library of Congress. The first two were published by Carros himself, the priest-linguist who served for many years among the northern Moba people. They are extremely well-organized, and each includes one hundred Moba proverbs (one per page), analysed both textually and linguistically, with key words indicating the message they intend to convey. The proverbs are also situated within the cultural context of the Moba people. Several indices are added, including one that links the Moba proverbs to their equivalents in French.

454 **Rapport entre la phonologie et la morphologie dans l'analyse linguistique: exemple du Tem.** (The relations between phonology and morphology in linguistic analysis: an example from the Tem language.)
M. Zakari Tchagbale. *Journal of West African Languages* (Dallas), vol. 14, no. 1 (April 1984), p. 19-38.
A linguistic analysis of the phonology and morphology of the northern Togolese Tem language.

455 **Renaissance du gbe: reflexions critiques et constructives sur l'eve, le fon, le gen, l'aja, le gun, etc.** (The renaissance of Gbe: critical and constructive reflections on Ewe, Fon, Gen, Adja, Gun etc.)
Hounkpati B. C. Capo. Hamburg, Germany: H. Buske, 1988. 234p. bibliog.
In this work Capo makes a study of the various dialects that comprise the Gbe cluster of dialects, in an effort to indicate their common roots, and suggest the linguistic standardization and modernization needed in order to allow the language's rebirth. The work contains an extensive bibliography (p. 220-33) and a comparative vocabulary of one hundred words in the different languages.

456 A study of the Ewe language.

Diedrich Westermann, translated by Aubrey L. Bickford-Smith. London: Oxford University Press, 1930. 258p.

Westermann's classic study of the Ewe language has been translated from the German and reprinted several times. The original was entitled *Grammatik der Ewe-Sprache*, and was published in 1907. Westermann has written various other works including: *Gbesela yeye, or English-Ewe*. Reprinted, Nandeln, Liechtenstein: Kraus-Thompson, 1973. 348p. bibliog.; and *Worterbuch der Ewe-Sprach* (Ewe dictionary). Berlin: Akademie-Verlag, 1954. 795p, bibliog.

457 Systematique phonologique et grammaticale d'un parler Ewe: le gen-mina du sud-Togo et sud-Bénin. (A systematic phonology and grammar of an Ewe language: the Gen-Mina of south Togo and south Benin.)

Rémy Bole-Richard. Paris: Harmattan, 1990. 350p. bibliog.

This work is a very thorough and useful linguistic analysis and brief dictionary to the Mina dialect that is spoken in the coastal areas of Togo and Benin.

458 The tonal structure of Ewe.

Gilbert Ansre. Hartford, Connecticut: Hartford Seminary Foundation, 1961. 39p.

Ansre examines the lexical and phonological aspects of the Ewe language. See also the same author's 'Reduplication in Ewe'. *Journal of African Languages*, vol. 2, no. 2 (1963), p. 128-32.

459 Vocabulaires comparés des langues de l'Atakora. (Comparative vocabularies of the Atakora languages.)

André Prost. *Bulletin d'IFAN* (Dakar), vol. 34, no. 2 (April 1972), p. 299-392; vol. 34, no. 3 (July 1972), p. 617-82; vol. 35, no. 2 (April 1973), p. 444-511; vol. 35, no. 3 (July 1973), p. 712-58; vol. 35, no. 4 (April 1972), p. 903-96; vol. 36, no. 3 (July 1974), p. 628-59.

Prost, the famous priest-linguist, provides the phonology and syntax of several languages spoken by a number of ethnic groups residing in the Atakora mountain chain, on both sides of the Benin-Togo border. One of the languages of principal interest to Togolese linguistics in that of the Somba or Battamaliba.

460 Vowel roundness in Gbe: a pandalectic approach.

Hounkpati B. C. Capo. *Journal of West African Languages* (Dallas), vol. 16, no. 1 (April 1986) p. 15-36. bibliog.

This is a linguistic study of the Gbe cluster of languages spoken in southern Togo. See also the same author's 'Vowel features in Gbe'. *Journal of West African Languages* (Dallas), vol. 15, no. 1 (April 1986), p. 19-30. bibliog.

Les bilingualismes littéraires: signification de la littérature orale tyokossi. (Literary bilingualism: the social meaning of Chokossi oral literature.) *See* item no. 138.

Contribution à un inventaire chronologique des ouvrages entièrement ou partiellement en langue Ewé. (Contribution to a chronological inventory of works entirely or partially written in Ewe.) *See* item no. 533.

Literature

461 **Akossiwa mon amour.** (Akossiwa my love.)
Victor Aladji. Yaoundé: Editions CLE, 1971. 52p.
This was the first novel by the Ewe author Aladji, who at the time worked for Togo's radio services. It is written as a monologue, recounting the passage from adolescence to adulthood and first love.

462 **Amegbetoa ou les aventures d'Agbezuge.** (Amegbetoa, or the adventures of Agbezuge.)
Sam Obianim. Paris: Karthala, 1990. 146p.
This is one of the more recently published novels by a relatively new Togolese author.

463 **Anthologie de la poésie togolaise.** (Anthology of Togolese poetry.)
Edited by Yves-Emmanuel Dogbé. Paris: Editions Akpagnon, 1980. 223p. bibliog.
Comprising selections from thirteen poets, including Dogbé, and in each case providing a concise biography, this book is an important anthology of Togolese poetry.

464 **Au pays des tortues qui chantes.** (In the country of singing tortoises.)
Alain Ricard. In: *Dramaturgies, langages dramatiques: mélanges pour Jacques Scherer* (Playwrights, dramatical language: collection for Jacques Scherer.) Edited by Jacqueline de Jomaron. Paris: Nizet, 1986. p. 99-103.
Taking inspiration from the title of one of Senouvo Agboto Zinsou's most-acclaimed plays for the title of this article, Ricard surveys modern Togolese theatre.

465 **Between resignation and refusal: francophone Togolese writers and the Eyadema regime.**
Guy Ossito Midiohouan, Camille A. Amouro. *Research in African Literatures* (Bloomington), vol. 22, no. 2 (Summer 1991), p. 119-33. bibliog.

This is a powerful article outlining the travails of writers, poets, musicians, artists and dramatologists under the repressive censorship imposed by the dictatorship of General Eyadema. Some have resisted it, and have been imprisoned or driven into exile; others have withdrawn from the literary and artistic scene, unwilling to join the expected sycophancy, and writing, but not publishing their works. For the majority, however, 'indifference to political problems remains the prevalent attitude' (p. 132). The authors illustrate their arguments with reference to some Togolese literature. On the issue of censorship see also Jean-Baptiste Dossé Placca, 'Is Togo television yours or mine?' *Index on Censorship* (London), vol. 13, no. 5 (1984), p. 21-24.

466 **Le bonheur à l'arraché.** (Happiness uprooted.)
Julien Guenou. Paris: Africa Media International, 1983. 163p.

This book is an autobiography that reads as fiction, about a handicapped individual who decides to proceed with his life ignoring his physical limitations, succeeding in his career and getting married. When he wrote the book the author was preparing for a law degree, and had already written a play that had been broadcast over Radio France International.

467 **Le champs littéraire togolaise.** (The Togolese literary arena.)
Edited by Janos Riesz, Alain Ricard. Beyreuth, Germany: Eckhardt Breitinger, 1991. 199p. bibliog.

Through the assembled thirteen essays the editors of this work present a veritable panorama of the rich corpus of Togolese literature and poetry. A number of chapters deal specifically with individual authors or works, some offer an overview of the first written sources (usually German) on Togolese history and culture, while others discuss the state of publishing in Togo prior to independence.

468 **Le Club.** (The club.)
Senouvou Agbota Zinsou. Lomé: Haho, 1984. 67p.

An acerbic play by Togo's most renowned playwright on the opulence and decadence of contemporary African élites.

469 **Le divin amour.** (Divine love.)
Yves-Emmanuel Dogbé. Paris: Editions Akpagnon, 1979. 111p.

This work, which won the Prix Vildrac in 1979, is a collection of sixty-six poems by one of Togo's greatest poets and literary figures. Born in Lomé in 1939 and with a PhD from the Ecole des Hautes Etudes en Sciences Sociales in Paris, Dogbé taught for a few years before returning to Togo. He was arrested by the Eyadema regime for writing a polemic against the latter's dictatorship, and when released promptly went into self-imposed exile establishing the Akpagnon publishing house in Paris. For Dogbé's novels see, in particular, *L'homme de Bé* (The man from Be). Paris: Editions Akpagnon, 1979. 44p.

470 **L'equilibriste.** (The equilibrist.)
Victor Aladji.   Yaoundé: Editions CLE, 1972. 52p.

The second work of Aladji, who studied journalism at the University of Lille, this is the story of the adventures of a young African devoted to the struggle against all forms of oppression. Aladji, who has since (and to date) published four books, is the sole Togolese author to have his literary output examined (p. 109-14) and biography included in Pierrette Hertzberger-Fofona, *Ecrivains africains et identités culturelles* (African writers and cultural identities). Tubingen: Stauffenburg, 1989. 124p.

471 **Essai sur L'esclave. Roman de Félix Couchoro.** (Essay on *The slave*. A novel by Félix Couchoro.)
Adrien Huannou.   Cotonou, Benin: ABM, 1987. 128p.

Couchoro, born in Benin, lived and wrote for most of his life in Togo. He wrote popular literature for the masses, was very widely read, and is considered the first of the African 'romancier' novelists. *L'esclave*, written in 1920 and republished in 1962 and 1983, was his first, and one of his most important books. Huannou, who is a Beninois scholar and author, studies and analyses Couchoro's main literary themes, and provides a bio-bibliography of his work. For another of Couchoro's influential books see *L'heritage, cette peste* (Heritage, that pestilence). Lomé: Editogo, 1963. 160p. For a literary analysis of Couchoro's work see: Sabit Adegbeyega Salami, 'Félix Couchoro: a Togolese novelist of the Onitsha school?' *Black Orpeus* (Lagos), vol. 4, no. 2 (1982), p. 33-45; Jean-Norbert Vignondé, 'Autour de *L'esclave* de Félix Couchoro'. *Research in African Literatures* (Dallas), vol. 16, no. 4 (Winter 1985), p. 556-63; and Jean-Norbert Vignondé, 'Les precurseurs: Félix Couchoro, Paul Hazoumé' (The precursors: Félix Couchoro, Paul Hazoumé). *Notre Librairie* (Paris), vol. 69 (1983), p. 33-40.

472 **Ewe comic heros: trickster tales in Togo.**
Zinta Konrad.   New York: Garland, 1994. 294p. bibliog.

This is a remarkable collection of Ewe folklore and tradition (from Togo and Ghana) in which tricksters play a major role. The work uses a semiotic approach, and is based on the author's PhD thesis. For additional folktales from Benin and Togo see Suzanne Lafage, *Ce que contait le vent en savane* (What the wind in the savanna recounts). Paris: Conseil International de la Langue Française, 1975). 143p.; Yves-Emmanuel Dogbé, *Contes et légendes du Togo* (Stories and legends of Togo). Paris: Akpagnon, 1981. 103p.; and Komla Agbétiafa, Yao Nambou, *Contes du Togo* (Folktales of Togo). Paris: CLE International, 1980. 111p.

473 **Expériences de ma jeunesse.** (Experiences from my youth.)
Koffi Koffi.   Lomé: Editions 1982, 1984. 119p.

This book is the autobiography of a journalist writing for Lomé's daily newspapers, followed by a collection of his poems.

474   **La fiction narrative dans la production littéraire Ewe.** (Narrative fiction in Ewe literature.)
Simon Agbeko Amegbleame.   *Africa* (London), vol. 50, no. 1 (1980), p. 24-36. bibliog.

In this article the author examines and compares two Ewe narrative forms, novels and stories, which he maintains are confused in literary analyses, partly because of the common tendency of Togolese authors to refer to their works as *nutunya*, a term that in translation means 'novel'. Using a structuralist approach, the author argues that the two literary forms are quite distinct, both in functional characteristics and in narrative approach. Stories, moreover, are deeply influenced by indigenous religion, are closer to oral legends and folktales, and have rural origins, while properly speaking, novels are a much newer phenomena, and urban in inception and concern.

475   **Le fils du fétiche.** (Son of the fetishist.)
David Ananou.   Paris: Nouvelles Editions Latines, 1955. 207p.

This novel is one of the classics of Togolese pre-independence literature, and reflects the social mores of that era and the tensions between tradition and modernity, fetishists and Christianity. It is the story of a man who repudiates his former two wives to marry a young girl, and the entanglements this results in for him, and for the son of this marriage, because of the involvement of fetish priests.

476   **Les grands jours.** (The great days.)
Nayé Théophile Inawissi.   Paris: Editions Akpagnon, 1983. 61p.

A collection of poems by a Togolese teacher, that has been assessed by one French reviewer/critic as 'remarkable'. Another collection of mystical poems is contained in Kris Wezin, *La puissance et l'eternité* (Power and eternity). Paris: Editions Akpagnon, 1985. 92p.

477   **Labyrinthe: poèmes.** (Labyrinth: poems.)
S. Tanella Boni.   Paris: Editions Akpagnon, 1984. 76p.

A collection of poems by a young Togolese teacher.

478   **La littérature togolaise.** (Togolese literature.)
Lomé: Institut National des Sciences de l'Education, 1987. 88p. bibliog.

Togo has a very rich modern literary tradition, and many established as well as budding authors and poets. This book is a series of ten brief essays, each written by a professor at the University of Benin in Lomé, dealing with various aspects of modern Togolese literature, fiction as well as poetry. Some essays analyse a specific work, several survey Togo's literary and poetry output in general, while others present interviews with specific Togolese authors.

479   **Morne sololoque, précédé de l'art de la nouvelle poèsie.** (Gloomy soliloquy, preceded by the art of new poetry.)
Yves-Emmanuel Dogbé.   Paris: Editions Akpagnon, 1982. 184p.

Written by one of Togo's greatest poets, this work is an introduction to the style of contemporary poetry, followed by a collection of new poems by the author about the

Soviet Union, pagan mysticism, and Africa. The collection is analysed in R. O. Elahoro, 'Une lecture de "Morne soliloque" d'Yves-Emmanuel Dogbé' (A reading of 'Gloomy soliloquy' by Yves-Emmanuel Dogbe). *Présence Africaine*, no. 144 (1987), p. 103-08. For one of Dogbé's novels see *La victime: roman* (The victim: a novel). Paris: Akpagnon, 1979. 237p.

480 **Naissance du roman africain: Félix Couchoro (1900-1968).** (The birth of the African novel: Felix Couchoro, 1900-1968.)
Alain Ricard. Paris: Présence Africaine, 1987. 228p. bibliog.

Ricard has carried out an exhaustive study of Felix Couchoro and his literary work, and the impact of his novels – written in the style of a typical populist French novel – on the evolution of future authors in francophone Africa. The author, who is a noted literary critic, also places Couchoro within the context of the evolution of literature in French Africa. He provides a bibliography of Couchoro's literary output, which is valuable since some works are serialized in Lomé's newspapers and are therefore not known in the West. See also the author's 'Du romancier au feuilletoniste: les limites de l'écriture de Félix Couchoro' (From novelist to pamphleteer: the limits of Felix Couchoro's writings). *Recherche, Pédagogie et Culture*, vol. 57 (1982), p. 47-56.

481 **La naissance du théâtre togolaise moderne.** (The birth of modern Togolese theatre.)
Senouvou Agbota Zinsou. *Culture Française* (Paris), vol. 3/4, no. 1 (1982/83), p. 49-57.

This is an overview of the emergence of modern Togolese theatre by Zinsou, the country's most talented and world-famous dramatologist, and winner of the African Grand Prize (1972) for his *On joue la comèdie* (q.v.).

482 **New plays: Togo, Madagascar, Mauritania: Afrique book two.**
New York: Ubu Repertory Theater Publications, 1991. 309p.

This collection of plays from francophone Africa includes for the first time in English two plays by Senouvou Agbota Zinsou: his world-acclaimed *The singing tortoise* (La tortue qui chante), p. 1-50; and *Yévi's adventures in monsterland* (Les Aventures de Yévi en pays des monstres), p. 277-309.

483 **On joue la comèdie.** (Putting on a play.)
Senouvou Agbota Zinsou. Lomé: Editions Haho, 1984. 62p.

Zinsou is recognized as Togo's greatest playwright. Written at the age of twenty-six, this play secured him a prize for drama, and a scholarship for higher literary studies in France.

484 **Regard sur le Togo ancien: histoire, économie, vie quotiodienne.**
(A look back at ancient Togo: history, economy, daily life.)
Kwassivi Amegan. Lomé: Goethe Institut, 1991. 58p.

This unusual play in five acts is a historical drama set in the days of German colonial rule.

485 **Sacrilège à Mandali.** (Sacrilege in Mandali.)
Adovi John-Bosco Adotevi.   Yaoundé: Editions CLE, 1982. 177p.
Written by a much-published Togolese journalist and correspondent for a variety of weeklies, this is a love story set against a religious background in a country embroiled in political strife.

486 **Semences nouvelles: poèmes.** (New seeds: poems.)
A. Ghan, et al.   Lomé: Editions Hao, 1986. 96p.
Brief biographies are provided for each of the nine Togolese poets, some of whom have not appeared in print before, who are represented in this collection of poems, or extracts from long poems.

487 **Togo.**
Locha E. Mateso.   In: *Anthologie de la poésie d'Afrique noire d'expression française* (Anthology of the poetry of francophone Black Africa.)   Paris: Hatier, 1987, p. 166-73.
This anthology of francophone poetry includes a section on Togo which contains thumbnail biographical sketches of six Togolese poets and a few of their poems.

488 **Togo.**
Alain Rouch, Gérard Clavreuil.   In: *Littératures nationales d'écriture française* (National literatures in French.)   Paris: Bardas, 1986. p. 462-70.
This book is a very valuable literary reference work on francophone literature. It is superbly organized by country, including a section on Togo, and internally subdivided into a general literary overview followed by specific analyses of key works of selected writers, including their biographies. The Togolese chapter focuses on David Ananou, and his *Le fils du fétiche* (1955); Yves-Emmanuel Dogbé, and his *L'incarcéré* (1980); and Julien Atsou Guenou, and his *Le bonheur à l'arraché* (1983).

489 **La vie ephemère d'un conteur public à Sansanné-Mango.** (The ephemeral life of a public story-teller in Sansanne-Mango.)
Diana Rey-Hulman.   *Cahiers de Littérature Orale*, vol. 11 (1982), p. 182-85.
Consists of a brief but fascinating look at the life of public story-tellers in Togo.

490 **La voix de l'ombre.** (Sound of the shadow.)
Victor Aladji.   Lomé: Editions Haho, 1985. 173p.
This is a novel about the death of a colonial soldier during the Second World War and the birth of his son after his death. It is the third book by a popular author who teaches developmental sociology at the University of Benin in Lomé.

Arts

Architecture

491 **Anatomy of architecture: ontology and metaphor in Batammaliba architectural expression.**
Suzanne Preston Blier.   Cambridge, England: Cambridge University Press, 1987. 314p. bibliog.

This remarkably erudite work is a veritable tour-de-force about the meaning of architecture to the Batammaliba (better known as the Tamberma or Somba) who are found in northern Togo and Benin and whose double-storied fortress-like domiciles are both a distinctive feature and a 'must' on any tourist circuit. To the Batammaliba, Blier notes, 'architecture is an important cultural priority' and because of this rich over-arching and multi-faceted meaning, Blier's book is equally a study of their 'cosmology, religion, psychology, society, politics' (p. ix). The work, replete with numerous plates, diagrams, and house-plans, includes a huge amount of original data drawn from extensive fieldwork among this highly individualistic ethnic group. This includes: building technology; village planning; rituals followed; and the significance of every stage in the construction and habitation of their domiciles which emphasizes the 'complementarity of house, family and tomb' (p. 189). See also the author's 'Houses are human: architectural self-images of Africa's Tamberma'. *Society of Architectural History Journal*, vol. 42, no. 4 (Dec. 1983), p. 371-82.

492 **L'architecture en Afrique noire.** (Black Africa's architecture.)
Masudi Alabi Fassassi.   Paris: Maspero, 1978. 198p. bibliog.

This is by far one of the best and most comprehensive studies of indigenous architecture and city-design in Africa. The book is replete with photographs, sketches and elevations. Togo, 'characterized by two types of dwelling' (p. 86), merits seven pages (p. 86-92) and these are largely devoted to the unique building style of its northern Somba people.

493 **Economie de la construction à Lomé.** (The construction economy in
Lomé.)
Akolly Adjavou. Paris: Harmattan, 1987. 203p. bibliog.

Supplemented by a surprisingly long bibliography (p. 159-67), maps, diagrams,
photographs and floor plans, this work is both a rare survey of the construction
industry in Togo and its unusual social and economic problems and limitations, as
well as of modern architecture in the country. The author discusses the construction
sector in a number of concise chapters on the major (mostly State) producers of
building materials, land developers and agencies involved in zoning issues and urban
development.

494 **Moral architecture: beauty and ethics in Batammaliba building.**
Suzanne Preston Blier. In: *Dwelling, settlements and tradition.*
Edited by Jean-Paul Bourdier, Nezer Alsayyad. New York: Lanham,
1989, p. 335-56. bibliog.

This is an important article that introduces new social meaning into architectural
styles. Blier maintains that 'aesthetic valuation reflects critical moral and social
canons of pragmatic efficacy and usefulness' (p. 352) and that 'the central tenets of
the society are expressed through the forms and meanings of their buildings' (p. 353).
She argues that, in this way, Batammaliba (or Tamberma/Somba) buildings 'serve as
forceful proponents of a moral code that reaches broadly into the society and that has
an impact on, and in turn is grounded in local politics, psychology, religion and
individual expression' (p. 352). Beautiful houses, seen in this society as both 'strong'
and 'youthful', extend these ideals to their inhabitants, in turn 'encouraging in them a
high valuation of youthful energy and hard work', so that 'each beautiful building
visually reaffirms the social mores and ethical values that help bind the communuity
together.' (p. 352).

495 **Rives coloniales: architectures, de Saint-Louis à Douala.** (Colonial
shores: architecture from Saint-Louis to Douala.)
Jacques Souilliou. Paris: ORSTOM, 1993. 316p.

Profusely illustrated, this is a study of the kinds of architectural styles (from the 15th
century to those of the 1960s) that co-exist throughout West Africa, from Saint-Louis
in Senegal to Douala in Cameroon. After a historical introduction, the author presents
specific material on several of the countries, including Togo.

496 **Technique de construction de cases et artisanats chez les Kabré.**
(Construction methods and artisans among the Kabre.)
B. Cridel. In: *Documents du centre d'études et de recherches de
Kara*, 1967, p. 37-38.

Despite its brevity this is a very useful source for the terminology of the construction
of dwellings in northern Togo.

Carvings and sculpture

497 Antelopes and anvils: Tamberma works of iron.
Suzanne Preston Blier. *African Arts*, vol. 17, no.3 (May 1984), p. 58-63. bibliog.

In this article Blier discusses the art of the Tamberma (or Somba) in northern Togo and Benin. As she notes 'western Tamberma traditions of forged iron are in many respects unique in African smithing technology' (p. 58) since they are geared to the production of jewellery and not agrarian implements. To the Tamberma, immersed in a world of symbolism, smithing is an art form, originating with the antelopes, a theme that Blier explores with the aid of many photographs and diagrams.

498 Ewe funerary sculpture.
Michelle V. Gilbert. *African Arts*, vol. 14, no. 4 (Aug. 1981), p. 44-46. bibliog.

Cement funerary art has evolved strongly among the coastal Ewe on both sides of the Ghana-Togo border. This article, which is illustrated with many photographs, focuses on the funerary statuary of the Anlo clan in Ghana, the most striking of which date to the period after the Second World War. These statues range from simple handstones to brightly painted commemorative statues, and can be extremely ornate, such as one of a soldier's memorial surmounted by a freestanding horse and aeroplane. The demand for these statues has spawned the need for the services of cement sculptors. Funerary art is often protected from the elements by a concrete blockshed in the family compound, and is not always easily seen by the casual observer.

499 Ewe sculpture in the Linden Museum.
Dzagbe Cudjoe. *Tribus*, vol. 18 (1969), p. 42-72. bibliog.

This article, which includes illustrations, assesses the items of Ewe sculpture that were collected during the German colonial era and can now be found in the Linden Museum in Stuttgart. Cudjoe places them in nine categories according to their function, and suggests that some were mislabelled by the curators. See also Jurgen Zwernemann, 'Un masque de laiton provenant du Togo au Linden-Museum à Stuttgart' (A brass mask from Togo in the Linden Museum in Stuttgart). *Notes Africaines* (Dakar), no. 101 (1967), p. 118; and Paul Ahyi, 'Sculptures en bois du Togo de 1894 à 1900' (Wood sculptures from Togo from 1894 to 1900). *Entente Africaine* (Nov. 1969), p. 66-67.

500 Die Gelbgusse des Ali Amonkiyi. (The yellow metal-casts of Ali Amonkiyi.)
Julius Gluck. *Jahrbuch des Linden-Museums*, vol. 1 (1951), p. 27-71.

A description and analysis of the provenance and use of a collection of masks in the museum in Basel from the German colonial era in Togo. See also Eberhard Fischer 'Die Gelbgussmaske des Ali Amonikoyi (aus Togo) im Museum für Volkerkunde in Basle' (The yellow metal-cast masks of Ali Amonkiyi (from Togo) in the museum for folk art in Basel). *Tribus*, vol. 15 (1966), p. 89-95; and Herta Haselberger, 'Au sujet des masques de laiton au Togo' (On the subject of brass masks in Togo'. *Notes Africaines de l'IFAN*, vol. 104 (Oct. 1964).

501 **Moba shrine figures.**
Christine Mullen Kreamer. *African Arts*, vol. 20, no. 2 (Feb. 1987),
p. 52-55.
In this article, which is accompanied by black-and-white photographs, the author
describes the carving and purposes of wooden shrine figures among the Moba in
northern Togo. These are produced to order for specific clients on the advice of local
diviners who may even specify the dimensions or sex of the carvings, some of which
may only be produced by the diviners themselves.

502 **Mystical protection among the Anlo Ewe.**
Michelle V. Gilbert. *African Arts*, vol. 15, no. 4 (Aug. 1982),
p. 60-66. bibliog.
One of the main branches of Ghana's Ewe are the Anlo, who have multiple links with
their kin across the Togolese border. This article describes the roughly modelled clay
or cement figures of simplified human form, which are less than a metre high, and
often adorned with pieces of cloth and palm necklaces, that flank the entrances to
many Ewe towns between the Togolese border and Anloga in Ghana. These are of
ritual significance as traditional representations of mystical powers guarding the
towns. Numerous plates illustrate these figures.

Artisanal art

503 **African majesty: the textile art of the Ashanti and Ewe.**
Peter Adler, Nicholas Barnard. London: Thames & Hudson, 1992.
129p.
This is a profusely illustrated book on the elaborate textiles of the Ashanti and Ewe. It
includes information both on their production and designs.

504 **Artisanats traditionnels en Afrique noire, Togo.** (Traditional
handicrafts in Black Africa, Togo.)
Jocelyne Etienne-Nugue. Dakar: Institut Culturel Africain, 1992.
bibliog.
Profusely illustrated with colour and black-and-white photographs and diagrams, and
part of a valuable series on the artisanal output of francophone Africa, this book is a
comprehensive enumeration of Togo's handicrafts. Covering a wide variety of crafts,
from musical instruments, textiles and saddles to boat making, the author also
provides a detailed listing of all market towns and market days in Togo, and the kinds
of indigenous handicrafts available. See also B. Benot-Latour, 'L'artisanat togolais'
(Togo's artisanal work). *Afrique Littéraire et Artistique*, vol. 30 (Nov. 1973), p. 40-42.

505 **Enquête sur l'artisanat: région de La Kara, région des Savanes.**
(Survey on artisanal art: the Kara region, the Savanes region.)
Togo, Ministère du Plan et des Mines. Lomé: Direction de la
Statistique; Ottawa: Centre de Recherches pour le Développement
International, 1989. 2 vols.

This work is a statistical compilation, and an analysis of the data obtained, and of the
nature and number of artisans and artisanal work in the northern Kara and Savanes
regions in Togo.

506 **Ewe weaving in the Volta region.**
Venice Lamb. In: *West African weaving.* London: Duckworth,
1975. p. 163-215. bibliog.

Lamb has produced an excellent detailed discussion of traditional and contemporary
Ewe weaving styles and designs, accompanied by diagrams and photographs.
Although the focus of this chapter is on the Ewe in the Volta region of Ghana, the
material is also relevant for the Ewe of Togo. Also of interest is the more general
work by John Picton, John Mack, *African textiles*. London: The British Museum,
1979. 208p. bibliog., which was reprinted in New York in 1989 by Harper & Row.

507 **Togo.**
Jacques Anquetil. Paris: Agence de Cooperation Culterelle et
Technique, 1980. 95p.

This profusely illustrated book is part of a series on the handicrafts and decorative
arts of francophone Africa. It covers all aspects of artisanal arts, such as: pottery;
textiles; culinary art; wood sculpture; architecture; and agricultural implements. The
book is organized by region and ethnic group.

508 **Traditional cloth from the Ewe heartland.**
Merrick Posnansky. In: *History, design and craft in West African
strip-woven cloth.* Washington, DC: Smithsonian Museum, National
Museum of African Art, 1988, p. 113-32. bibliog.

A description of textile designs and cloth names in Ewe country.

509 **Yoruba sculpture of West Africa.**
William Fagg, John Pemberton, Bryce Holcombe. New York: Knopf,
1982. 209p. bibliog.

This book is a vivid representation of the rich Yoruba art, illustrated by numerous
plates, many of which are in stunning colour. The Yoruba are found primarily in
Nigeria, but considerable numbers are also resident in Benin and Togo. The text
describes the art presented, and its ritual purpose.

Music and drama

510 **Le concert-party: une pedagogie pour les opprimés.** (The concert-party: a pedagogy for the downtrodden.)
Togoata Apedo-Amah. *Peuples Noires - Peuples Africains*, vol. 8, no. 44 (Jan.-June 1985), p. 61-72.

The author, who teaches at the University of Benin in Lomé, reports on 'the concert party', or popular theatre, a unique form of entertainment in Togo, which can also be found throughout Africa, right down to Malawi. This is a major departure from normal theatre on several grounds: the language used is either in the vernacular, in French, or in street-language; the plot is an everyday one that everybody can identify with; and the play does not happen on 'stage' but in the open with the active participation of the playwright, actors and 'audience'. One such play is analysed in this article.

511 **Concours et concert: théâtre populaire et théâtre scolaire au Togo.** (Shows and concerts: popular theatre and scholarly theatre in Togo.)
Alain Ricard. *Revue d'Histoire du Théâtre*, vol. 27, no. 1 (1975), p. 44-86.

Using examples, Ricard describes and differentiates between several different popular and classical forms of theatre in Togo. See also Senouvou Agbota Zinsou, 'La naissance du théâtre togolaise moderne' (The birth of modern Togolese theatre). *Culture Française*, Special issue, no. 3, 1984; and René Gouellain, 'Recherche anthropologique et théâtre akposso' (Anthropological research and Akposso theatre). *Documents de Centre d'Etudes et de Recherches de Kara*, Piya, Togo. vol. 3 (1968), p. 27-34.

512 **Mister Tameklor, suivi de Françis-le-Parisien, par le Happy Star Concert Band de Lomé, Togo.** (Mister Tameklor, followed by Francis the Parisian, by the Happy Star concert band of Lomé, Togo.)
Transcribed, translated, annotated and recorded by Noble Akam, Alain Ricard, Jean Charron. Paris: SELAF/ORSTOM, 1981. 289p.

This is a remarkable package: a critical historical review of Togolese popular music is followed by two musical librettos in their original Ewe language and in French translation, with brief summaries in English, German, Russian and Spanish. Two attached cassettes provide recordings of the two 'concert party' plays. These are an original form of cabaret-theatre, that has spread to Togo from Ghana. See also the same author's 'Reflexions sur le théâtre à Lomé' (Reflections on the theatre in Lome). *Recherches, Pedagogie et Culture*, vol. 57 (1982), p. 63-70.

513 **Petit recueil de chants et rythmes populaires togolais.** (A small collection of popular Togolese songs and tunes.)
A. Ketoglo. Lomé: Institut Pédagogique National, 1974. 189p.

A variety of songs and melodies from several parts of the country, and which are often sung during communal work are included in this book. See also Pierre Sallée, 'Improvisation et/ou information: sur trois exemples de polyphones africaines'

(Improvization and/or information: on three examples of African polyphony). In: *L'improvisation dans les musiques de tradition orale*, edited by Bernard Lortat-Jacob. Paris: SELAF, 1987. For three works in English see David Locke, *A collection of Atsiagbeko songs 1975-1977*, Legon: University of Ghana Institute of African Studies, 1980. 119p. The latter includes the full text of the Ewe songs with English translation. See also the more technical ethnomusicological articles by V. Kofi Agawu: 'Variation procedures in northern Ewe song', *Ethnomusicology*, vol. 34, no. 2 (1990), p. 221-44; and 'Tone and Tune: the evidence for northern Ewe music', *Africa* (London), vol. 58, no. 2 (1988), p. 127-46. bibliog. For an important and very thorough early German article on Ewe songs see Ant Witts, 'Lieder und Gesange der Ewhe-Neger (Ge-dialekt)' (Songs and singing of the Ewe-blacks [of Ge dialect]), *Anthropos*, vol. 1, no. 1/4 (1906), p. 65-81, 194-209.

514 **Théâtre littéraire et théâtre populaire: l'exemple des Ewe du Togo.** (Literary and popular theatre: the example of the Ewe of Togo.) Alain Ricard. In: *L'invention de théâtre: le théâtre et les comédiens en Afrique noire.* Lausanne, Switzerland: L'Age d'Homme, 1986, p. 40-59.

Presents a description of the origins and evolution of the concert-party, or popular theatre, where in open-ended contexts the public participates in the 'play'. The author also discusses the role of the Happy Star Group in popularizing this form of popular theatre in Togo.

Painting

515 **La peintre Emmanuel Dabla.** (The painter Emmanuel Dabla.) *Espoir de la Nation Togolaise* (Lomé), vol. 19, no. 4 (Aug. 1986), p. 49-51.

This is a brief article on one important modern Togolese painter.

Museums

516 **Hubert Kponton (1905-1982). Erfinder, Kunstler und Begrunder eines ethnographischen Privatmuseums in Lomé, Togo.** (Hubert Kponton [1905-1982]. Inventor, artist and establisher of a private ethnographic museum in Lomé, Togo.) Gerhard Kubik. *Archiv fur Volkerkunde* (Vienna), vol. 40. (1986), p. 157-71. bibliog.

Brief references to Hubert Kponton exist in French but this is the only detailed article, illustrated with photographs, to treat the Togolese traditional leader. He was also an artist of many talents, as well as an inventor (of a musical instrument), who assembled in his private home a museum of traditional artifacts (including agricultural implements) and slave era memoriabilia that was bequeathed on his death to the State, which now runs his museum.

Bibliography of art and architecture in Togo.
See item no. 529.

Media and Publishing

517 **La presse au Togo (1911-1966).** (The Togolese press [1911-1966].)
Raymond Guillaneuf.   Dakar: Faculté des Lettres et Sciences
Humaines, 1968. 526p.

This work, the author's dissertation for a higher degree at the University of Dakar,
provides an incredibly rich, thorough and definitive overview of the history of the
press in Togo. The work is organized into chronological chapters covering the periods
1911-1940, 1943-1958, and 1958-1966. All newspapers and other publications that
appeared in Togo during these periods are presented, along with details which are
impossible to obtain except in the archives in Lomé. A complete alphabetical list is
appended at the end. See also John Dovi Madjri, 'Audience et impact d'un media
rural africain: le journal *Game Su* au Togo' (Audience and the impact of rural African
media: the journal *Game Su* in Togo), *Communication et Information*, vol. 2, no. 1
(1977), p. 127-34.

518 **Publishing and literature in Togo.**
Jan Kees van de Werk.   *African Book-Publishing Record* (Oxford),
vol. 11, no. 4 (1985), p. 201-04.

Little has been published in any language on the publishing scene in Togo, so this is a
valuable review of the topic. The author is the co-founder of the Editions Haho in
Lomé, an autonomous project of the Eglise Evangelique du Togo and financially
backed by Dutch and German Protestant Churches. Since inception Haho Press has
published numerous literary works that would normally be published in Europe, thus
depriving Togolese readers of easy (and inexpensive) access to its own national
literary output, while imposing Eurocentric marketing and editorial criteria. The
author notes that in Togo there are no publishing houses that cater for literary works,
and those that exist, still using old presses that are memoriabilia in Europe, are
involved in commercial work. The article, translated from Dutch, is also a survey of
the evolution of literature in Togo. It is not as cursory as its brevity might suggest,
since both a surprisingly large amount of material is included in it, and the page-
format is long.

519 **Togo Presse.**
Lomé. 1962- . daily.

Togo Presse was established as a weekly newspaper on 26 April 1962, as the epistemological successor to a previous weekly publication. Within a few years, however, it became a daily and throughout the years has had several different names. Published with between four and eight pages (and lengthier on special occasions), it has always included a surprising amount of foreign news, and a section in Evegbe for its Ewe readers.

Bibliographies and Reference Works

520   Africa: a guide to reference material.
John McIlwaine.   London: Hans Zell, 1993. 507p.

This is a valuable, up-to-date reference work that provides a broad overview of multiple sources of information (other than bibliographies) on Africa. These are found in, for example, encyclopaedias, almanacs, yearbooks, dictionaries, gazetteers and other directories.

521   Africa Bibliography.
Edited by Hector Blackhurst.   Edinburgh: Edinburgh University Press, 1990- . annual.

Published by Manchester University Press between 1985 and 1989, this is one of the two most comprehensive annual bibliographies on Africa. It lists, one or two years in arrears, all the books and articles available on the continent, arranging the material by region and indexing by subject and author.

522   Africa Research Bulletin.
Edited by Pita Adams.   Oxford: Blackwell, 1964- . monthly.

This absolutely indispensible periodical for the serious student of Africa is by far the best English-language research tool for Africanists in general, and especially for those interested in francophone Africa who do not speak French. Issued monthly in two series, one on essentially economic issues, and the other on political and international developments, the material is grouped both by theme and by country, making it very easy to use and catch up on developments in the preceding month. In essence, the publication consists of abstracts (some lengthy) of news items and articles published in dailies, weeklies and monthlies, including translations of items from foreign languages.

523 **African libraries.**
Glenn L. Sitzman.   Metuchen, New Jersey: Scarecrow Press, 1988.
486p.

A comprehensive guide to the libraries and librarianship in Africa. The book includes
a number of general essays and a country-by-country listing in which those on Ghana,
Togo and Benin are of use for researchers on Togo.

524 **Afrique Contemporaine.** (Contemporary Africa.)
Paris: La Documentation Française. 1962- . quarterly.

This official French publication, which was originally published more frequently, is
one of the best reference sources on francophone Africa, and virtually indispensible
for any serious student of these countries. It contains articles of topical interest,
including full texts of important documents (such as constitutions), chronologies of
quarterly events on each country, an important review of (mostly French) literature
recently published, and (until a few years ago, grossly de-emphasized) invaluable
biographies of either new African leaders, or obituaries of recently deceased ones.

525 **American and Canadian doctoral dissertations and master's
theses on Africa, 1974-1987.**
Joseph J. Lauer, Gregory V. Larkin, Alfred Kagan.   Atlanta, Georgia:
Crossroads Press, 1989. 377p. bibliog.

This book is an annotated listing of 8,537 theses, of which some three-quarters are
doctoral dissertations, completed between 1974 and 1987. The dissertations are
arranged by geographical region and country, with data on degree-granting
institutions and indices. It is a follow-up to Michael Sims, Alfred Kagan, *American
and Canadian doctoral dissertations and master's dissertations, 1886-1974*,
Waltham, Massachusetts: African Studies Association, 1989, 365p., of which an
earlier edition exists, and is itself periodically updated through listings by Lauer in
ASA News (Atlanta), a quarterly newsletter of the African Studies Association of the
United States.

526 **Bibliographie des travaux en langue français sur l'Afrique au sud
du Sahara.** (Bibliography of works in French on Africa south of the
Sahara.)
Zofia Yaranga.   Paris: Centre d'Etudes Africaines. irreg.

This is one of the best comprehensive French bibliographies on Africa.

527 **Bibliographie Deutschsprachiger Literatur zur Ethnographie und
Geschichte der Ewe in Togo und Sudostghana, 1840-1914,
annotiert.** (Annotated bibliography of German-language literature for
the ethnography and history of the Ewe in Togo and south-east Ghana,
1840-1914.)
Christine Seige, Wolfgang Liedtke.   Dresden, Germany: Staatliches
Museum für Volkerkunde Dresden, 1990. 404p. English section.

A very valuable bibliographical work, this covers the early German anthropological
and historical research in Togo (primarily on the Ewe and Mina) and the

neighbouring Ewe regions in Ghana. Entries are annotated, and there is an introductory and explanatory section in English.

528 **Bibliographie evhé (Ewe) en Afrique occidentale.** (Bibliography of the Ewe in West Africa.)
Krzystof Zielnicka. Vienna: Institut für Volkerkinde der Universität Wien, 1976. 178p.

This is a comprehensive bibliography on all aspects of the Ewe people, comprising 1,281 items alphabetically listed by author. There is an index in three languages, including English.

529 **Bibliography of art and architecture in Togo.**
Thomas McDonald Shaw. *Africana Journal*, vol. 8, no. 2 (1977), p. 131-35.

This is a useful bibliography of forty titles on Togo in a field that is difficult to research. Many are in German.

530 **Bibliographie rétrospective du Togo 1950-1970.** (Retrospective bibliography of Togo 1950-1970.)
Lomé: Bibliotheque Nationale, 1974. 169p.

Produced by Togo's national library, this bibliography covers items published during the critical 1950-1970 period. It includes many items published locally, and/or in vernacular languages, that do not appear in other bibliographies.

531 **Bibliographies for African studies, 1970-1986.**
Yvette Scheven. New York: Hans Zell, 1988. 615p.

Much useful information is contained in this most current and substantial bibliography of bibliographies in African Studies, which cumulates the author's several earlier volumes for 1970-1975, 1976-1979 and 1980-1983, with additional data for 1984-1986. The work excludes African-language works, but includes those in major European languages, giving a total of 4,500 annotated entries. It is organized by themes/subjects and is indexed at the end by author/topic/country. The material for Togo is found on page 531.

532 **Contribution à la bibliographie du Togo: inventaire bibliographique d'archives, de services administratifs et de bibliothèques de Lomé.** (Contribution to a bibliography of Togo: a bibliographical inventory of archives, of administrative services and of the libraries of Lomé.)
Danielle Noel, Michele Santraille. Lomé: Direction des Etudes et du Plan, 1971. 139p.

This is an early bibliographical inventory of Togo's Union catalogues, including those in the national archives and administrative divisions. Another still useful early survey is G. Wesley Johnson, 'Archival system of former French West Africa', *African Studies Bulletin* (London), vol. 8, no. 1 (April 1965), p. 45-58. See also

J. Fontvieille, *Togo. Les bibliothèques: enquêtes et propositions de développement*, Paris: UNESCO, 1977.

533 **Contribution à un inventaire chronologique des ouvrages entièrement ou partiellement en langue Ewé.** (Contribution to a chronological inventory of works wholly or partly in the Ewe language.)
Suzanne Lafage. *Annales de l'Université d'Abidjan* (Abidjan), vol. 7, no. 1 (1974), p. 169-204; vol. 8, no. 1 (1975), p. 159-89.

This chronologically arranged bibliography of Ewe works is organized in two parts: the period 1857 to 1973 which lists 323 titles; and the period 1867 to 1974 which includes 191 titles specifically on Ewe culture.

534 **Country Report. Togo, Niger, Benin, Burkina.**
London: The Economist Intelligence Unit, 1986- . thrice-annually.

The section on Togo in this work is usually only eleven pages long, but it is nevertheless the best summary in English on recent events. This is a valuable, succinct but remarkably accurate report, including forward forecasting, of economic and political conditions in the four countries concerned. It includes valuable statistical tables, and a list of cabinet members. Since 1986 the Unit has also published an annual *Country Profile. Togo, Benin*, that provides a summary (in the case of Togo of about twenty-two pages) of the previous year's quarterly reports, but with greater emphasis on economic developments.

535 **Dictionnaire des oeuvres littéraires négro-africain de langue française, des origines à 1978.** (Dictionary of Black African literary works in the French language, from their origins to 1978.)
Edited by Ambroise Kom. Sherbrooke, Canada: Naaman, 1983. 668p.

This book provides a comprehensive compendium of descriptions and assessments of the key literary writings of francophone African authors. Arranged alphabetically by title of work, the entries, which are quite detailed, cover the most important Togolese authors.

536 **Documents et travaux inédites ESACJ-ESTEG.** (Documents and unpublished works of the ESACJ-ESTEG.)
Kwam Kouassi. *Annales de l'Université de Bénin* (Lomé), vol. 2, no. 1 (Dec. 1978), p. 153-66.

In this bibliography Kouassi lists one hundred Master's theses concluded between 1976 and 1977 at the university in Lomé. The main fields represented are public administration, local economy, social issues and international relations.

537 **Elements de bibliographie du Togo.** (Elements for a bibliography of Togo.)

A. Othily.   Lomé: ORSTOM, 1970. 2 vols.

Each volume in this two-volume bibliography (258p., 102p.) is individually alphabetized, including a total of some 2,800 entries, and making it one of the most comprehensive bibliographies on Togo. However, Othily does not include many items published in English not found in local archives. For a more recent bibliography see Catherine Cipot, *Togo 1990, références bibliographiques* (Togo 1990, bibliographical references). Paris: Ministère de la Coopération et du Développement, 1990. 120p.

538 **Elements d'une bibliographie Ewe.** (Elements for an Ewe bibliography.)

A. M. Aduayom, N. L. Gayibor, A. Amegbleame.   Lomé: Université du Bénin, Institut National des Sciences de l'Education, 1983. 168p.

This volume is a remarkable testimony to both the considerable academic interest in the Ewe people, culture and language, and to the vibrant vernacular Evegbe literature that has developed in Togo and Ghana. The bibliography, which stresses publications in German, French and English, and of course Ewe, is composed of a section of 617 items from the periodical literature (p. 1-59), another 772 items (p. 61-127) that are books and brochures, and a triple index. Entries are not annotated and not all entries are fully documented: some, for example, merely list the name of the author and the title of the book or periodical. The bibliography is also somewhat lean on more contemporary material that might best be traced using other sources.

539 **French colonial Africa: a guide to official sources.**

Gloria D. Westfall.   London: Hans Zell, 1992. 244p.

An indispensable guide to the material of the colonial era in francophone Africa, this reference work covers the various bibliographies, guides, manuals, directories, censuses, publications, serials and repositories of official and quasi-official literature in both Africa and France. It deals with both the two large colonial federations, and their individual components, and concludes with a twenty-five-page index.

540 **Le guide bancaire du Togo.** (The banking guide to Togo.)

Jacques Alibert.   Paris: EDITM, 1988. 87p.

This is a banking manual that includes a useful assembly of information about Togo's various banks. It is especially pertinent to those contemplating trade with the country.

541 **Historical dictionary of Togo.**

Samuel Decalo.   Metuchen, New Jersey: Scarecrow Press, 1987. 2nd ed. 331p. bibliog.

Scheduled to come out in a third updated and much-expanded edition at the end of 1995, this reference work is part of a fifty-volume series on individual African states. The book consists of a broad introductory essay, a list of acronyms, statistical tables and maps, a lengthy alphabetical 'dictionary', a brief assessment of the literature on Togo and a bibliography of over 1,700 items. The dictionary includes entries, ranging from a few lines to seven pages, on most of the key historical and contemporary social, political, economic, military and religious personalities, groupings, structures, political parties and events in Togo. The bibliography that follows is comprehensive and multilingual (p. 216-331), arranged by subject headings. In common with most of the works in this series, and especially those dealing with francophone Africa, the book is a synthesis of a wide range of information not found in any one source, and not at all in the English language. Two other dictionaries in this series, dealing with countries neighbouring Togo, also contain information relevant to Togo. See: Samuel Decalo, *Historical dictionary of Benin*. Metuchen, New Jersey: Scarecrow Press, 1995, 550p. bibliog.; and Daniel Miles McFarland, *Historical dictionary of Ghana*. Metuchen, New Jersey: Scarecrow Press, 1985 (third edition forthcoming). 356p. bibliog. For some additional political biographies on Togolese personalities see: *African Biographies* (Bonn, Germany: Verlag Neue Gesellschaft, 1971. looseleaf.; *Les élites africaines* (The African elites). Paris: Ediafric, 1971. 328p.; *Personalités publiques de l'Afrique de l'Ouest* (Public figures of West Africa). Paris: Ediafric, 1968. 300p.; and John A. Wiseman, *Political leaders in Black Africa*. Aldershot, England: E. Elgar, 1991. 249p.

542 International African Bibliography.
Edited by David Hall.   London: Hans Zell, 1971- . quarterly.

This quarterly publication is the continuation of the bibliography originally published (until 1970) in *Africa*, the quarterly journal of the International African Institute, and later for over a decade published by Mansell. Produced at the School of Oriental and African Studies, it is one of the two most comprehensive ongoing bibliographies in African studies. Listed are books and articles that are arranged by regions, and then by country.

543 International guide to African studies research.
Edited by Philip Baker.   London: Hans Zell, 1987. 2nd ed. 264p.

Some 1,100 sources of use to research in African studies are included in this guide which has four indices (p. 217-64).

544 Le livre ewe: essai de bibliographie. (Ewe books: bibliographical essay.)
Simon Amegbleame.   Bordeaux, France: Institut d'Etudes Politiques, CEAN, 1975. 72p.

This is a survey of book-publishing in the Ewe vernacular, and an introductory bibliography of such literature. Some 408 titles are included, with a subject index.

545 Marchés Tropicaux et Mediterranéens. (Tropical and Mediterranean Markets.)
Edited by F. Gaulme.   Paris, 1945- . weekly.

Appearing over the years with a slightly changed name, this influential weekly is by far the premier journal for ongoing economic matters relating to francophone Africa. Though brief news items predominate, including coverage of topics such as industrial projects, contracts awarded, and development plans, there are also very frequent in-depth and comprehensive surveys of an entire country's economy or market, rendering the journal invaluable. Several years ago an English version was launched. While the latter would be valuable to those with linguistic difficulties in French, the English version, a monthly, is a rather abridged and poor substitute for the French original.

546 **Materials for West African history in French archives.**
P. Carson. London: Athlone Press, 1968. 170p.

This is a very useful source-guide for students and scholars contemplating research in France. The material that is listed includes records of traders, chambers of commerce, as well as libraries and archives of the various French ministries concerned with Africa.

547 **Répertoire bibliographique.** (Bibliographical index.)
Lomé: Ministère du Plan et des Mines, Centre de Documentation Technique, 1988. 4 vols.

This four-volume bibliographical set is an inventory of books, government reports and documents available in the country's regional branches of the Ministry of the Plan's statistical offices, except for the La Kara region, where the resources are in the Rural Development Regional Headquarters. Each volume covers one of four regions (Centrale, La Kara, Plateaux, Savanes), with entries grouped under the issuing organ, and separately (but hardly adequately) indexed at the end by topic. The largest office is for the Plateaux region (83p.).

548 **Répertoire des activités commerciales, industrielles et agricoles de la République togolaise.** (Directory of commercial, industrial and agricultural activities in the Togolese Republic.)
Lomé: Chambre de Commerce, d'Agriculture et d'Industrie du Togo, 1984. 135p.

Intermittently published by Togo's Chamber of Commerce, this is an invaluable directory of all economic enterprises and professional services in Togo. It provides names of the company/enterprise and their director or owner, street and postal address, telephone number, and a brief description of its activities. The roughly 1,000 entries in this volume are organized under several broad categories of enterprise.

549 **Répertoire des memoires soutenus à l'Ecole des Lettres et déposés à la bibliothèque universitaire, 1978-1985.** (Index of theses defended in the School of Letters and deposited in the university library, 1978-1985.)
Lomé: Université du Bénin, Bibliothèque Universitaire, 1987. 54p.

Much important research is conducted at the Master's level at the University of Lomé, especially in the fields of history, ethnology, demography and linguistics. This listing is an index of theses available in the library for the period in question. There are many other listings of dissertations, some periodically updated. For French dissertations in the fields of law and politics see Mireille Lafond, *Recueil des thèses africanistes: droit et science politique, 1967-1984.* (Collection of Africanist theses: law and political science, 1967-1984.) Paris: Université de Paris I, Pantheon-Sorbonne, Centre d'Etudes Juridiques Comparatives, 1985. 183p.

550 **République togolaise.** (Togolese Republic.)

In: *Guide ouest africaine* (West African guide.)   Paris: Diloutremer, 1973. p. 429-52.

Originally a yearbook of francophone Africa, this last issue is still valuable despite being badly dated, since it provides information which is not available elsewhere, or very difficult to collate. The volume covers every region, district, subdistrict and (where applicable) village in Togo, and provides a compendia of all kinds of information on: government services, offices, hospitals, clinics, schools, post offices, and barracks; private and public enterprises, including factories, stores, petrol stations, and garages; and professionals and traders in every town and village. Although obviously much has changed in Togo since the early 1970s, including the administrative organization of the country itself, and a plethora of organizations, structures and traders have appeared on the scene, a surprising amount of the data is still current, and of use if one keeps in mind that the yearbook only provides a snapshot of conditions in 1973.

551 **République togolaise.** (Togolese Republic.)

In: *L'Afrique d'expression française et Madagascar.*   Paris, special annual issue of *Europe Outremer.*

In 1987 the long-established *Europe Outremer* ceased publication. Prior to this, however, a special annual issue provided very authoritative compact reference material on every francophone country in Africa, including by far the best maps available. The annual sections on Togo, of around ten pages long, contain information on all aspects of the country, including a list of cabinet ministers, and an especially valuable and detailed outline of the economy. Although other reference works exist, this issue of Europe Outremer has always been among the best. Monthly issues have also at times included special issues on Togo, with an array of brief articles on various aspects of the country.

552 **République togolaise: annuaire économique officiel, 1982/83.**

(Republic of Togo: official economic annual, 1982/83.)

Paris: ABC, 1982. 300p. bibliog.

Intermittently published by various publishers, and not always easily available, this is Togo's official economic annual. This particular issue outlines, in condensed form under four broad sections, the nature of the country's constitution, government, RPT party, the country's geography, people, commercial structures, industry, tourism, banks, development plan, agriculture, the investment code, and a telephone directory of 'useful numbers'. The bibliography is sparse and unalphabetized.

553 **The SCOLMA directory of libraries and special collections on Africa in the United Kingdom and Western Europe.**

Edited by Harry Hannam.   Oxford: Hans Zell, 1983. 188p.

This is the second edition of an invaluable guide to sources of African documentation in Western Europe. The work was sponsored by the Standing Conference on Library Materials on Africa, and lists 142 collections in Great Britain and 133 in the rest of Western Europe.

554 **Theses on Africa 1963-1975 accepted by universities in the United Kingdom and Ireland.**
John McIlwaine.   London: Mansell, 1978. 123p.

In this work McIlwaine lists 2,231 dissertations (from bachelor to doctoral) by geographical region and country and with indices. It was produced on behalf of SCOLMA – the Standing Conference on Library Materials on Africa – and is a follow-up to a previous volume compiled by SCOLMA, *Theses on Africa accepted by universities in the United Kingdom and Ireland.* Cambridge, England: Heffer, 1964, 74p., covering the years 1920-1962. It is supposed to be periodically updated.

555 **Togo.**
Dakar: Banque Centrale des Etats de l'Afrique de l'Ouest, Statistiques Economiques et Monétaires. quarterly.

This is by far the most comprehensive, authoritative and up-to-date compilation of statistics on all aspects of Togo's domestic economy and international trade published by the central bank of most of francophone West Africa. Each thirty-six-page issue (separate ones are published for each member-state) contains only statistical data organized in tables on items such as: local staple crops; cash crops and minerals produced; volume of trade; trading partners; levels of imports and exports and their breakdown by commodity; aeroplane traffic and vessels arriving; number of vehicles registered in the country; consumer prices and salaries.

556 **Togo.**
Samuel Decalo.   In: *The Oxford companion to the world.*   New York: Oxford University Press, 1993. p. 151-56.

This is a brief overview of Togo's socio-economic and political evolution in a compact reference guide to the world.

557 **Togo.**
Sean Moroney.   In: *Africa.*   New York: Facts on File, 1989.

This is a useful overview of Togo's social, economic and political development up to the late 1980s, covering the country's peoples, economy and political evolution. In view of the major political changes in the country in the 1990s some of the information is currently dated.

558 **Togo.**
In: *Africa Contemporary Record.*   Edited by Colin Legum.   New York: Africana Publishing, 1966-1989. annual.

Until it was sadly discontinued, this was one of the best sources of information in English about the previous year's developments in each African state. Preceded by a hefty segment of articles dealing with thematic issues relevant to the entire continent ('China's year in Africa' 'France in Africa' 'The Sahel Drought' and 'Refugees in Africa', for example) each country section summarizes in a succinct but informative and accurate manner the social, economic and political events of the preceding year, followed by statistical tables. Togo's entries were usually on the shorter side (six pages) but nevertheless valuable.

559 **Togo.**
   In: *Africa south of the Sahara*.   London: Europa Publications, 1971- .
   annual.

This important annual provides a country-by-country survey of Africa. Each volume
includes a number of intermittently revised overviews of the country's history,
economy and politics, which are followed by much statistical data about the country,
including a 'Directory' of the cabinet and other lists, and a ten-item bibliography.
Sections on Togo have numbered around sixteen pages.

560 **Togo.**
   In: *L'economie des pays d'Afrique noire* (The economy of the
   countries of Black Africa.)   Paris: Ediafric, 1987.

Until it closed down in 1989 Ediafric published this volume at intermittent intervals
starting in 1979. It provides a useful guide to the economies of all countries of
francophone Africa, with compact data on trade, commerce, agriculture, mining and
developmental plans, and listing the major enterprises in each economic sector.

561 **Togo.**
   Paul Clifford.   In: *Francophone West Africa: Cameroon, Gabon,
   Ivory Coast, Guinea, Senegal, Benin, Togo: business opportunities in
   the 1980's*.   London: Metra Consulting Group, 1982. p. 293-320.

This is a businessman's guide to francophone Africa. Metra Consulting is a subsidiary
of Metra International and publishes, *inter alia*, business feasability studies and
engages in consultancy work on the part of foreign companies thinking of entering
African markets. The Togolese section includes a list of useful addresses and
telephone numbers of various government agencies, and concise information about
banking, commerce, the investment code, tariffs, the economic infrastructure and
business climate. The bulk of this book of 347 pages is on Gabon, Cameroon and
Ivory Coast.

562 **Togo.**
   Edited by Ralph Uwechue, et al.   In: *Know Africa: Africa today*.
   London: Africa Books, 1991, 2nd ed., vol. 1, p. 1,851-74.

A comprehensive compendium of useful historical, political and economic
information about Togo, including statistical tables. An equally large second volume
is devoted to biographies of African leaders. These are alphabetically listed, but as
entries do not give prominence to the nationality of the individual, the volume is
somewhat cumbersome to use except where specific information is sought. Half the
entries are on Nigerians, and many of the Togolese biographies have not been
updated since the 1970s.

563 **Togo.**
   In: *Répertoire des centres de documentation et bibliotheques*.
   (Directory of documentation centres and libraries.)   Abidjan: Conseil
   de l'Entente Service de Documentation, 1980. p. 223-50.

Covering Benin, Côte d'Ivoire, Burkina Faso, Niger and Togo, this work is an
invaluable guide to repositories of documentation, including banks, cultural centres,

and libraries, in the states of West Africa's Conseil de l'Entente. The Togolese section provides concise data on the country's twenty-five libraries and documentation centres. Each is presented on a separate page with its civil status, address, telephone number, name of head librarian, indication of approximate number of volumes held (the largest is the University library with 40,000 books and 700 periodicals) and hours of operation.

564 **Togo.**

In: *Sociétés et fournisseurs d'Afrique noire* (Societies and suppliers of Black Africa.) Paris: Ediafric, annual to 1987.

Defunct since 1987 when Ediafric closed down, this is a trade directory of francophone Africa. Arranged alphabetically by country, the Togo section usually consisted of around twenty-three pages that provided concise information on all private and mixed economy companies in the country (some 120 in total), with their addresses, telephone and fax numbers, capitalization, name of managing director and equity share of their owners. In a separate section are listed all major European companies involved in trade with French Africa, with similar data on them.

565 **Togo.**

In: *Sources d'information sur l'Afrique noire francophone et Madagascar: institutions, répertoires, bibliographies* (Sources of information on francophone Black Africa and Madagascar: institutions, catalogues and bibliographies.) Paris: La Documentation Française, 1988, p. 305-11.

This reference work provides comprehensive information about research institutions and governmental organs in Togo, their libraries and publications, and general as well as specialized bibliographies on the country.

Connaissance du Togo. (Knowledge of Togo.)
See item no. 1.

The People's Republic of Benin and the Republic of Togo.
See item no. 9.

Togo.
See item no. 10.

Le Togo aujourd'hui. (Togo today.)
See item no. 18.

Togo. Les hommes et leur milieu. (Togo. The people and their setting.)
See item no. 19.

Togo: official standard names approved by the United States Board on geographic names.
See item no. 39.

Contribution aux études éthnobotaniques et floristiques au Togo.
(Contribution to ethno-botanical and flower studies in Togo.)

See item no. 45.

Flore analytique du Togo. (Analysis of Togo's flora.)
See item no. 48.

Code des investissements. (Investment code.)
See item no. 276.

Directoire des industries et activités du Togo. (Directory of industries and activities in Togo.)
See item no. 392.

Bibliography of Gbe (ewe, gen, aja, xwala, fon, gun, etc.): publications *on* and *in* the language.
See item no. 417.

Indexes

There follow three separate indexes: authors (personal and corporate); titles; and subjects. Title entries are italicized and refer either to the main titles, or to many of the other works cited in the annotations. The numbers refer to bibliographical entry rather than page numbers. Individual index entries are arranged in alphabetical sequence.

Index of Authors

175

Index of Titles

186

Index of Subjects

Map of Togo

This map shows the more important towns and other features.

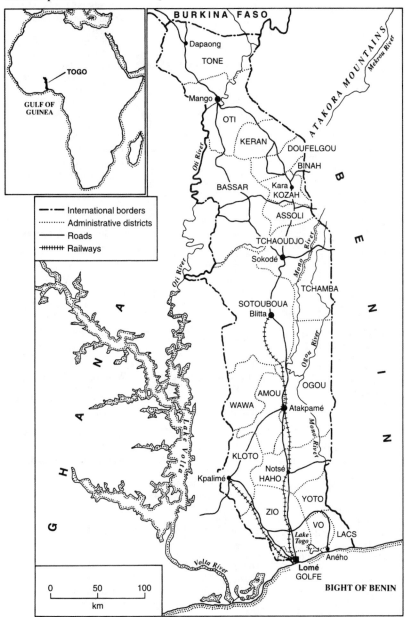

ALSO FROM CLIO PRESS

INTERNATIONAL ORGANIZATIONS SERIES

Each volume in the International Organizations Series is either devoted to one specific organization, or to a number of different organizations operating in a particular region, or engaged in a specific field of activity. The scope of the series is wide-ranging and includes intergovernmental organizations, international non-governmental organizations, and national bodies dealing with international issues. The series is aimed mainly at the English-speaker and each volume provides a selective, annotated, critical bibliography of the organization, or organizations, concerned. The bibliographies cover books, articles, pamphlets, directories, databases and theses and, wherever possible, attention is focused on material about the organizations rather than on the organizations' own publications. Notwithstanding this, the most important official publications, and guides to those publications, will be included. The views expressed in individual volumes, however, are not necessarily those of the publishers.

VOLUMES IN THE SERIES

TITLES IN PREPARATION